SHARED SERVICES

SHARED SERVICES

Adding Value to
the Business Units

Donniel S. Schulman
Martin J. Harmer
John R. Dunleavy
James S. Lusk

JOHN WILEY & SONS, INC.
New York • Chichester • Weinhein • Brisbane • Toronto • Singapore

This publication is designed to provide accurate and authoritative information in regard to the subject matter covered. It is sold with the understanding that the publisher is not engaged in rendering legal, accounting, or other professional services. If legal advice or other expert assistance is required, the services of a competent professional person should be sought.

Library of Congress Cataloging-in-Publication Data

Shared services : adding value to the business units / Donniel Schulman . . . [et al.].
   p. cm.
   Includes bibliographical references and index.
   ISBN 0-471-31621-0 (cloth : alk. paper)
   1. Shared services (Management) 2. Reengineering (Management)
  3. Decentralization in management. I. Schulman, Donniel.
  HD62.13.S49 1999
  658.4'02—dc21   98-44990
                                              CIP

Printed in the United States of America.

10 9 8 7 6 5 4 3

About the Authors

Donniel S. Schulman

Donniel Schulman, a Partner in PricewaterhouseCoopers, L.L.P., is the Americas Theater Leader for the Finance and Cost Management practice. Mr. Schulman has 18 years of industry and consulting experience in areas of reinventing the office of the CFO, business process reengineering and shared service implementation. He is the leading expert in assisting companies increase shareholder value by improving working capital management. His principal focus is to help companies forge a strategic and operational partnership between the finance function and the business units. This partnership can maximize shareholder value, reduce SG&A, increase profitability and improve customer retention.

Mr. Schulman has worked across industries including Manufacturing, High Tech, Consumer Products, Chemicals, Media, P&C Insurance, and Telecommunications. Mr. Schulman has frequently been quoted as an expert in Financial Management processes in CFO Magazine, Chemical Weekly, Industry Week, Global Telecoms Review and other trade publications.

Martin J. Harmer

Martin Harmer is a Managing Associate in PricewaterhouseCoopers, L.L.P., Finance Cost Management practice, where his primary focus is shared services consulting. He has over 20 years of combined industry and professional experience in international finance and accounting. His previous responsibilities have included: Pan-European Financial Shared Services; Business Process Reengineering; Financial Analysis & Reporting; International Mergers and Acquisitions; and Auditing. In particular, his audit experience has been gained in numerous business environments (spanning more than 30 countries), encompassing both Public Accounting and Internal Auditing.

Mr. Harmer has worked across a number of different industries during his extensive commercial and professional career, covering manufacturing (particularly Automotive components); Oil & Gas; Advanced & Engineered Materials; Process Chemicals; Electronics & Instrumentation; Aerospace; Construction; and Service Organizations. Mr. Harmer has been a guest speaker at a number of International Conferences and forums on the subject of Pan-European Shared Services, where his experiences were widely recognized as breaking new ground.

James S. Lusk

James Lusk is Vice President and Controller of Lucent Technologies. He has played a key role in the largest IPO in U.S. history, which successfully launched Lucent Technologies. Mr. Lusk created and launched Lucent Financial Services, which provides all of the "high volume/low cost" accounting and financial transaction processing to Lucent. Additionally, Mr. Lusk is leading a Corporate Center-wide reinvention effort focused on ensuring that all corporate functions provide value-added partnership to the entire Lucent enterprise.

Prior to his current position, Mr. Lusk was CFO for Network Systems North America, a global business generating a $9 billion revenue stream. He was part of a team responsible for implementation of the new Customer Architecture Business Model. As CFO for AT&T Computer Systems, he provided financial direction for a $1 billion operation heightening emphasis on a worldwide asset management process. Mr. Lusk has worked across industries including banking, retail, health care, energy and manufacturing. In May of 1998 Mr. Lusk was named Financial Executive of the Year by the Institute of Management Accountants.

John R. Dunleavy, C.P.A.

John Dunleavy is a partner in PricewaterhouseCoopers, L.L.P. specializing in the communications finance and accounting fields.

Mr. Dunleavy has extensive experience in consulting to the telecommunications, food processing, broadcasting, and education industries in the areas of international transfer pricing, management reporting, financial planning control, and product management and marketing information systems.

He is a Visiting Lecturer at Tuck School of Business and has been co-author to two books, *Reinventing the CFO: Moving from Financial Management to Strategic Management,* and *SAP*—An Executive's Comprehensive Guide.

Foreword

As we prepare to enter the new millennium, businesses are moving at a frantic pace to develop and capitalize on the competitive advantage that sets them apart from the rest of the field. Additionally, companies have stepped up their globalization efforts to take advantage of opportunities in emerging markets throughout the world. As a result, we have seen a rush of mergers, acquisitions, and divestitures, as well as downsizing, rightsizing, and restructuring, all in an effort to position businesses to leverage their competitive advantage and build greater shareholder value.

Lucent Technologies was spun off from AT&T for that reason—to increase the shareholder value that had been unrealized as part of AT&T. Bob Allen, then Chairman of AT&T, took a bold and courageous strategic step in unleashing the power of Lucent. The shareholder value that has been created is confirmation of his wisdom. We had to deliver on that promise of growing shareholder value. Achieving this meant growing the business profitably and developing best-in-class systems and processes to support the new company. In addition, we had to create a compelling vision that would drive a major change in our operations, moving us toward a high-performance operating environment.

It was clear that we needed to drive revenue growth by allowing our business units to focus on what they did best, leveraging our competitive advantage. Our benchmarking convinced us that moving to shared services within our finance function was a business imperative required to achieve best-in-class margins, a companion objective to revenue growth. We knew that moving high-volume transaction-processing activities into a shared service environment would create the core competency of a dedicated transaction processing organization.

Engaging in shared services is a complicated process, from developing an understanding of shared service concepts, through the decision-making process, and to successful implementation. The transition must be managed without losing focus on either external customers or internal business unit partners.

Jack Dunleavy, Martin Harmer, Jim Lusk, and Don Schulman have given us a framework for understanding the process. They have provided a broad overview and detailed discussion of the design and implementation of a shared service organization, including program and project management, the creation of appropriate service-level agreements, and development of metrics to measure success after implementation.

One of the key drivers to the successful implementation of shared services at Lucent was the contextual change driven by Jim Lusk, Vice President and Controller. I worked closely with Jim and his consulting team during the implementation. Jim created a compelling vision of why the Lucent finance organization needed to utilize shared services and to change the way we thought about our finance function. This was a critical factor in our successful implementation as the shared vision was essential to overcome organizational resistance.

This book provides invaluable guidance on the wide array of issues that develop before and after the decision is made to implement shared services. Reading it can help you capitalize on your company's competitive advantage and unleash shareholder value from within your business.

Henry Schacht
Former Chairman & CEO
Lucent Technologies

Preface

As our shared service practice at PricewaterhouseCoopers has come together over the last months and years, two things have become apparent to us. First, this is an incredibly powerful tool, especially for the world's largest companies. Second, we assist companies to get the most leverage possible out of shared services through some innovative and cutting-edge techniques and practices.

It became clear over time that we could provide serious thought leadership in this area, especially if we worked together closely with a client such as Lucent Technologies.

This book is the result of articulating on paper what we had previously only done in presentations and client field work. It is also a chance for a participant in a large and dynamic shared service implementation to stake his and his company's claim to leadership in this area.

While there are only four names attached to this book, three from PricewaterhouseCoopers and one from Lucent, the book was truly a team effort by many players. We are grateful to them all and wish to acknowledge them.

Acknowledgments

Firstly, to the PricewaterhouseCoopers global shared services leaders: Clive Johnson, Karen Nold, Yvonne Welch and Richard Sandwell, who worked with us to develop the framework for this book and who provided, with the help of their teams, valuable insights and views on the implementation of shared services.

Secondly, to the many subject matter experts; James Bramante (performance management), John Lerch (call centers), Marc Holloway (business process outsourcing), Judy Reach (human resources) and many more, who provided the indepth knowledge that make this book so powerful.

Thirdly, to the many people who have supported us in bringing this book to life: Judy Spartling, Bonnie Platt and Martin Wong for keeping us organized, the creative services team for helping us communicate complex ideas through simple images, and Sheck Cho and team at John Wiley & Sons for keeping us focused on the end goal.

Special thanks must also go to Alan Kilyk (Lucent) and Mila Schulkleper (PricewaterhouseCoopers) who worked side-by-side with us to push forward many of our ideas. They demonstrated immense creativity and their help was invaluable.

Much gratitude also goes to Cedric Read, Bob Leach and Doug Simpson, the global leadership team of PricewaterhouseCoopers Financial and Cost Management consulting practice, for their guidance and support in writing this book.

Finally, to Jon Zonderman. His professionalism and patience have been critical to this book. As we would say, at the end of a long hard day discussing one of the chapters in this book, "he brought clarity to our ramblings." Thank you.

Introduction

As businesses enter the new millenium, there is an increasing clash of competitive forces. Telecommunications and information technology are clearly making the world "one market" and allowing customers to obtain goods and services from providers located anywhere. Companies are feeling compelled to grow horizontally in order to provide customers around the world with goods or services.

At the same time, individuals are encouraged to be more entrepreneurial in the way they chart their careers and their lives. Those with the right mix of expertise, combined with the willingness and ability to continually learn new tasks, are thriving in businesses that are allowing for more employee decision making at all levels.

One of the ways companies are looking for competitive advantage in this frenetic environment is through the reenginnering or redesign of their core business processes, the end-to-end processes that touch customers and through which a company can make strategic changes. Another way is through the use of a tactical technique called shared services. In a shared service environment, a company pulls activities that support core business processes out of each business unit and consolidates them into a separate operating unit that runs these supporting processes as its core business process.

Shared services is not for the faint of heart. Moving to a shared service method of operation entails a huge culture change for an organization. The entire business context must be changed. It takes time, effort and vast amounts of management energy to move from a mindset of purely decentralized management of support activites within each business unit or centralized management of support activities at the corporate level to a mindset of partnership between business units and the consolidated, shared service organization.

There are a number of reasons companies are turning to the shared service model. These reasons are described in detail in the early chapters. One underlying reason all companies embark on shared services is to create more of a "one company" mindset among often disparate business units. In today's truly "small world," this desire to show a consistent face to clients and customers, vendors and suppliers, shareholders and potential shareholders is becoming of paramount importance.

Acting as one company provides increased flexibility to all of the business's operations. It allows corporate leaders to maintain a global perspective while at the same time allowing regional and country-specific business unit leaders to take strong, local customer-focused actions.

In this book, we bridge that chasm between the theory of how a shared service operation "ought to" work and the practical issues involved in how to make it work—how to carry out a successful implementation of a shared service operation in your business.

This book is meant to be read by a number of different constituencies within a company: the corporate leaders who will make the decision to move to a shared service model; the business unit executives; and those who currently hold "corporate" jobs in areas such as human resources, finance, information technology, and legal services who will become the shared service operation executives—those who will have to make the arrangement work; and those in the ranks of support process management who will become the program managers and project managers of the implementation effort itself.

The book is divided into four parts. The first two parts are a theoretical examination of the macro issues facing executive decision makers who are having their company embark on a "shared services journey." Parts Three and Four get into the details of implementation and lend themselves to a wider readership.

Throughout these last two parts, one of the co-authors, Jim Lusk, Vice President Controller of Lucent Technologies, narrates the story of how his company dealt with all of these implementation details.

At the end of the book are a number of appendixes we hope you will find useful, including service-level agreements between shared service operations and their business unit partners, and templates for baselining and benchmarking.

We often refer to a company as "embarking on a shared service journey." To emphasize this metaphor, we have created a pathway to shared services, which is seen in Figure I.

Along this pathway, each of our chapters is a paving stone. At the top of each chapter, that chapter's paving stone is "exploded" graphically to show the topics that will be covered in that chapter. At the end of each chapter is a checklist of items for review and to be used as a "cheat sheet."

Figure I   Pathway to Shared Services

Mobilize

What is Shared Services All About? • What's the Compelling Business Reason for Pursuing Shared Services? • Is Shared Services Right for You? • International Challenges

Assess

Considering Outsourcing • Shared Services and Its Relationship with Information Technology • Shared Services and Its Relationship with Process Reengineering and Redesign

Design

Getting Started • Planning and Approach • Selecting the Location • Setting Up the Infrastructure • Service-Level Agreements & Pricing Issues • The Final Business Case

Implement

The Global Potential and the Virtual Potential • Performance Measures and Continous Improvements • Barriers to Implementation and Change Management Solutions • Program and Project Management • Partnering for Success: Proceed with Care When Choosing a Consultant • Defining and Setting Up the Project

Contents

Contents

Contents

Contents

Contents

xxiii

Contents

Contents

Part One

Mobilize

In this part, executives are invited to mobilize an effort to create a shared service operation in their company by asking themselves a series of questions. These are the three questions we are often asked the first time we talk to executives about moving to shared services:

1. What is shared services all about?
2. What is the compelling reason for pursuing shared services?
3. Is shared services the right approach for our company?

Part One stresses that shared services is an approach to doing business that takes from each business unit many of the activities within support processes and brings them together to achieve critical mass. Too often, the supporting processes in a business are seen by executives and senior managers as "non-value-added"; because of this, they often receive little management attention and result in being too costly. However, in many companies, when these processes are operated as a free-standing business unit and "run like a business," they do indeed add value by freeing up the time and management resources of management in business units throughout the company.

For shared services to be successful, the operation must be seen by corporate executives as a way to solve business problems through the consolidation—but not centralization—of transaction-oriented processes that are repetitive and are much the same for each business unit. In order to do that, corporate leaders must articulate for management as well as employees a compelling business reason for pursuing what will clearly be a challenging organizational change effort.

While shared services presents a company with a challenge under any circumstances, it is especially so for companies seeking to implement shared services on an international scale, as discussed in Chapter 4.

Before chief executive officers commit the management time of their most senior people to this long-term and time-consuming effort, they must be clear that shared services is indeed the proper approach. We believe that for most large corporations it is.

1

What Is Shared Services All About?

- Enhancing corporate value
- Searching for strategic growth
- Creating new management responsibility
- Focusing on partner service and support
- Allowing business units to focus on strategic aspects of operations
- Transferring secondary activities of SBU into care processes of shared services
- Providing concentration of resources that perform the same support activities
- Providing supporting activities at lower cost with higher service levels
- Leveraging technological investments
- Focusing on continuous improvement

In today's increasingly competitive environment, there is constant pressure for corporate leaders to add value to their companies by streamlining processes that are not central to the company's operations and concentrating on strategic, or core, processes. Chief executive officers (CEOs) are confronted with multiple business units that have duplicative supporting processes and staffs. They are faced with a need to modernize computer systems and telecommunications. They are also faced with increasing global pressures.

3

They have a mandate to reduce sales, general and administrative (SG&A) expenses as a percentage of revenue. They are searching for a way to allow strategic operations to grow more rapidly without being burdened by distractions and extra support loads. The question is how to accomplish this.

One way companies are increasingly looking to solve this dilemma is through bundling some of those supporting processes and nonstrategic activities into a separate organization, which in turn treats those processes and activities as the core of its own business. This concept is known as *shared services.*

Shared services. What could be more natural?

The idea behind shared services is that to get more bang for the buck, you share some common elements of every business unit. And what could be better to share than support services—processes and activities that are, by definition, not core to the business unit's strategy.

Consider Figure 1-1. The goal of the company is growth, and the way the company focuses on meeting its goal is through the value chain. In order to do this, executives and management must solve business problems. In order to solve business problems, they need to look at enhancing business processes and making them more effective. They cannot just consider process efficiency; neither can they consider functional enhancement.

Corporate support services are tactical in nature. They are necessary, and doing them well helps support the corporate strategy. However, in and of themselves they are not strategic. By collecting these nonstrategic processes and activities into a common organization, under its own management, the management of all the individual business units can be freed up to manage their goals. This, in turn, allows business unit management to focus on solving business problems by enhancing the business unit's core processes, thus enhancing the value chain and in turn leading to growth.

Clearly, though they are tactical, supporting activities need to be done well in order to increase the company's ability to meet its strategic goals, increase corporate value, and in turn increase shareholder value.

Putting services together into an independent organization also allows employees and managers who work in the service unit to see di-

Figure 1-1   From Business Problem Solution to Goal Attainment

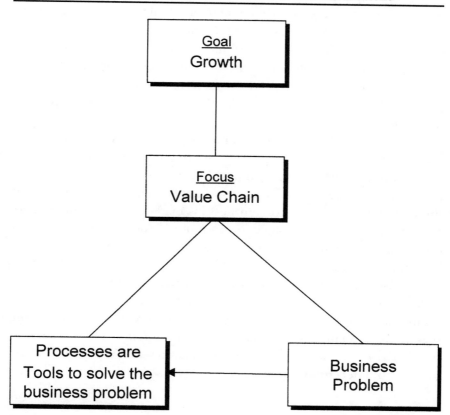

rectly how they drive the top line of revenues. This, in turn, allows them to shake the feeling that they are "low-value-added" employees performing "cost center" functions.

Sales may seem more important than paying a vendor, or making sure an employee's expense reimbursements are done properly, or that an employee's benefits are calculated correctly, or that a computer workstation is functioning correctly. But if you don't pay the vendor, reimburse the employee appropriately, calculate the benefits correctly, or fix the workstation, management time, effort, and energy is expended solving a problem and taking away from the ability to sell product or perform work. (It is interesting to note that in some consumer products companies, where sales is seen as tactical and brand management is the strategic process, companies are looking to create a shared services operation out of disparate salesforces.)

The job of shared service management—and by extension, the job of each individual who works in the shared service organization—is to free up salespeople to spend as much time with their customers as possible, and to free up those salespeople's managers to help them make those sales.

Business really is a team sport rather than a series of individual efforts. Like any other team sport there are visible stars and there are those who make it possible for the visible stars to perform up to their potential. In soccer, the strikers score, but somebody has to get them the ball. A shared service organization is made up of the midfielders and defenders, who work hard to position the team so that the scorers—the sales and marketing force—can be most effective.

Yet there is, in every company that moves to a shared service mode, opposition. The opposition comes about because to many, especially to business unit management, shared services smacks of centralization and corporate control. However, when created for the proper reason, implemented appropriately, and run *as if it were a business unit, and for the benefit of business-unit partners*, shared services is actually a key to successful decentralization.

PARTNERS, NOT CUSTOMERS

Throughout this book, the focus is on business units as "partners" with shared services, not customers of shared services. This is done for two reasons.

First is the concept of "internal customers" that became popular in the late 1980s during the last great wave of total quality management (TQM) implementations in the United States and Europe. It creates more confusion than it solves in discussions, trying to distinguish between internal customers, external customers, and end users.

Second, and more important, the relationship within a company between those who perform a task and those for whom the task is performed is not a simple transactional relationship. It is a relationship of members of a team, who know or should know that the company's value chain is only as strong as each individual link. It is a partnership relationship.

CHARACTERISTICS OF COMPANIES THAT GET INTO SHARED SERVICES

Shared services are most often seen in larger and more complex organizations—those with over $2 billion in revenue and with multiple business units. The services that are most often carved out of individual business units and put into the shared service organization are elements of finance, information system management, and human resources. Some others have added such staff functions as legal and communications. A few companies at the cutting edge are moving into shared services for supply-chain management.

In some companies, all of the services that are to be shared are collected into one organization. For instance, Monsanto moved most professional staff positions into its Monsanto Business Services shared service organization. The "group" layer of management was eliminated; staff who serve the CEO and board directly were retained; and support staffs within the 15 business units were transferred to Monsanto Business Services, except those who directly support manufacturing. The company believes it saved $80 million in its first year, after start-up costs.

AlliedSignal Business Services, started in 1994, has taken 75 separate business functions and consolidated them into one support business unit. The company says it saves $70 million annually, not least of all because the work is done with 60 percent of the former workforce when the effort was spread out (productivity increase), but also because of the increased span of control that service unit management has to solve problems.

Tenneco put its finance, human resources, information technology (IT), and some other common functions together for its North American operations into Tenneco Business Services in 1995. The company estimates three-year savings at $120 million.

One of the world's largest pharmaceutical companies created a European shared service organization.

The company has global revenues of more than $15 billion. R&D, manufacturing, distribution and marketing are all carried out on a worldwide basis. The corporate culture is derived from the U.S., although throughout Europe there is a strong country focus with equally strong local management structures.

Creation of shared service operations worldwide were one of more than 10 major initiatives the company undertook simultaneously. Others included business process reengineering and implementation of enterprise resource planning (ERP) software, in this case SAP R/3 software.

Throughout the 13 European countries in which the company had operations, there were many disparate finance functions, systems and processes.

Goals of the effort were to create a "working across Europe" face, both inside the company and to customers. This would be done by standardizing processes and integrating the SAP approach, which until then had been implemented on a rather ad hoc basis. It was hoped that establishment of a European Financial Shared Service Center that took repetitive transaction processing and reporting out of all business units would have the effect of:

- Reducing finance and related costs in information technology (IT) and administration by a cumulative 30-40 percent;
- Improving reporting and processing to ensure quality and consistency of information; and
- Refocusing management attention onto the business and reemphasizing the role of local finance to decision support and analysis.

The scope of what would be in the shared service organization included the discreet activities of accounts payable, accounts receivable, general accounting, travel and entertainment, fixed-asset accounting, and bank and cash management. It was hoped that over time the operations could mature to encompass the entire order-to-cash process, the strategic purchasing and procurement process, and demand management for manufacturing.

Tax, legal, treasury and audit issues were addressed locally, and some services were outsourced. Because of heavy organizational resistance to the shared service concept, it was decided to move the shared services center to a green field location in Chester, England and a major locating exercise was undertaken.

We have seen examples where each individual type of service becomes its own shared service organization; a financial services business unit, an IT services business unit. AMOCO tried this approach, but it did not work as well. First, it overlays many managements where only one is necessary. Second, companies find that support processes are tightly interlinked; there really are synergies in managing them all under one umbrella organization.

Even companies that start out with piecemeal service operations—for philosophical or internal political reasons—find over time that the natural evolution of a shared served operation is to go to one unified shared service organization. The question then becomes: Do we do it all at once as a "big bang" or over time, adding new services into the organization? This will be discussed in detail later.

Some companies are finding that as they bring service processes and activities together, traditional definitions no longer work. At Lucent, whose story is followed throughout this book, the company is working to create nomenclature for these new groupings of service activities, testing such terminology as *knowledge partner* activities and *employee care* activities.

A WORKING DEFINITION OF SHARED SERVICES

Shared services can be defined broadly but needs to be tailored to each organization. However, before looking at the way shared services can be tailored, it is important to have a common working definition. We define shared services as:

> The concentration of company resources performing like activities, typically spread across the organization, in order to service multiple internal partners at lower cost and with higher service levels, with the common goal of delighting external customers and enhancing corporate value.

From this concentration of resources comes a concentration in focus and an ability to keep all of the organization's goals in management's line of sight. Finally, all of those disparate activities and operations that have been seen by business unit executives as "back office" and secondary to the core business processes are being treated as if they themselves were the core processes. In a shared service organization, they are the core processes.

Some of the attributes of a shared service operation are:

- It operates as a stand-alone organization.
- It is process oriented and focuses on specific activities within processes.
- It is driven by market competitiveness. The services are the organization's "product." No one has ever thought of accounts payable, or benefits management, or IT data warehousing as a product before, or as a real priority. If it sits within each strategic business unit (SBU), finance or human resources or even IT is often an "also ran" in the competition for management attention. But in the shared services organization, it's the primary focus.
- It leverages technological investments.
- It focuses on service and support to "business partners," which goes beyond even the traditional notion of "customer service" or "client support."
- It focuses on continuous improvement.

Does Stand-Alone Mean Self-Governed?

In a word: yes. The ultimate goal of shared services is for the organization to be self-governed. This may not be the case initially; the shared service operation might report to the controller, or to another senior corporate official—there have been cases in which shared services reported to materials management. But the best case is for the shared service organization to be truly self-governing.

What Shared Services Is Not

Notice that in our definition the words *concentration of company resources* were used rather than centralization of company resources. That is deliberate. Shared services is by no means centralization, although when it is described, many people mistake it for centralization.

Centralized processing brings with it a "corporate" mentality. The focus is oriented upward to corporate headquarters. Service providers are located at corporate headquarters. They bundle services and standardize them. The business unit takes what it gets, lives with it, and has no recourse. There is little accountability by corporate staff for costs or service levels.

In a shared service environment, the service providers are oriented outward toward the business units to whom they provide services. The individual business units are the shared service organization's partners, and they have the right to demand the appropriate service level. Services are separated by customer set; not all business units need all of the same services, so they get more customized products and pay more appropriate prices.

Figure 1-2 shows how shared services captures the best elements of both centralization and decentralization, while leaving behind the problems. Connecting these "best of" elements with the attributes discussed earlier makes shared services all the more powerful.

In a shared service environment, service providers can be centrally located, located in centers of excellence, or embedded into each business unit in a physical sense, although they all report to the shared service organization's management, rather than to the individual business unit management or to corporate management. Finally, there is joint accountability for costs and quality through agreements that stipulate service level and pricing.

In some corporations, business units are allowed to opt out of shared service arrangements, performing the services themselves or contracting with an outside provider (outsourcing.) See Chapter 7 for a discussion on outsourcing.

It is increasingly common practice for corporate executives to say to business unit executives that they must use the shared service busi-

11

Figure 1-2   The Best Elements of Centralization and Decentralization

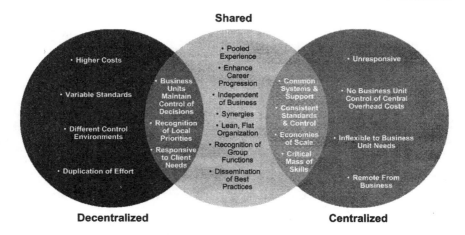

ness unit for two to three years, then evaluate the service level. Then they are allowed to make a decision about whether they want to bring the activities within the shared service organization back in house, maintain the relationship with the shared service organization, or go to an outsourcing provider.

Corporate leadership needs to be careful about how it urges or even mandates shared services. At one U.S.-based global manufacturing company, a new CEO mandated shared services in the early 1990s. Two years later, he found that the operation was not bringing in nearly the benefit he had thought it would.

When he explored why this was, he found from the leaders of operating business units that the shared service organization was not truly partnering with the business units and that service levels were subpar. More important, there was no mechanism for business-unit partners to air grievances. The shared service organization still had a "corporate" take-it-or-leave-it mentality toward the business unit partners since they were compelled to use the shared services operation. Business unit executives believed there was no point in pushing the shared services management to improve. As "captive customers" rather than true partners, they felt, they had no leverage.

The CEO acted on these findings. Over the next few months he determined that operating business unit executives and shared service executives had to work together and in partnership agree to service-level agreements that clearly define what the shared service business unit had to do to meet its partners' requirements. Satisfaction of the business unit partners became the mantra for the shared service organization and became the leadership's objective. What the CEO effectively did was continue to support the shared services philosophy, while putting the onus of quality and competitiveness squarely on the shared service organization by making it "sell" its services to business unit partners.

Service levels did improve over time, and the shared service approach is now accruing benefits that are increasing all the time.

SHARED SERVICES GOES HAND-IN-HAND WITH DECENTRALIZATION

Shared services, when performed correctly, actually enhances a decentralized corporate operation. It allows each business unit to focus on the strategic parts of its operation, putting more of its energy into performing strategic tasks, while carving out necessary but nonstrategic and noncore processes to the shared service unit. In effect, each SBU "outsources" these services, not to a third-party provider but to another organization under the same corporate umbrella. Some call the concept *insourcing*.

Figure 1-3 shows both the tangible and the intangible benefits of a shared service approach.

Looking at all of the attributes, benefits, and elements of centralization and decentralization discussed so far, one can see that some are related to efficiency—pooling resources, leveraging technology, and creating economies of scale—while others are related to effectiveness—creating standard processes, sharing expertise, and enhancing service. In fact, a shared service environment moves beyond the notion of efficiency and effectiveness to one of value.

Figure 1-3   Tangible and Intangible Benefits of Shared Services

Benefits are achieved:

Pre-Shared Services

Tangible:
- Expense reduction
- Increased productivity
- Economies of scale
- Leveraged technology
- Improved spans of control
- Working capital improvements
- Leverage purchasing from consolidated vendors

Intangible:
- Enhanced customer services
- Standardized processes & pooled resources
- One-company approach
- More rapid transition by focusing on "added value"
- More effective maintenance of standard "code block"
- Improved accuracy and consistency of information
- Better leverage of learning curve

Post-Shared Services

Efficiency is a step function; only so many costs can be eliminated at any one time. Gains in efficiency occur in blocks: reducing staff headcount, reducing supervision headcount through increased span of control, improving systems, and so forth. However, effectiveness can be improved in a linear way by working with partners to define standard processes and to correct information transfer problems at the source. Constantly sharing expertise among centers within the shared service organization and between the shared service organization and its partners also improves effectiveness over time. Together, step-function efficiency gains combined with continuous increases in effectiveness over time leads to increased value to the company's customers and ultimately to shareholders.

A concentration of company resources does not have to mean one location. There is nothing in the definition of shared services that mentions physical location. Processing centers can be anywhere in the world, and there can be any number of centers. Management of the shared service operation does not even have to be physically located at one of the processing centers, although as with any other "multinational," the management of a multicenter shared service operation by off-site leadership is more challenging than being onsite and managing a single processing center. There are any number of reasons for locating a processing center in any particular location, including workforce education levels, pay rates, and tax considerations. Location decisions are discussed in detail in Chapter 10.

RATIONALE FOR SHARED SERVICES: FINANCE EXAMPLE

Research has shown that 80 percent of traditional finance organization activities do not add value to the business. Flipping this equation on its head—creating a finance organization in which 80 percent of activities *do add value*—is one of two key tasks being given to CFOs and their finance organizations as we enter the 21st century. The other key task is to reduce the cost of the finance organization as a percentage of corporate revenues.

In order to do this, the Office of the Chief Financial Officer (OCFO) is being asked to shift resources away from simple transaction processing and controls, and to put those resources into becoming a partner with business unit and corporate leadership by providing business case analysis and decision support synthesis. They are being asked to do this while simultaneously reducing cost, with the goal being a finance organization that costs 1 percent of revenue or less, as opposed to the more than 2 percent of revenue that many finance organizations now cost to operate. Cutting-edge CFOs have looked to many tactical tools to do this, as discussed by PricewaterhouseCoopers colleagues in two books, *Reinventing the CFO: Moving From Financial Management to Strategic Management* and *CFO: Architect of the Corporation's Future.*

The shared services concept allows the OCFO to become a better strategic player for the benefit of the CEO and business unit leadership by moving transaction processing into a separate shared services organization and managing that organization as a business with a need to maintain low-cost, high-quality products and services. Although the financial shared service operation is not truly a "profit center," the goal is to create appropriate pricing to meet actual costs.

In fact, the shared service organization can, itself, become more of a strategic player. This will be discussed in detail later, but it is possible for the shared service operation to move further up the value chain than simple transaction processing. For instance, rather than just handling accounts payable and collections, a financial shared service organization might pick up the customer billing activity. However, this is an activity very close to the external customer, and as such is quite sensitive. Depending on the corporate culture, a shared service organization might or might not take on the customer billing activity as part of its original brief; in other businesses it would evolve to pick up this sensitive activity over time in discussion with and agreement with its business unit partners. Increasingly, especially in commodity businesses, shared service operating units are picking up the billing process immediately.

OTHER BENEFITS OF A SHARED SERVICE APPROACH

Companies that are currently undertaking shared services are constantly accruing benefits, many tangible but others intangible. These benefits go far beyond headcount reduction. It is important that we talk about companies that are undertaking shared services because, as of 1999, there are no companies who believe they have garnered everything possible from a shared service approach—even those companies that have been doing it for a decade or more.

Some of the more tangible benefits are:

- Leveraging purchasing by consolidating vendors in order to negotiate better terms and prices.
- Creating working-capital improvements from standardizing, concentrating, and netting treasury activities, as well as from operating receivables, payables, and inventory management in a center of expertise. This creates economies of scale and improves span of control, and thus decreases expenses.
- Increasing productivity; doing more with less.
- Consolidating transactions of common customers and vendors who deal with more than one SBU. This provides for economies

of scale and standardization of process and experiences as they pertain to these customers/vendors.

Many of these benefits are accrued through leveraging technology. Among the intangible benefits are:

- Promoting the "one company" approach. This can be seen internally, where employees all feel as if they are members of one company, as well as in the way outsiders see the company as a single entity.
- Driving the effort to more rapidly transform the business, focusing on adding value.
- Enabling the effective maintenance of standard transaction processes throughout the organization.
- Leveraging and speeding the adoption of best practices and thus the learning curve.
- Improving accuracy and consistency of information.
- Allowing SBUs to do more of what they do to earn money and to service their customers better.
- More effective maintenance of standard "code block" throughout the company.

Companies that create a shared service organization as part of an overall business strategy achieve a higher level of tangible results to intangible results. Those that "hop on the bandwagon" and hope for the best often see the intangible results, but do not really achieve many of the tangible benefits.

The following short case study is of a clearly tangible result from good positioning of shared services into an overall strategy. It pertains to the issue of working capital.

When a new CEO came into a well-known larger corporation, the company set about to do some process rationalization and redesign. As a natural outgrowth, a shared service center was set up for working capital management. Accounts receivable had previously been handled in each sales office.

Today, there are 10 centers in the United States; one center in each European country; and a regional center for Asia. The activities and processes associated with working capital management were cleaned up in their sites, then transferred to the shared service operation, then further refined. The company plans to consolidate further, to three centers in the United States and a pan-European center. In the first two years of operation, the shared service organization saved $3 billion.

The efforts of this and other companies to create "pan-European" shared service centers should be enhanced with the advent of the Euro in 1999. While there will not be a physical Euro currency until 2002, beginning in 1999 the first 11 European countries to join the common currency—the European Monetary Union (EMU)—will perform their business transactions in the new monetary unit, which eventually will reduce the difficulties and expense of working in multiple currencies. The implications of the Euro will be discussed in more detail later.

INTANGIBLE BENEFITS DEMAND CHANGE MANAGEMENT

Change management is discussed in detail in Chapter 17; however, it is important to note here that in order to achieve the full intangible benefits, companies must actively manage the expectations of individuals as their roles within the business change.

When the transactional aspects of human resources or finance are removed from a business unit, that does not mean that there is no need for a head of business unit human resources or finance. Rather, it means that these people will be able to take new and different roles in the business unit, roles in which they act more as strategic business advisors with the business unit head. But many of these senior functional managers are more comfortable managing the transactional aspects of their jobs than they are in being business analysts and business advisors.

Managing the change in the roles of these senior functional managers whose transactional activities are moved to a shared service organization is as important as managing the change encountered by those who go to the shared service organization.

QUANTIFYING BENEFITS DEMANDS METRICS

In order to know the benefits that are accruing through a shared services effort, it is necessary to create a set of metrics. People manage to what they can measure, and to what they are measured by. A company cannot truly get into shared services until it figures out what it wants to improve and how to measure whether that improvement is indeed taking place.

Appropriate metrics are an essential ingredient to an efficient and effective shared service organization that focuses on continuous improvement. They establish the "baseline" performance levels from which to improve, and provide fact-based support in discussions with both business unit partners and end-user customers of the business units.

These metrics must be visible and transparent to all. They will change over time, but all those who are measured by them need to understand what they are, when they will change, what they will become, and why they are changing.

Metrics include the qualitative performance of shared services as well as some hard, quantifiable numbers. These include cost, cycle time, productivity, and quality.

Figure 1-4 lays out how typical metrics need to evolve for successful operation and enhancement of shared services.

At the bottom tier of the first pyramid, a company needs fundamentally good performance in place at the grass roots level before it can try to measure at a higher level. The ability to adopt best practices is, to some degree, dependent on good operating levels at this tier. For example, payment on receipt is highly dependent on good purchasing and receiving discipline.

Certain metrics are of interest to business units, while others are more important to the shared service organization itself. In the second pyramid are the "best practices" metrics that the shared service management (at each processing center) will look at. Meeting goals and targets for these measures is how they will be judged.

Moving to the top of the second pyramid are metrics that business management are interested in. These are appropriate to shared

Figure 1-4 Hierarchy of Metrics

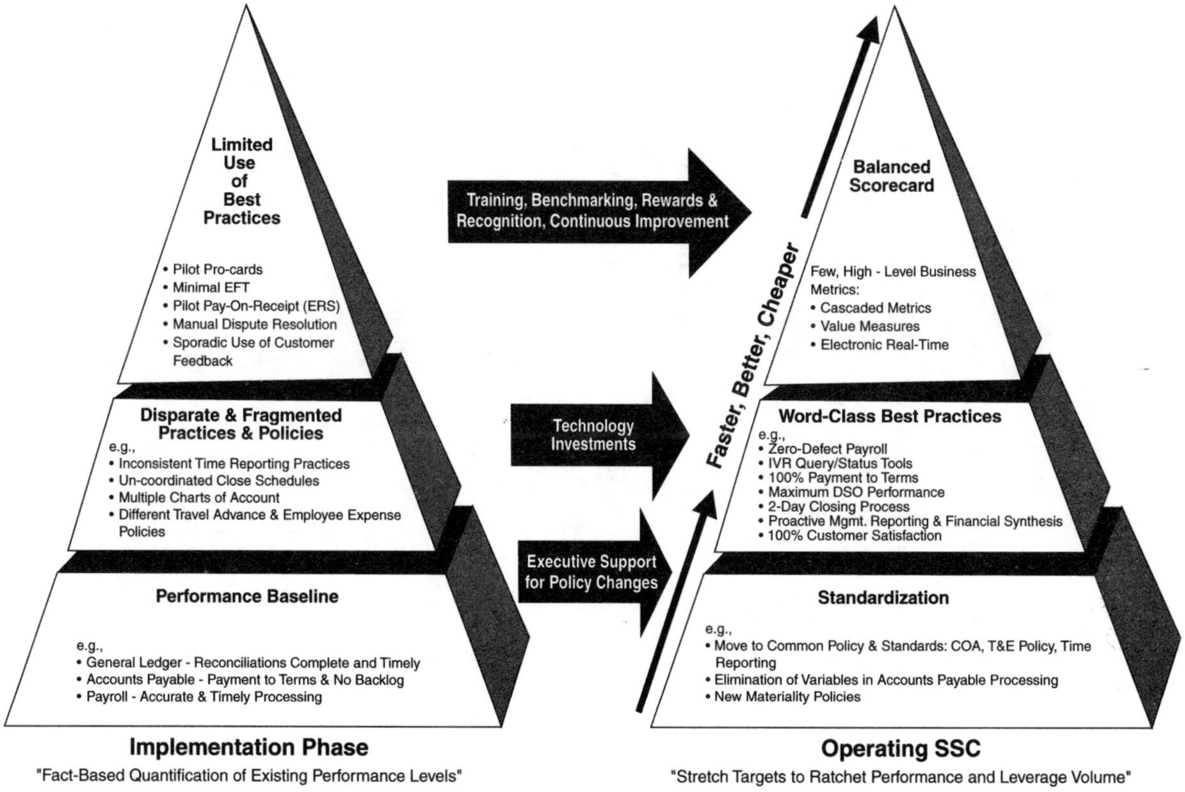

Faster, Better, Cheaper

Limited Use of Best Practices

- Pilot Pro-cards
- Minimal EFT
- Pilot Pay-On-Receipt (ERS)
- Manual Dispute Resolution
- Sporadic Use of Customer Feedback

Disparate & Fragmented Practices & Policies

e.g.,
- Inconsistent Time Reporting Practices
- Un-coordinated Close Schedules
- Multiple Charts of Account
- Different Travel Advance & Employee Expense Policies

Performance Baseline

e.g.,
- General Ledger - Reconciliations Complete and Timely
- Accounts Payable - Payment to Terms & No Backlog
- Payroll - Accurate & Timely Processing

Implementation Phase

"Fact-Based Quantification of Existing Performance Levels"

Training, Benchmarking, Rewards & Recognition, Continuous Improvement

Technology Investments

Executive Support for Policy Changes

Balanced Scorecard

Few, High - Level Business Metrics:
- Cascaded Metrics
- Value Measures
- Electronic Real-Time

Word-Class Best Practices

e.g.,
- Zero-Defect Payroll
- IVR Query/Status Tools
- 100% Payment to Terms
- Maximum DSO Performance
- 2-Day Closing Process
- Proactive Mgmt. Reporting & Financial Synthesis
- 100% Customer Satisfaction

Standardization

e.g.,
- Move to Common Policy & Standards: COA, T&E Policy, Time Reporting
- Elimination of Variables in Accounts Payable Processing
- New Materiality Policies

Operating SSC

"Stretch Targets to Ratchet Performance and Leverage Volume" service organizations that are "post-reengineering," and that therefore can be focused on high-level metrics.

The top level is the aspiration that many organizations seek to attain. These metrics, once in place, will show at a glance how a shared service organization is performing?

Maintaining Accountability in Business Units

Just because business units are turning over the operations of activities within supporting processes to a shared service organization does not mean that business unit management abdicates ultimate responsibility and accountability for the performance of those activities.

However, the management responsibility becomes different. Rather than managing the actual activities and the individuals who perform those activities, business unit managers now manage a relationship with a business service partner, in much the same way they would manage the relationship between any other service-providing vendor such as a consultant, auditor, or outside legal counsel.

SHARED SERVICE GEOGRAPHIC MODEL: A KEY CHOICE

There are five possible geographic models for a shared service operation, for a global organization, as shown in Figure 1-5. These options are all equally valid, and all are used by some companies who are today engaged in their shared service journey. However, as companies move their processing centers to locations chosen for reasons of personnel cost, workforce education, and taxes, the regional or even global options are increasingly becoming the options that are aspired to, if not already in place, even if the company has no operating unit in the country where the transaction processing center is located.

Choosing which of these geographic models to pursue is a key first step in implementing a shared service organization. The choice of geographic model drives many other choices one will make. The steps and thinking involved in making this choice are detailed in Chapter 10.

Figure 1-5   Possible Geographic Models for a Shared Service Organization

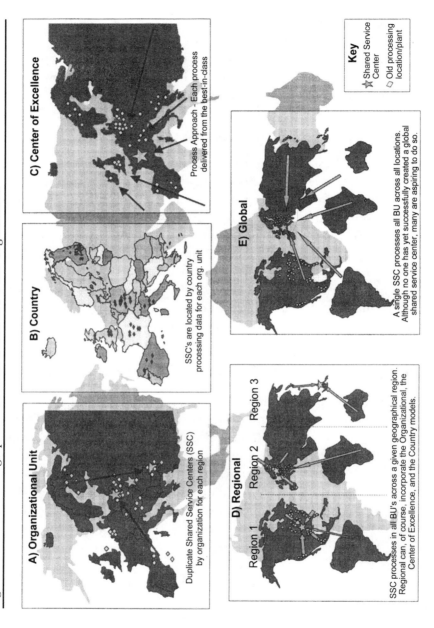

A) Organizational Unit

Duplicate Shared Service Centers (SSC) by organization for each region

B) Country

SSC's are located by country processing data for each org. unit

C) Center of Excellence

Process Approach - Each process delivered from the best-in-class

D) Regional

Region 1   Region 2   Region 3

SSC processes in all BU's across a given geographical region. Regional can, of course, incorporate the Organizational, the Center of Excellence, and the Country models.

E) Global

A single SSC processes all BU across all locations. Although no one has yet successfully created a global shared service center, many are aspiring to do so.

Key

☆ Shared Service Center
◇ Old processing location/plant

22

DO NOT ALWAYS START WITH FINANCE

The concept of shared services can be applied to areas other than finance, although many companies use finance processes as the starting point of their shared service effort. Figure 1-6 shows the major areas of corporate support that are most appropriate for setting up shared services or incorporation in a business services unit, as well as the processes within those areas that are ripe for sharing services.

In addition to finance, areas companies look toward to incorporate in shared services are information technology, human resources, legal, and communications.

When thinking of shared services in an IT context, it is important to push the organization to create a truly partner-focused, service-oriented view. If an IT shared service organization is allowed to exist without strict partner-service requirements, it will end up looking like the old data processing departments that did not provide service effectively.

Some argue that IT is the natural place to implement shared services first, but many companies have had to break apart entrenched, centralized IT organizations in the past. The move to decentralize IT to the business units was often a long, hard battle. Because of this, many business unit executives are loath to give up control of IT. Some, however, have been very successful in doing so and moving to a shared-service IT model.

Creating IT shared services is made easier in an atmosphere in which a company has successfully installed an enterprise resource planning (ERP) software package, such as SAP, Baan, PeopleSoft, or Oracle, as discussed in detail in Chapter 6.

10 KEY QUESTIONS

Figure 1-7 shows the 10 questions most commonly asked about shared services, its potential, and how to go about undertaking the effort to develop a shared service business unit. By the time this book is completed, answers to all of these questions will have been provided, or at least the tools with which to answer them will have been discussed.

Figure 1-6 House of Shared Services

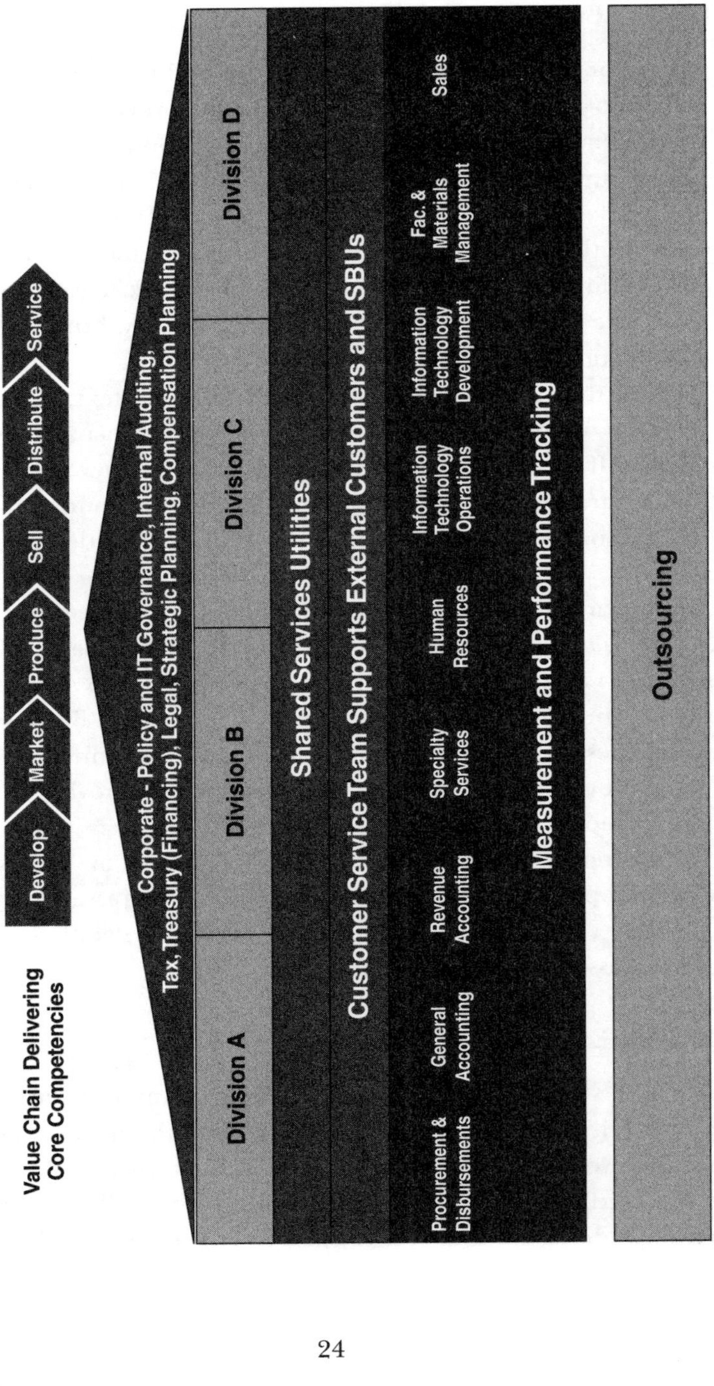

Figure 1-7 The Ten Most Challenging Questions about a Shared
Services Implementation

- How can Shared Services do it for less than what we do it for today?
- How many Shared Service centers should there be?
- Where should the Shared Service centers (SSCs) be located?
- What processes and activities should be included and what are the criteria for inclusion?
- How do we link Shared Services to our I.T. strategy?
- Should I consolidate business unit activities first or reengineer in-place?
- Should we migrate all processes for one business unit at once or implement by process/activity?
- How do we resource our implementation and what role should outside consultants play?
- How do we liquidate our costs equitably while encouraging the right behaviors?
- Where does it end and how do I keep people in the SSC motivated?

Think of the effort to create a shared service organization in your company as a "journey," rather than a project. Journey implies travel over time, adventure, and, to some degree, the necessity of flexibility in your schedule.

The larger your company, the greater the potential for significant savings and streamlining from shared services. However, the larger your company, and the more complex your company in terms of operating units, product lines, and global reach, the more challenging the journey to shared services will be.

ISSUES TO CONSIDER

☐ CEOs are searching for a way to allow strategic operations to grow more rapidly.

☐ Shared services enhances a corporate operation by allowing each business unit to focus on the strategic parts of its operations, putting more energy into performing strategic tasks while moving necessary but nonstrategic and noncore processes to the shared service business unit.

☐ Shared services takes all of those disparate activities and operations that have been seen by business unit executives as "back office" and secondary to the core business processes, and treats them as if they themselves are the core processes.

☐ The shared services operation should strive to be self-governed.

☐ The advent of the Euro will require a certain amount of transactional and system rationalization.

☐ This new relationship requires a new management responsibility, where business unit leadership no longer manages activities but rather a relationship with a business service partner.

2

What Is the Compelling Business Reason for Pursuing Shared Services?

- Customer demands
- Business partner demands
- Globalization
- Transactional efficiency
- Process effectiveness
- Consolidate activities
- Rationalize support activities
- Service to business unit partners
- Benefits outweigh costs
- Business units are partners with the SS operation
- Business unit partners help define service levels
- Career progression

The compelling reason for pursuing a shared service environment is simple: Customers and the business environment are demanding it. Global competition is forcing every company to be more competitive and adaptive.

Perhaps the best example can be seen in Europe, with the introduction of the single-market European Union (EU) and a single currency, the Euro. Companies are facing the specter of customers consolidating across countries and cherry picking their suppliers because supplier companies cannot unify their processes fast enough.

What exactly is meant by this? In the old, fragmented Europe, most businesses built, marketed, and sold on a national basis. A company built as many units in each country as it could, tailoring product variations to local preferences and creating products that could only be sold in that country.

Beginning in the 1980s, companies manufactured regionally for the European market but still marketed and sold locally. Today, consumers and business customers realize they no longer must shop locally and are scouring the continent for the best purchase price (including value-added tax [VAT] and currency differentials). With open trade throughout the EU, there are no longer tariffs on goods produced within the Union. With the advent of the single currency, currency differentials will fall by the wayside, but until tax rates are harmonized throughout the continent, customers will still be able to search for price.

In this new world, customer profitability analysis will have to have a wider focus. Companies must combine information from multiple business entities throughout the continent. Transactional efficiency and support process effectiveness are increasingly important in this environment.

In short, the environment cries out for consolidation of supporting activities and processes into shared service centers. Companies must create more unified systems and processes to gain a continent-wide, and indeed a global, customer view.

Enterprise resource planning (ERP) software affords an opportunity to do this from a technical perspective. However, companies must put in place process and organizational structures that enable them to respond globally to the global information they consolidate.

Shared services is a vehicle to accomplish this. It permits the concentration of focus necessary. It permits the reduction in costs that customers demand and facilitates support for companies' customer-facing units. Shared services not only produces the cost-saving efficiencies that customers are demanding, but it also provides the uniformity and focus needed to serve them effectively. Higher education, hospitals, and other not-for-profit corporations are also exploring shared services within their organizations.

STRATEGIC VISION

Corporate leaders must convey this new business imperative to their companies. The most important first step for the leaders of the various organizational groups in which a shared service environment is envisioned (chief financial officer [CFO], vice president of human resources, chief information officer [CIO], etc.) is to communicate this imperative to both their peers in the executive suite and to the organization they lead. These leaders and their functional organizations must boldly step into the future.

Lucent Technologies has taken this approach. Figure 2-1 shows the strategic architecture developed by Lucent's CFO. This strategic architecture envisions what the features should look like first, then identifies the steps to get there. Once the endpoint vision of becoming a "high-performance company" is engaged, the CFO can then lay out the transformation that will have to take place. Lucent describes this in terms of its CFO value proposition; how the organization wants to be

---

Figure 2-1   Strategy—For CFO to Power the Business

Take a Bold Stand - Create Strategic Intent and Conditions of Satisfaction
Drive Results, Not Just Activities
Assume Accountability for Making **_the_** Difference

"It is not just what we accomplished, but the context that we created"
Stages of the CFO Evolution

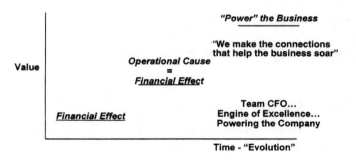

29

perceived; and which major functions it needs to alter. This is shown in Figure 2-2.

Finally, in order to make this happen, the office of the CFO itself will need to be "reinvented." Lucent's plan for this is shown in Figure 2-3.

FROM STRATEGY AND VISION TO BUSINESS CASE

The decision to pursue a shared service environment can be justified through the development of a business case. How to develop that business case will be discussed in detail in Chapters 8 through 13. In short, the business case should be developed around the following notions:

- Consolidation of activities, not centralization of functions
- Rationalization of lower-value-added activities in order to allow for:
  - Strategic business units (SBUs) to focus on customer-facing activities
  - Lower-value-added activities to receive the undivided attention of a dedicated management

Figure 2-2   Strategy: A Story of Transformation

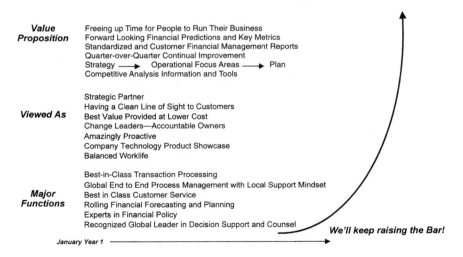

Figure 2-3 CFO Context—The CFO Reinvention

- Foundation - People/Assets/Technology
- Vision - Stand from the Future (Context)
  - Strategic Intent - Team CFO ... Engine of Excellence ... Powering the Company
  - Conditions of Satisfaction

- Creating a Results-Oriented Culture
  - Drive, Don't Walk
  - Accountability - Not Just Authority
  - Cross Organizational Team Engagement

- Our Organization - The CFO Model
  - Know the business, the industry, our competition, and the technology
  - Shared Service Model

Changing Context: The Most Critical Component

- Service to business unit partners
- Benefits that outweigh costs; rewards that outweigh risks

Conduct Shared Services "Like a Business"

In order to create a shared services operation, one must first get beyond the duality of centralization versus decentralization. For 30 years or more, business leaders debated the virtues of centralization—the corporate-office-down model—versus decentralization—the conglomerate model.

In order to run a shared service operation like a business, shared service management must have what is called an "it's a business" mindset, shown in Figure 2-4.

At Lucent, leaders gained the attention of the shared service managers and employees by using this "it's a business" mindset, getting them to focus on the fact that they are running a business that provides

31

Figure 2-4   "It's a Business" Mindset

- **It Is a Business - Run It Like A Business!**
  - Strategic Plan
  - Delivery Channel/Cycle Time
  - Product Plan & Offerings
  - Key Metrics
  - Continuous Benchmarking
- **Incredibly Awesome Partner Service**
- **On Time, At Cost, At Quality, Ahead of Competition**
- **Results Focused, NOT Activities**
- **Line of Sight to the Customer**
- **Driving the TOP Line**
- **Showcase of Company Products**
- **Focused on the Entire Value Chain**

a service. This helped to galvanize some of their entrepreneurial instincts and create a partner focus that did not exist before.

Only in the last few years, by stepping back and looking at what we call the "continuum of business improvement," have business leaders been able to see that the centralization versus decentralization debate is a false dichotomy.

Continuum of Business Improvement

The continuum of business improvement is the collection of strategies and tactics developed to enhance nonfinancial aspects of business that affect the bottom line, such as the following:

- Quality initiatives, including formal total quality management (TQM), determining cost of quality, quality circles, and a host of other techniques
- Process reengineering, redesign, and enhancement

- Just-in-time (JIT), lean plants, Kanbans, bottleneck/nonbottleneck determination, and constraint management
- Self-directed teams, worker involvement, job enrichment, and cross-training
- Customer focus through "voice of the customer" and other techniques
- Enterprise resource planning solutions and other information technology (IT) improvements such as electronic data interchange (EDI) and the Internet.[1]

This toolbox is constantly being added to with both new tools and refinements of these tools to meet the changing needs of businesses in a more global and increasingly competitive world.

Shared services is a concept that integrates many of these tools and puts them into a context of strengthening internal "back office" operations to enhance the ability of customer-facing SBUs to do more of what they do—produce, sell, and take care of their customers.

False Dichotomy

Why is centralization versus decentralization a false dichotomy? The business history of the last 30 years has shown that neither of these models—the totally hierarchical, top down, command and control centralization, as well as the free-for-all, local office or business unit decision making—work in an environment of global competition and instant communication/total information.

Companies decentralized because centralization led to a monolithic and insensitive corporate culture with little regard for customer needs. But decentralization led to the need to create duplicate infrastructures within each operating unit in order to conduct support functions and processes.

Over time, people realized that the ideal structure would be one in which some activities were concentrated (not centralized) and others were distributed (not decentralized). In order to do this, it became necessary to define which activities are appropriate for concentrating.

The way to do this is to define what activities áre unique to the business unit and strategic to the business unit's relationship with its customers, and what activities are common to all business units and nonstrategic. These common activities are the ones business unit leaders often consider non-value-added or low-value-added.

These common activities are ripe for consolidation into a shared service operation. They fall into two categories: high-volume transaction processing and specialized professional services. A powerful tactical weapon that allows the business to reach its strategic goals can be created by taking all of these nonstrategic activities and putting them into a "shared service house" (see Fig. 2-5).

Partnership and Service are the Key Differentiators

The key differentiators between a consolidated shared service environment and a centralized corporate staff environment are the notions of

Figure 2-5   House of Shared Services—Detailed View

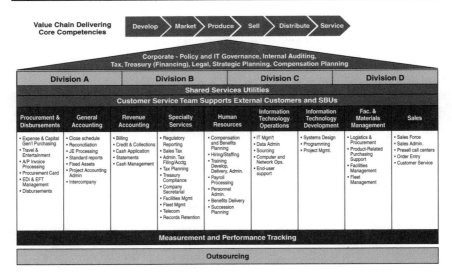

partnership and service. Business units are seen as partners to the shared service operation. It is a notion of doing things "for" and "with" the SBU, rather than doing things "to" it.

Business unit partners participate in defining the services required from the shared service operation and the service levels that are expected of it. Measures of service level are created and included in the business case.

With regard to external customers, business unit management is freed up from managing the time-consuming transactional chores and other activities they are not good at, and are allowed to focus their managerial attention on customer-facing activities integral to customer satisfaction and business unit success.

SHARED SERVICES BY ITSELF IS NOT STRATEGIC

When building the business case, it is important not to fall into the trap of trying to argue that shared services is strategic. Shared services is tactical. It is the consolidation and improvement in both the efficiency and effectiveness of nonstrategic activities. By consolidating and improving these activities, business unit and corporate managers can devote their full time and energy to strategic activities. In this way, the tactical operations of a shared service operation are a key factor in the company's being able to reach its strategic goals.

While shared services is not in and of itself strategic in nature, the creation of a tactical unit to perform shared services is a strategic decision and should be undertaken as a part of the company's overall strategic vision.

The business case consolidates all associated benefits and costs and projects a tangible, financial return. Note that in Figure 2-6 the proposed implementation becomes positive in terms of financial return some time in the second year.

While the benefits shown in Figure 2-6 are tangible and quantifiable, there are also some intangible, qualitative benefits that will accrue from a shared service operation. These mostly have to do with the workplace within this new shared service operating unit, which is run

Figure 2-6   The Business Case

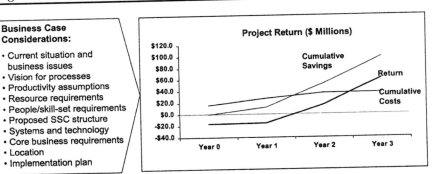

Business Case Considerations:

- Current situation and business issues
- Vision for processes
- Productivity assumptions
- Resource requirements
- People/skill-set requirements
- Proposed SSC structure
- Systems and technology
- Core business requirements
- Location
- Implementation plan

The business case will vary, but should be dependent upon and address management's vision and demonstrate significant improvement potential

as a stand-alone entity, as if it were a profit center. (It is important, in order not to artificially inflate business unit costs, that shared services be run as a "break-even" proposition, pricing its services to cover actual costs rather than to make a profit.)

Profits should not be kept in a support organization. The creation of profits for a support organization can skew the profitability of customer-facing business units, causing the management of these business units to make incorrect decisions. An example of this is the experience of a large telecommunications company that decided to set up its real estate subsidiary as a profit center. Attempts by the real estate subsidiary to generate profits put profits of the operating units that were its lessees under pressure. Business unit managers were required to cut costs. They did this by laying off sales staff (which reduced sales). At the same time, competitors were putting "feet on the street" by hiring these salespeople and gained market share at the company's expense.

The question of workplace atmosphere and career path within a shared service organization is also important. Some companies that have moved to a shared service environment report that those employed in shared services have a better perception of their work than they did when they were "support" within a business unit. They believe their work is valuable and that they are part of a larger corporate team. Many also appreciate the cross-training that goes on in order to enable them to handle many tasks—a necessity in a lean operation. In addition, there is better career progression; as individuals move up to management within the shared service operation, they acquire skills that can be transferred into management of a profit-making business unit.

The flip side of this is that in some shared service organizations, many employees have the feeling of being in limbo, having lost the close connection to a business they felt when they were working within a business unit. This emphasizes the need to make the connection between the work of the shared service unit and the business units explicit for all employees.

A number of major corporations are on the path to creating shared services. Pioneers include companies in many different industries who have markedly different strategies. Some of the earliest proponents of shared services are listed in Figure 2-7.

A FINAL WORD

Increasingly, a company's customers will be dealing with it as a global business. They will expect the company to provide its products at a reasonable cost, wherever in the world they purchase them. The pressures of the "business ecology" in which one works are myriad, as seen in Figure 2-8.

Shared services is a vehicle to reduce these costs by reducing the cycle time, cost, and error rate of high-volume, standard transactional and other activities formerly carried out by individual business units. It also provides a unified information base that allows a company to be more responsive to its customers.

Figure 2-7   Twenty Percent of *Fortune* 500 Companies Are Actively
Pursuing Shared Services

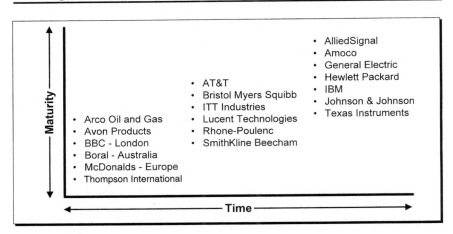

Typical savings from shared services implementations are in the 25–50% range.

Figure 2-8   Business Ecology

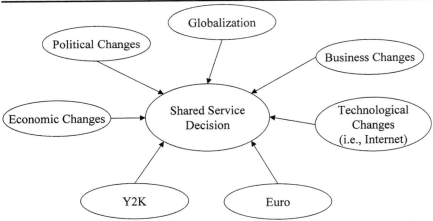

ISSUES TO CONSIDER

- ☐ Global competition is forcing companies to be competitive and adaptive in their relationships with their customers and business partners.
- ☐ Shared service organizations address and meet the emerging requirement from globalization: transactional efficiency and support process effectiveness.
- ☐ Activities that are appropriate for concentration into shared service centers can be identified by first deciding which activities are unique to the business unit and strategic to the business unit's relationship with its customers. The company can then identify activities that are common to all business units.
- ☐ Because business units are partners to the shared service operation, they participate in defining the service level required from the shared service operation, and the service levels that are expected of the shared service operation. Measures of service level are created and included in the business case.
- ☐ Shared service centers should be run as break-even propositions, and therefore will not skew profitability of customer-facing businesses, causing incorrect decision making.
- ☐ Positions at shared service organizations will provide better career progression for employees.

NOTE

1. These tools and techniques are all described in detail in other PricewaterhouseCoopers LLP books. An annotated bibliography appears in Appendix A.

3

Is Shared Services Right for You?

- **Do you need to minimize SG&A?**
- **Do you need to free up SBU management to focus on customer-facing activities?**
- **Do you need to create critical mass for support activities?**
- **Are you able to tie infrastructure together across SBUs?**
- **Are you able to provide management time and commitment?**
- **Are you able to address issues around responsibility?**

As stated earlier, a shared service environment accomplishes three important goals:

1. It minimizes sales, general and administrative (SG&A) costs by capitalizing on economies of scale, while improving service quality for common support activities.
2. It frees up divisional and strategic business unit (SBU) management resources and permits them to focus on customer-facing activities (selling, producing, after-sale servicing).
3. It provides a critical mass to the support activities that are consolidated, enabling them to receive attention in a more professional environment and to obtain more experienced management.

While these three advantages accrue, there are three major areas of potential hazard to the creation of a shared service operation. They are:

41

1. Infrastructure across SBUs must be tied together.
2. Migrating to a shared service environment takes management time and commitment and assumes a certain level of performance inherent in the activities as they exist today.
3. If there are issues around where accountability lies in certain processes, these arguments will become emotional barriers to the process.

If infrastructure cannot be tied together, or management cannot commit the time and effort, or there are too many conflicts regarding accountability of the processes that will be affected as activities are pulled out and placed in the shared service operation, then shared services is not for you.

However, if infrastructure can be tied together, and management is willing to put the time and effort into the migration process, and accountability is clear so that activities can be taken out of processes and consolidated, then shared services is right for you.

What exactly is meant by each of these three challenges?

TYING INFRASTRUCTURE TOGETHER

Tying the infrastructure together means that all SBUs must be working with the same, or a limited number of, common hardware, software, and programmatic platforms.

For instance, if some activities within human resources, such as benefit reporting, are to be put in shared services, then all the SBUs must use a common benefit package, or one of a few packages. If the shared service operation has to run a different benefit reporting system for each SBU, there is no gain in efficiency from moving to shared services.

In a similar way, if the accounts payable (A/P) system of each business unit is done on different hardware platforms with different software, there is less benefit to merging the activity. Benefits enhanced by the A/P systems are all put on a common information technology (IT) hardware/software platform, or one of a few platforms. In Europe especially, because of labor rate differentials, you can achieve significant benefit through physical consolidation first, then system consolidation.

If IT is moving to a shared service environment, each SBU cannot be using different software packages on different hardware. Before or during the migration into shared services, this must be rationalized.

Sometimes, a multitude of systems—either hardware, software, or work processes—have grown up over time, either through acquisition of businesses that then become SBUs or because of an era of complete decentralization, when all decision making was left to SBU executives. There are other times when the corporate strategy explicitly creates the opportunity for multiple systems to proliferate.

For instance, one client was looking to reduce general and administrative (G&A) expenses and considered shared services as a vehicle to accomplish this. The company had over 200 independent businesses that it managed in a portfolio manner. Although the business case suggested that there was a significant opportunity to save money, moving to shared services would have required that each business unit select from a few common systems and standardize their interfaces with the shared service center (e.g., general ledger systems and types of accounts). The company would have had to go from 50 or 60 different hardware and/or software platforms to no more than a handful of each.

The company was in a period of rationalization, looking to divest itself of businesses that did not meet its strategic goals. Moving to shared services would have meant significant investments of both management time and money in all 200 business units, including those that were on the sales block and could be sold at any time. In addition, restricting business unit management's choice of systems conflicted with the company's corporate strategy of allowing each business unit to operate completely autonomously.

The issue of infrastructure rationalization is especially difficult to deal with in global corporations, where different national organizations are sometimes wedded to their locally developed hardware, software, and work systems. See Chapter 4 for a detailed discussion.

Another important point is that moving to a shared service environment, rationalizing infrastructure, and transferring activities within processes to the shared service center creates an inability to explicitly identify all the resources that support a particular activity for a particular business unit.

For instance, Jack Johnson, who used to be in charge of accounts receivable (A/R) from distributors, and Doris Smith, who used to be in charge of A/R from retailers, have both been moved from your SBU to the shared service operation. They are now part of a team that does A/R work for all of the eight SBUs within the corporation. But Jack and Doris no longer work on "your" accounts, because the shared service group has been organized in a different way. Jack now does A/R for all the SBUs from California accounts, and Doris has Canadian A/R for all the SBUs.

You no longer have the ability to identify exactly who "works for you"; instead, you now have a "partner service rep" at the shared service organization who is your "go-to guy" when you need information or assistance.

MIGRATING TO SHARED SERVICES

Since the 1980s, companies have been working hard at increasing productivity, reducing cost, and improving management of SG&A. A shared service operation has become an exciting and logical next step in this process.

However, making the jump to shared services assumes that those corporations have done other things first. We have created a "hierarchy of operations and process improvement" that allows you to determine whether you are ready to attempt a shared service implementation. There are three levels to this hierarchy; each level contains three items that must be fulfilled in order to move to the next level.

These levels are:

1. *Responsibilities.* Within this level are:
   - Governance, that is, the creation of strategies and goals.
   - Accountability, that is, the clear definition of who is responsible for delivery of what product. This is more than revenue targets.
   - Measures, that is, measures to create accountability.

Only when these building blocks are in place can one move to driving process improvement through the second level of the hierarchy.

2. *Efficiency.* Efficiency gains are achieved through three areas:
   ○ Processes
   ○ Systems
   ○ Economies of scale

To achieve these efficiency gains, companies delve into process reengineering, process redesign, and/or process enhancement. They also look at upgrading, rationalizing and improving their hardware and software systems, possibly moving to an enterprise resource planning (ERP) system. Finally, they look at ways to reduce headcount. Both responsibilities and efficiencies are preconditions to moving to the third and final level of the hierarchy of improvement.

3. *Effectiveness.* Within effectiveness are three areas:
   ○ Skills
   ○ Service delivery
   ○ Organization

To move up this hierarchy takes management that is dedicated and willing to spend the time and the human and financial resources that are necessary to do the job in an orderly manner.

Shared services has within it many efficiency elements; done well, it takes an organization into the realm of effectiveness. In Chapters 5 and 6 we will take up the "chicken or egg" type of questions that are invariably asked when discussing the relationship between shared services and IT improvements, and between shared services and reengineering. Both IT improvement and reengineering also propel a company into the effectiveness domain. After this package of initiatives—IT improvement, reengineering/redesign, and shared services—is successfully completed, in whatever order, a company has reached a very high level of both efficiency and effectiveness.

Although it would appear from the way we have constructed our hierarchy—efficiency before effectiveness—that both IT and reengineering would be a necessary precondition to shared services, as shown in the discussion in Chapters 5 and 6, depending on the individual company's circumstances, attempts to increase efficiency and effectiveness can be done simultaneously or sequentially, flipping repeatedly between gains in one and gains in the other.

In addition, there are some companies that are simply not ready, willing, or able to move into either gains in efficiency or effectiveness. These companies are:

- Small and/or fast growing, where all attention is focused on growth or sustaining the business.
- In an industry that is rapidly consolidating, where the company may be bought or may be buying others at any time.
- Very entrepreneurial, where in order to sustain the business it must constantly be focusing on the organizational rules of governance, accountability, and measures.

CLEAR ACCOUNTABILITY OF PROCESS ACTIVITIES

One of the most difficult tasks of moving to the shared service environment is determining accountability for process activities and determining which activities should appropriately be moved into the shared service environment.

All business activities fall within one of three categories:

1. *Policy.* Policies are corporate level activities. They deal with strategy and governance, and rightly belong to the "central" corporate headquarters.

2. *Customer/product.* There are many activities that fall within the processes where SBUs or divisions deal directly with customers. In addition, activities such as product development and manufacturing need to stay within the SBU from which the product emanates.

3. *Support services.* These provide support for SBUs in their dealings with customers, vendors, or internal operations.

Processes that are candidates to be consolidated into a shared service operation are either customer facing or support service. Deciding which activity from these processes belongs where is crucial. Figure 3-1 shows this graphically. This will be discussed in detail in Chapter 8.

SBU management needs to become comfortable with the concept that losing the activity does not mean losing control. If taking away the activity removes accountability from the SBU, there is an issue that must be addressed clearly and early on.

People are measured by performance. People often feel that if there are activities that are physically out of their purview, they are out of their control. If at the same time they are being held accountable for performance of those activities, the loss of control—real or perceived—is threatening.

In strong SBU corporate cultures, SBU management is accustomed to nearly total control, and comfortable with the complete accountability that comes with that. Because they have complete

Figure 3-1   For Each Process, Identify Where Activities Will Be Performed

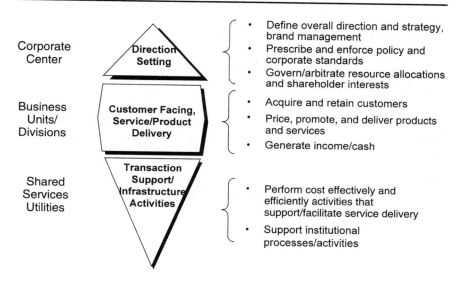

control, they can easily be measured on the performance of an identifiable group of people. A shared service operation by necessity "dethrones the SBU kings" by moving some activities that had previously been within their span of control into the shared service operation.

This plays itself out especially clearly in companies like a $2 billion plus chemical company. The company has long worked on a country operation basis. Each country SBU has an executive whose job it is to run the company's business however he or she sees fit, from customer to product. He or she can build plants to manufacture individual products or product groups for customers within the company's country.

The company has for some time been trying to reorganize to a more regional model, in order to rationalize production facilities and cut attendant costs. Shared services is a critical tactical ploy in this company's reorganization. By taking away important support activities, the company is able to loosen country executives' stranglehold on the SBUs.

Pass-Through Accountability

The question remains, however: If the activity is passed to the shared service organization, how does the SBU executive maintain a willingness to take on accountability despite having given up day-to-day control to the shared service organization? The answer is by developing a sense of partnership and comfort with each other.

This is done through negotiating exactly what activities within which processes will be passed to the shared service organization, and then negotiating a service-level agreement, which essentially says that XYZ services (support activities, transaction processing, etc.) will be carried out for ABC cost. The parts of a service level agreement and the negotiations involved in creating a service level agreement are discussed in detail in Chapter 12.

In this way, the SBU leadership knows what the cost will be ahead of time. He or she no longer has to "manage" these support costs; the shared service management is doing it.

IN THE FINAL ANALYSIS

Timing, approach, and planning are critical to success in developing a shared service organization. Every solution will be unique according to the company's conditions and the business environment in which it operates. The only generalization that can be made is that properly undertaken, shared services can provide huge advantages for those who are ready and able to enter into this realm.

ISSUES TO CONSIDER

☐ Shared services may be right for you if you have the following three goals:
   1. Minimize SG&A.
   2. Free up SBU management to focus on customer-facing activities.
   3. Desire to provide critical mass for support activities, enabling them to receive attention from a more professional and experienced management.

☐ However, for shared services to address the above concerns, you must avoid potential hazards by:
   1. Tying infrastructure together across SBUs. All SBUs must be working with the same, or a limited number of, common platforms, unless significant cost-reduction exists through work relocation.
   2. Defining management time and commitment:
      Responsibility (governance, accountability, measures)
      Efficiency (processes, systems, economies of scale)
      Effectiveness (skills, service delivery, organization)
   3. Understanding issues around responsibility:
      Determine which activities should appropriately be moved into the shared services environment.
      Losing the activity does not mean losing accountability for SBU managers.
      Negotiating exactly what activities within each process will be passed to the shared service organization and then negotiating a service level agreement.

4

International Challenges

- **Cultural boundaries**
- **Complexity**
- **Infrastructure**
- **Time zones**
- **Legal issues**
- **Government**
- **Stability**
- **Security**
- **Weather**
- **Currency**

There is a popular European joke: In heaven, the French cook, the Italians are lovers, the Germans are the police, and the British are the managers. In hell, the British cook, the Germans are lovers, the French are the police, and the Italians are the managers.

Of course, this is a stereotype, but it points out a serious lesson. There are *real differences* in the way people see the world and the way organizational cultures work in different countries, regions, and even in different regions or cities within a country.

The decision to create a global shared service organization must be made after careful consideration of a host of complications that arise when trying to lump common business activities across often disparate national business cultures. Taking into consideration where a company does the majority of its business in a particular region and balancing that with the realities of business climate are necessary in undertaking a cross-border shared service operation. You probably will not find heaven, but if you work at it, you will not be stuck in hell either.

It is important to understand in conceptual terms the challenges faced by any attempt to share services globally before one can discuss the ins and outs of just exactly where to locate. Figure 4-1 shows what might be called the business ecology within which the global corporation finds itself when making decisions about locating regional shared service operations.

While communications and information technology (IT) are globalizing business, and political and even monetary boundaries are falling, cultural boundaries continue to exist. Even among the 11 countries that will soon give up their national currencies and transact business using the Euro, they will continue to abide by vastly different business practices. These countries will continue to compete, as all countries do, rarely sharing common interests.

The decision making is especially hard for companies that have a small business presence in many disparate countries. When there is a

Figure 4-1 International Business Ecology

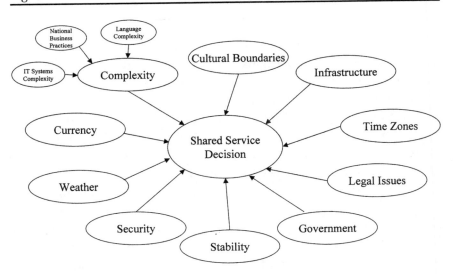

critical mass of personnel or business in one country, there is a natural tendency to use that country as a "hub" of operations; but when there is little presence in many countries, there is no natural point of regional leadership.

Business practices that are common in some countries, such as holding all accounts payable at the end of the year, are anathema in others. In some cultures, the handling of cash is a sensitivity. Some countries' business practice is to pay against an invoice, whereas others pay against a statement. Start times and end times of the workday vary, as does the timing and length of the lunch "hour." In predominantly Moslem countries, the "weekend" is from noon Thursday through Saturday morning, and in Israel the weekend runs from Friday at about 2:00 P.M. until Sunday morning.

Reconciling the national and religious holidays in each country being consolidated into a regional service center calls for some juggling when determining when transactions will occur.

Despite seeming political and even military closeness today, the legacy of the two world wars fought in the 20th century are real and cannot be ignored, both in Europe and in Asia. Certain cultures mesh well and others do not. Cultures vary in terms of work ethic, education, and the ability to behave and work cross-culturally.

Even in the United States, cultures vary greatly, for instance, among Texas, California, and New York. It is interesting to note that the three "hottest" areas in America during the 1990s for creating shared service centers are the Research Triangle area of North Carolina; Nashville, Tennessee; and Phoenix, Arizona. All three of these areas have seen enormous population growth since the early 1980s, with individuals from all over the country, thus creating a "national" population instead of one that is wedded to the cultural norms and historic business practices of these regions.

COMPLEXITY

There are three major challenges of complexity a company must overcome when organizing a global shared service operation:

1. National business practices
2. Language complexity
3. IT systems complexity

National Business Practices

Some national business practices are legislatively driven. For instance, Italy still requires paper records for every transaction. Every transaction must be recorded in a hard-copy general ledger, which must be examined and stamped by a tax examiner.

Other national business practices are driven by simple custom and past practice. For instance, Germans are still resistant to using credit cards, as are Japanese. It was noted by television commentators during the 1998 Winter Olympics that businesses in Nagano, Japan, had been scurrying for weeks to have extra telephone lines put in so they could handle credit card approvals for the thousands of foreigners who would be using credit cards.

Some business practices are driven by industries despite national preference. For instance, the automotive industry was into the electronic data interchange (EDI) game early on and forced subsidiaries and suppliers to use EDI even in countries where the practice would normally be shunned.

Finally, there are national business practices that are driven by the tax and legal structure. For a host of reasons such as value-added tax (VAT) rates, taxation of branch offices, and the complexity of managing contracts through branches, throughout Europe the practice is not for companies to sell directly across country lines, but rather to sell through in-country representatives. There are also unique situations in the way payroll is handled in different countries. These all add immensely to complexity.

The Euro. The advent of the Euro in 1999 and the potential that all of Western Europe will join the European Monetary Union (EMU) and use the Euro within 10 years opens the door to enormous shared service opportunities. Among them are the following:

- Companies will be able to access larger capital markets.
- A singular Euro-zone will eliminate currency risk and provide price transparency.
- Financial instruments will be quotable and tradeable across borders without currency risk.
- Access to new markets and new investors will broaden products.
- Efficiencies in operations will result in reduced costs and higher margins.

In short, the millions of people hours that are devoted annually to foreign exchange transactions will now be free for other, more productive work. The Euro will provide a strategic business opportunity for companies to increase market share, gain competitive advantage, and introduce new products in one of the world's largest economic regions. Companies will gain an advantage if they are ahead of their competitors in being Euro compliant; have customer support facilities to provide Euro-based information; and can manage the requirements of conversion and adapt to changes for customers and suppliers.

To date, 11 countries have agreed to join the first wave of Euro adoption. Three member countries of the European Union (EU) that were elegible decided not to join immediately. In addition, at the start of 1999, there were three countries whose applications for EU admission were pending and another 10 countries who have the potential to become EU members in the early part of the 21st century. If all of these countries were to gain admission and join the EMU over time, by the second quarter of the twenty-first century, there could be as many as 27 countries in Western and Central Europe using the Euro.

However, for at least the first few years of Euro, there will be many decisions to be made and much confusion. Any European regional shared service operation will face a number of questions, such as:

- What is the base currency of operation?
- What currencies are paid out?
- What banking relationships support the shared service operation's payment and receipt structure?

Early in the transition, most of these companies are continuing and will continue to compute their transactions both in local currency and in Euros, unless customers specifically ask to be billed in Euros or suppliers specifically ask to be paid in Euros. This is actually causing more processing work per transaction. Over time, local currency billing will end.

What makes the Euro such a powerful transformation is the sheer size of the market that will be covered by one currency when the transition is complete sometime in the first decade of the 21st century. By creating the EMU, the countries that have banded together instantaneously created the world's largest economic force. At the start of 1999, the EMU's share of world trade was estimated at 20.9 percent, while the United States' share was estimated at 19.6 percent. It is estimated that at the end of the EMU transition, the EMU will be twice the size of the United States in terms of percentage of world trade.

A certain amount of transactional and systems rationalization needs to be accomplished by both European-based corporations and others with large European operations during this transition to full monetary union. It is the ideal time to move to both a shared service method of operation and an enterprise resource planning (ERP) software environment. Many of the costs—financial and organizational— are already being incurred in order to position the company for monetary union.

Language Complexity

What is the language of business? That depends. In order to be truly pan-European, a shared service center needs personnel able to speak, at a minimum, three languages among French, German, Spanish, Italian, and English. Increasingly, knowing an Eastern European language or two is also helpful. (The need for Scandinavian language proficiency is less important because those countries have essentially adopted English as their language of business.) Some European-based global businesses, such as the Swedish/Swiss company ABB Asea Brown Boveri Ltd. (ABB), have done the same, declaring English the company's official language around the world.

In South America, there is a battle for language supremacy. While the entire continent save Brazil speaks Spanish, Brazil is the largest economy, followed by Argentina. The Brazilians are very proud of their heritage as a Portuguese-speaking country. Personnel in any pan-South American service center must speak both languages fluently.

In India, there are hundreds of local dialects, and there is currently a political debate about what the country's official language should be. Some believe it should be English, specifically because it is becoming the language of global business and India wishes to join the ranks of the fully developed global economy. Others believe English remains the "language of the colonial oppressors" and that the country's official language should be Hindi.

Even among those from English-speaking countries, there is some language complexity. Do you put your bags in the boot of the car or the trunk? Is the head of finance in your company the finance director (FD) or the chief financial officer (CFO)? Who takes care of your employees, the personnel office or human resources?

IT Systems Complexity

Chances are that if you visit the country business units of a global company, you will find dozens of different computer hardware platforms being used. For many years, it has been a point of pride to purchase IT equipment from a company based in one's home country. So you will find Nixdorf/Siemens equipment being used by German business units, Olivetti in Italy, Bull/Honeywell in France, and ICL PLC (ICL) in England. In many instances, the software used with these machines was custom written, and communication among the various national business unit's computers was next to impossible.

As software products become global and non-hardware-platform specific, especially those that offer ERP solutions, the opportunities for shared services in IT explode. Such companies as Systemanalyse Und Programmentwicklung AG (SAP), Baan, Oracle, and PeopleSoft have spent millions of dollars on research and development (R&D), creating software that links these disparate platforms and translates into a coherent, unified record-keeping infrastructure.

However, because hardware choice has, over time, been very nationalistic in many countries, there is still the need to force some business units in a global company to drop their present IT hardware infrastructure in order to move to a shared service environment where there are no more than a handful of hardware platforms. (See Chapter 6 for a more detailed discussion.)

Other Infrastructure Issues

When looking to create regional shared services, it is also important to consider a host of other infrastructure issues, such as banking, communications, utilities, roads, and airports. This is not only important in the question of where to locate the regional shared service center, but in the entire question of whether it is possible to link some offices to that shared service center.

In some regions of the world, the telecommunications infrastructure is still not sophisticated. It is possible to get around this for voice transmission by using cell phones (an increasing phenomenon in many countries). It is projected that by 2000, one in every six people around the world will own a cell phone. However, this still does not solve many business problems. For example, without high-speed data lines, it is impossible to implement electronic funds transfer (EFT). In addition, businesses cannot transfer information electronically, and daily records would have to be flown to the shared service center to be processed.

TIME ZONES

Time zones are another issue global businesses must deal with. For instance, a single American shared service center would have to deal with five hours of time difference, from the East Coast to Hawaii or Alaska. A pan-European center would have to deal with a three-hour difference, from Ireland or the United Kingdom to Ankara, Moscow, or Tel Aviv (there is not much business east of Moscow that is still in Europe). An Asian center would have to deal with a five-hour time difference, from Calcutta to Brisbane.

This means having to run customer support help lines, technology support, and other operations for at least 12 to 14 hours a day. Other operations, such as disaster recovery, must be 24-hour-a-day operations.

To add to the natural time differences, some countries go onto Daylight Savings Time in the summer, while some do not. And then there are the savings time quirks.

○ Portugal, for instance, moves the clocks forward one-half hour for the summer.

○ The United States goes to Daylight Savings Time the first weekend of April, while Europe begins the last weekend in March.

○ In Israel, the religious parties are pushing for a floating end to Daylight Savings Time, having it end the week before the High Holy Days, so the Yom Kippur fast day will end one hour earlier. (It would float, because the Jewish calendar on which the holy days are calculated is a lunar calendar.)

To add yet another layer of complexity to time, it can be said without too much exaggeration that "every day there is a holiday somewhere in the world." Then there is the weekend issue. Determining when information transfers, payments, invoices, and other material *should not* be sent to one country or another is a complicated task. Working this out for critical payments such as employee travel and expense can be especially difficult.

Time differences can sometimes be advantageous. Many companies—most notably, global pharmaceutical companies, automotive companies, and telecommunications equipment companies—have created 24-hour R&D operations by having teams in Asia, Europe, and the United States working on the same problem. At the close of business in one region of the world, the team literally hands its work off to the next team to continue in a "westward" fashion—Asia to Europe to the United States to Asia.

It is possible also to move work eastward. U.S. airlines in the early 1990s began to use workers in Ireland to perform billing tasks. Sales records would be put on the overnight flights from New York to Ireland, arrive "the next morning," be processed in Ireland, and sent electronically back to New York by the beginning of the business day. This got millions of dollars of billings posted "a day early" from a New York point of view—a big advantage.

LEGAL ISSUES

Businesses that operate in many countries already know that global operations create a legal minefield. There are literally hundreds of legal requirements, many of them seemingly nitpicky. For instance:

- In Italy, payments of over 20 million lira (not much more than $10,000) must be logged and reported to the authorities.
- In France, certain professional fees require that income tax be deducted and remitted at the source (withheld and paid by the party hiring the service).
- In the United States, there are 50 different state sales tax rates, running from 0 to 9 percent. In addition, some counties and/or cities impose an additional sales tax. Some cities or counties do not levy a general sales tax but do have food and lodging taxes.

Other legal issues include the following:

- Electronic direct deposit payments. In some countries, such as the United Kingdom, it is illegal to force either vendors or employees to receive payment electronically; they must agree to it.
- European countries especially often have complicated data protection laws. When making cross-border data transfers, it is important that they not violate the laws of either country.

Of course, the largest issue for companies looking to consolidate support activities are the laws surrounding employees whose positions are eliminated in the consolidation. This gets a company involved in the entire gamut of European labor laws, including unions, work councils, redundancy payments, worker representation on boards, and the issue of whether to relocate workers across national borders to the shared service center or recruit locally. Many times, a location is chosen specifically because there is an educated labor pool willing and able to work in less restrictive conditions for lower total compensation (wages, health benefits, and labor-related taxes).

The bottom line is that transparency is the key to handling legal issues. It is always better to ask and argue the case for why you would like to do something and why you believe it fits the spirit of the law than to just do it, then argue after the fact. For instance:

- Is it "legal" to maintain books and records for a German operation outside of Germany in a shared service center, closely linked to the German operation by modern communications?
- What exactly is a general ledger? Does it have to be paper? Is it the magnetic tape that holds the information? Is it the general ledger software?

GOVERNMENT

Issues of government will be discussed in much more detail when the specifics of how to choose a location for a shared service operation are examined in Chapter 10. For now, it is important to say that government issues include not only legislation, but regulation and taxation.

Some countries offer investment incentives for companies to build, for worker training, or for general support. A number of countries are creating incentives in an attempt to become home to the "Silicon Valley of Europe."

Some countries offer different grants in an effort to get companies to locate in particular parts of the country. The Welsh Development Authority is an example of this, as well as Ireland's incentives for companies to move to the West (including continued expansion of Shannon Airport and the road infrastructure to the airport).

Other countries offer tax holidays. One of Ireland's largest draws as a location for shared services is the country's 10-year, 10-percent-a-year corporate tax rate for new investments.

Payroll costs, including the tax treatment of benefits, as well as reporting requirements, are also large issues. For example, there is a lower rate of social security tax in the Mezzo-Giorno region than in the rest of Italy.

STABILITY AND SECURITY

Political stability and personal security are always issues when businesses locate any operation in a country without a strong and long democratic and capitalist tradition. Following the wave of independence of African, Asian, and Middle Eastern countries from European colonial holders that has occurred since the end of World War II, there have been instances of corporate operations, whole companies, and indeed entire industries that are being nationalized.

Business conditions can change very quickly in such countries. In the 1960s, Beirut was known as "The Paris of the Middle East," but by the 1970s, it was engulfed in a civil war from which it has not completely recovered. Only a decade after hosting a Winter Olympic Games event, Sarajevo became a city in which no global company wanted to risk doing business. Today, companies are unwilling to locate in Lima or Bogota despite their reputation 20 years ago as hospitable to business. This is not just a matter of potentially being mugged outside one's office; there is the possibility of being caught up in a war—official or unofficial.

When looking to consolidate regional support operations, it is important to look beyond the possibility of war and government failure. Security of the banking, telecommunications, and roadway systems is important. Also, weather and a propensity for natural disaster are not to be taken lightly.

The irony is that as the security and stability of a country's systems increases, so do the general business costs. However, there is usually a period of time during which the country is moving from a less stable environment to a more stable one—a period when a country is "emerging," when it is ripe for attracting shared service operations. Education levels are rising, but wage levels are still relatively low by the standards of industrialized countries. Spain would have been such a country in the first 10 to 15 years after the death of Francisco Franco in the mid-1970s, but shared services was not a viable concept until the late 1980s.

A similar set of circumstances can be found in countries or regions where young people are willing to put up with lower wages and less "opportunity" in order to take advantage of "quality of life" or remain close to family. This is true of such places as Ireland and the eastern provinces of Canada (Newfoundland, Nova Scotia, and Prince Edward Island).

CURRENCY

Currencies are as diverse and varied as languages. Until the late 1980s, currency differences made it nearly impossible to consolidate support activities across countries.

IT software that is hardware–platform independent and can calculate in numerous currencies (ERP software) is one piece to enabling shared services to become a reality. Another piece is banking that is becoming more global. Ironically, although there are no "pan-American" banks, it is American banks such as Bank America and Citibank that are leading the way in becoming truly global players.

On the opposite end of the currency spectrum from the strict inflation guidelines set for admission into the EMU Union are countries where there is hyperinflation. Hyperinflation in such countries as Brazil and Russia forces individuals and companies to pay in cash and to change their entire decision-making process to one based on the instability of the currency over the long, medium, and short term.

IN CLOSING

Setting up a shared service operation on a global basis is much more difficult than it is to set one up on a U.S.-only basis. Although no company has yet been successful in creating a completely global shared service organization, it is still a worthy goal.

The complexities are different in different regions. For instance, in Latin America, many of the complexities center around critical mass: Is there really enough business, and enough of a workforce, in any one place to set up a shared service center? In Asia, the issue of critical mass is magnified by the sheer size of the region, the language differences, and the differences in business practices among countries. In the United States, the complexities revolve around political and cultural issues and how those affect the potential workforce. In Europe, complexities abound because of the multinational and multicultural nature of the region.

These complexities will be discussed in more detail in Chapter 10, when the particular decision making involved in locating a shared service operation is examined.

ISSUES TO CONSIDER

☐ There are considerable differences in the way people see the world and the way organizational cultures work in different countries, regions, and even in different regions or cities within a country.

☐ The reason to consider these issues is not only to decide where to locate regional shared service centers, but rather whether it is or will be possible to link some/SBU offices to those centers.

☐ Issues:

Cultural boundaries

Three challenges of complexity

1. National business practices
   Drivers: legislation, customs and traditions, best practices, industry, tax, legal structure
2. Language complexity
   The language of business depends on where you are and with whom you are dealing
3. IT systems complexity
   Long-term point of pride to purchase IT equipment from a company based in one's home country
   Other infrastructure issues (banking, communications, utilities, roads, and airports)

Time zones
Legal issues
Country/state specific
Government
Stability and security
Currency

All of these issues can be mitigated by:

1. IT software that is hardware–platform independent and can calculate in numerous currencies
2. Global banking
3. Breaking down of currency exchange controls

Part Two

Assess

In this part the assumption is made that an executive has decided to pursue shared services. In Chapters 5 through 7, we discuss how tightly intertwined shared services is with two other major business improvement schools of the last decade—process improvement through business process reengineering (BPR) or process redesign; and information technology (IT) improvement through the implementation of enterprise resource planning (ERP) software.

Some companies contemplating moving to shared services for noncore supporting processes are already in the midst of BPR or ERP efforts, while many others are not. Some companies are already pursuing both BPR and ERP.

The question of which effort to pursue first is a tricky one. In some instances, pursuit of shared services "forces" a BPR or ERP effort to be undertaken in order for the shared service effort to be successful. In other instances, executives realize that for a company to really achieve all the possible "bang" from a BPR or ERP effort, it must be complemented with shared services. In Chapters 5 and 6, these three intertwined issues are gently pulled apart, and some hints are given about when and under what circumstances each should drive the others.

In Chapter 7, a simple question is asked: If my company is going to consolidate support processes, why should I spend the time and money to create a new shared service business unit when there are already companies out there who perform these services on an outsource basis, possibly cheaper than my company ever will?

This question is logical, but for many companies it is probably advantageous to pursue the "insourcing" of shared services for a host of reasons that are unrelated to cost.

5

Shared Services and Its Relationship with Process Reengineering and Redesign

- Process reengineering/redesign is usually a requirement
- Will reengineering be worthwhile
- Pick "low-hanging fruit"
- Pick up incremental improvement
- When to reengineer prior to fully implementing shared services
- When to reengineer after implementing shared services
- Corporate culture issues
- New human resource structure
- Additional reengineering opportunities upstream and downstream
- When to hire new staff/utilize existing staff

Companies undertaking the creation of a shared service organization always confront the issue of the relationship between shared services and process reengineering/process redesign. Although *process reengineering* is *not a requirement* of engaging in shared services, *process redesign* is a requirement at some point in the journey to a fully operational shared service organization. The reason for this lies in the fact that shared services is involved with activities within processes, although it may not be involved with the entire end-to-end process.

Once processes are broken down to the activity level and some activities within particular processes are consolidated from business units to shared service operations, the shared service personnel become major champions of the process. This is because in order for them to carry out their mission of efficiency and effectiveness of the portion of the process they control, the entire process must be as efficient and effective as possible.

Companies must engage in process reengineering in order to improve an entire core business process, from where it touches the customer back upstream to its headwater. Companies have opportunities to redesign processes that are not core or redesign portions of processes, such as the activities within the support processes that will be collected in a shared service operation.

In short, reengineering can play a key enabling role in moving to a shared service method of operation. Whereas some process areas can be consolidated immediately and then reengineered, others can often benefit from reengineering prior to consolidation. Figure 5-1 shows this.

Figure 5-1   When to Reengineer, When to Consolidate, and When to Do Both

	• Input Mobility	• Economies of Scale/Critic
	• Input Quality	• Service Levels
	• Interdependencies	• Standardization
	• Technology	• Strategic Importance

	High	"Consolidate as Appropriate"	"The Consolidatables"
"Ability" to Consolidate		• Fixed Assets • Local Tax Reporting	• COD - Check Sorting • AP - Contracts, Direct Shipment • IS - Help Desk • Fleet Administration
		"Reengineer Only"	"Reengineer, Then Consolidate"
	Low	• AP - Claims Audit • Payroll - Time & Attendance • IS - Hardware Support	• GA - Closing and Reporting • AP - Local purchase, exp. accounts • Collections

Low   "Need" for Consolidation   High

The key is to time the two change efforts correctly so that they complement each other, not detract from one another.

BASIC DEFINITIONS

A simple set of definitions is necessary to understand the difference between reengineering, redesign, and shared services.

Shared services is:

> The concentration of company resources performing like activities, typically spread across the organization, in order to service multiple internal partners at lower cost and with higher service levels, with the common goal of delighting external customers and enhancing corporate value.

Process reengineering is:

> Fundamental analysis and radical redesigning of business practices and management systems, job definitions, organizational systems, and beliefs and behaviors in order to achieve dramatic performance improvement.

Process redesign is:

> Changing strategic value-added business processes and the systems, policies, and organizational structures that support them, in order to optimize productivity and the flow of work.

A key driver in both shared services and process reengineering or redesign is the need to improve the company's financial performance by improving operational performance. It is a realization that "the numbers" do not magically appear, and that long-term financial gains can occur only when a company delivers increasing customer value while simultaneously lowering the cost of delivering that value.

Shared services and process redesign or reengineering all aim at four things simultaneously: a reduction in process costs and time and a simultaneous improvement in quality and customer service. This is what is called the *value equation.*

$$\text{Value} = (\text{quality} \times \text{service}) / (\text{cost} \times \text{time})$$

where

quality × service = effectiveness, and cost × time = efficiency.

In addition, this must all take place in a context of alignment to the company's vision and strategy.

ASSESSING WHETHER TO REENGINEER

The processes involved in supporting core business processes—the activities of which are at the heart of a shared service effort—are processes that have usually been overlooked in the last decade as companies have undergone business process reengineering (BPR). Because of this, it is tempting when starting a shared service operation to get caught up in thinking about how to reengineer these processes.

When you are looking to build shared services, you need to realize that the activities that will be incorporated into the shared service operation probably touch on only a small piece of a particular process—say, payment processing as a part of the entire purchase-to-pay process. The temptation may be to fix the entire purchase-to-pay process, but the opportunities to improve the process are probably upstream (the way the company purchases), and not in the activity that is going to be in the shared service center (payment of bills).

Figure 5-2 shows in which corporate function different activities within particular processes reside. From this, one can get an idea of which activities might be candidates to move into a shared service operation, and which must be maintained within strategic business unit operations.

Before you dive into reengineering, you need to ask two questions to determine whether the effort will be worthwhile.

First, has the process been part of a previous reengineering effort?

Figure 5-2   Residence of Activities within Corporate Functions

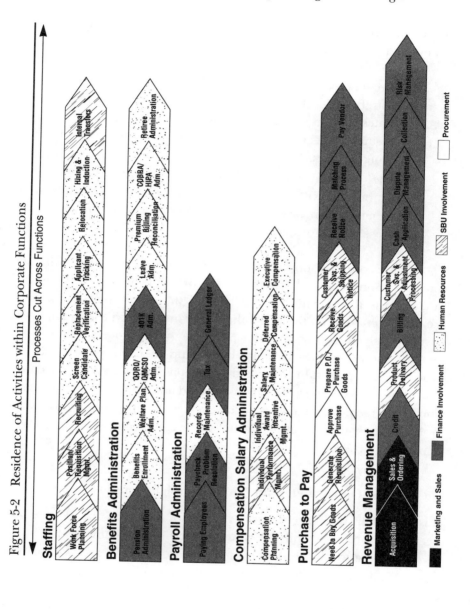

There are two reasons why support processes would have already been reengineered.

1. The company has been under huge pressure to increase shareholder value, either by reducing cost or increasing revenues, so that reengineering was conducted not only on core business processes but also on support processes in order to wring out costs.

2. The company has already installed an enterprise resource planning (ERP) software solution. ERP software forces you to reengineer in order to match your process definitions with those of the software.

The second question is whether the reengineering effort will pay for itself in one year or less. Most of the time, the answer is that it will not, because the activities that will fall in the shared service purview are not far enough up the value chain. For instance, in the example of payment activities as part of the purchase-to-pay process, the shared services operation must be created first and then the portion of the process encompassed by those activities reengineered. At a later date, after those activities have been consolidated and efficiencies have been won, it may be possible to work with purchasing departments upstream in the business units or at the corporate level to reengineer the entire purchasing process.

Do Not Miss Opportunities for Quick Redesign Victories

It is important to realize that even if the company has already reengineered the process within which the shared service activities lie, or if reengineering would not pay for itself, there are valid reasons for redesigning the piece of the process that the shared services activities encompass.

In the course of moving to a shared service environment, one may find hugely inefficient processing and moving activities, which would be expensive to maintain in the shared services center. In this case, take the opportunity to pick this "low-hanging fruit" and do some rapid redesign before moving to the shared service environment.

In other words, do not miss opportunities to pick up incremental improvement through process redesign prior to moving a particular set of activities into the shared service environment or immediately after setting up the shared service organization. However, do not put aside the real work of going to a shared service environment in order to engage in deep and difficult reengineering.

ASSESSING WHETHER REENGINEERING SHOULD BE DONE BEFORE OR AFTER MOVING TO SHARED SERVICES

There are some valid reasons for engaging in a more all-encompassing reengineering effort, either preceding or following the implementation of a shared service operation.

If there are significant benefits to be gained from reengineering, but not specifically for the shared service effort, the reengineering should be considered by others as a separate project. However, if there are specific benefits to the shared service operation, reengineering should be undertaken in the context of the shared service implementation.

Three Clear Reasons to Reengineer Before Implementing Shared Services

There are three circumstances under which the decision to reengineer prior to fully implementing shared services is clear:

1. When volumes or productivity are out of control
2. When the company is replacing its information systems, especially if moving to an ERP system
3. When a company is in a postmerger/acquisition position and needs to integrate the activities of an acquired company or many acquired companies

VOLUMES OR PRODUCTIVITY

When a company begins looking into shared services, a common step is to find the baseline measures of time, cost, and error rate to process particular items within its own company; then compare those internal measures against those of companies that are better—an effort known as *benchmarking*. A company should baseline and benchmark three basic metrics: cycle time, cost, and volume.

Too often, management will say, "we have too many people processing payroll." But headcount is a symptom, not a cause. "We can do it with fewer people" is true only if you can get the process under control, so that fewer people can handle the appropriate volume.

If people are a symptom, what are the causes? The causes of long cycle times, and therefore of a lot of increased costs, as well as of some increases in volumes, are the same:

- Errors
- Rework
- Lack of information
- Poor communication

If it takes three tries to process a change in life insurance beneficiary for an employee, the volumes are going to reflect that—three transactions; the costs are going to reflect that—three times the cost of a transaction; and the cycle time is going to reflect that—cycle time measured from the time the first processing attempt starts until the third attempt is successful.

However, some cost and volume will reflect work made necessary by other internal issues. For instance, if a company's manufacturing operation works on a just-in-time (JIT) basis and demands hourly shipments from suppliers, it may also be getting invoices for each hourly shipment. That will drive up volumes and consequently the costs to process those volumes.

However, just because you get hourly deliveries does not mean that you need hourly paperwork. You can reengineer the payment process to receive weekly or even monthly cumulative invoices and pay once a week or once a month.

SYSTEM REPLACEMENT

Until recently, even companies that were successful in radical reengineering of processes had a difficult time creating effective information technology to work with those processes in a timely manner. The pace of business change always seemed to outrun the pace of enabling software development.

Today's sophisticated ERP software provides automation for the tedious, low-value-adding reporting and documenting of business activities. An entry at the operating level automatically courses its way through the information technology (IT) veins of the company and posts the resultant data into all of the appropriate places: general ledger postings, reduction in inventory, generation of new order for material, generation of payment for approved invoices, and the like.

In this way, for the first time, one really can reengineer and automate on a large scale at the same time, without having to shut the business down in order to do it. In fact, to get the most out of ERP software, it is necessary to reengineer processes so that they match up with the way the ERP software envisions them.

Enterprise resource planning software defines standard processes and what they entail. There is a language in which process terms mean the same thing to everyone using the software. Armed with the knowledge of what the software tool can do to eliminate the non-value-adding activities (e.g., rekeying data) and automate a lot of the low-value-adding reporting (e.g., three-way matches), frees one up to examine how the value-added aspects of the process can be enhanced.

POSTACQUISITION INTEGRATION OF LIKE ACTIVITIES

A company that purchases other companies often finds that each company purchased maintains processes to accomplish common functions that are fundamentally different from the way other companies do it.

In this instance, it makes sense to reengineer the processes of each newly acquired company to match the way the acquiring company operates, let the newly acquired company run the reengineered process for six months to one year, and then bring the process into the shared services operation.

Key Reason to Reengineer After Creating Shared Services

The best reason to reengineer after creating shared services is the need to simply pull the disparate groups together as soon as possible in order to get the activities under control. This is the case in which a company is not immediately worried about maximum efficiency but has a crisis of another sort it needs to deal with and believes that pulling activities together can help. In this instance, a shared service management must go into existence with the attitude of "We know everything is out of control, but just give us the garbage as it is and we'll pull it together over time."

For instance, a global cosmetics company decided to move its European financial organization to a shared service method of operation. Profits were falling, and volumes and costs were both out of control. Every European country managed its financial processes differently. Rather than try to reengineer all, or even a few, of the disparate country operations, the company simply pulled the entire mess into one organization, upset all of the apple carts at once, and then reengineered the processes once they had been coalesced into a shared service operation.

DO NOT FORGET CORPORATE CULTURE ISSUES

Too often, those who head up process reengineering, systems enhancement, shared services, or other major change efforts leap right to working on the processes or the systems without giving enough consideration to the effects that the effort's outcome will have on the people who ultimately will have to do the work within the process or who work with the system. In order to understand the effort's impact on individual employees, one must break down processes into their activity components and determine how those activites are being run and how they should be run in the future.

Coincident with the design of the process at an activity level, a new human resource structure must be designed, role by role. In addition, one must have an understanding of what the costs will be to train individuals and to manage the change in terms of reduced productivity during the period of change—counseling, retraining those who will stay, separating those who will not, and hiring those who bring new and necessary skill sets to the reengineered or redesigned processes.

You must understand the corporate culture in the context of the change you desire—why people do what they do, and why you want them to do it differently.

In fact, culture is only one of the six points of analysis it is necessary to undertake for each candidate process to be reengineered, and for each candidate activity to be moved into a shared service operation. In Figure 5-3, the vertical columns are the points of analysis, and the horizontal arrows are the processes being analyzed.

Each Circumstance Is Unique

A large U.S. insurance company will serve as an example. The company had for years processed receivables at dozens of offices around the country. The total employees responsible for accounts receivable at all of the various centers was between 400 and 500.

The company decided to consolidate receivables into a shared service environment, with one service center. The U.S. managers also realized that the process needed to be reengineered to take out redundancies and eliminate unnecessary handoff volumes. The question was whether to reengineer before or after creating the center.

A decision was made to reengineer after creating the center, for a few reasons. First and foremost was that most of the individuals working in accounts receivable (A/R) decided not to take the company up on its offer to relocate them to its processing center, to be located in New Hampshire.

This decision by employees allowed the company to consolidate first, hire temporary employees at the new processing center, then

Figure 5-3 Regardless of Process, Same Level of Activity Analysis Needed

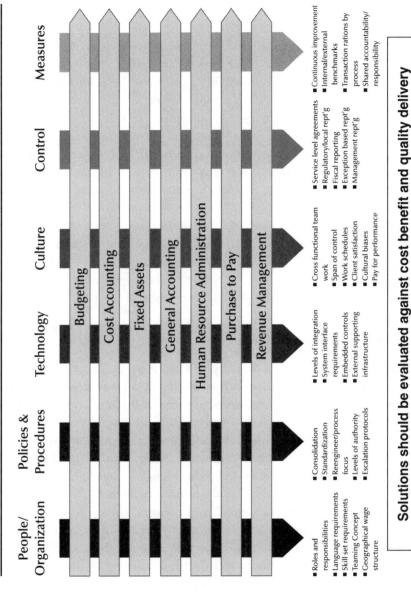

Solutions should be evaluated against cost benefit and quality delivery

80

reengineer the process and reduce headcount simply by reducing the staffing from the temporary agencies being used.

Had the company reengineered first, it would have pushed the shared service project back in time and spent a lot of time, effort, and psychic pain getting people to change the way they did business, even though those people would be leaving the company as soon as the reengineered process was moved.

MORE REENGINEERING OPPORTUNITIES UPSTREAM AND DOWNSTREAM

Another way to look at the question of whether to reengineer is to ask how much of the process in question the shared service organization will handle and whether the shared service organization will be responsible for the "customer-facing" part of the process. The greatest opportunities for increasing competitiveness through reengineering occur at the parts of the process all the way downstream that face the customer, as well as the parts of the process further upstream that are at the company's strategic center.

Stated simply, the more of the process the shared service organization owns, the more opportunities it has to reengineer the process.

If the shared service organization is in charge of only collections and A/R transaction processing, there is not much opportunity to reengineer the process. To be sure, there is opportunity to gain efficiencies in processing the transactions by reducing handoffs and internal transactions, consolidating and co-locating collections and receivables personnel, optimizing supervision, and the like, which increases efficiency. However, if the shared service organization is responsible as well for the actual billing, then there is an opportunity to reengineer the billing-to-collection process and achieve major increases in effectiveness.

The same is true of the purchase-to-pay process; running the accounts payable as a shared service does not provide much reengineering opportunity, but running purchasing as a shared service does.

As shared service organizations move farther upstream toward the vendor or farther downstream toward the customer, they have the opportunity to become strategic shared services.

GOOD SHARED SERVICE OPERATIONS LOOK FOR REENGINEERING OPPORTUNITIES ON AN ONGOING BASIS

Once the shared service operation is up and running, there is the opportunity to identify reengineering possibilities that were not apparent when the effort was being planned. This comes because suddenly there are dedicated professionals focusing on the processes within the shared service organization as core business processes, not merely as processes that support the company's core processes.

These processes have never before had champions looking to make them best in class. Continuous improvement of these processes leads to lower costs to business unit customers.

Sometimes continuous process improvement is mandated. At AlliedSignal, for instance, the business services unit has the same mandate as other business units, to increase productivity by 8 percent year-on-year. Whereas business units that produce goods and services for external customers show their progress in increased profitability, the business services unit shows its progress in lower transaction costs to business unit partners. This can be achieved both by increasing volumes and/or decreasing costs.

Some chief financial officers (CFOs) are finding that in a shared service environment they suddenly have line responsibility, with hundreds of employees reporting to them as the head of a shared financial service operation. They are finding ways to literally cut millions off corporate costs by more effective use of working capital.

GOOD SHARED SERVICE OPERATIONS LOOK TO SPARK REENGINEERING IN THE BUSINESS UNIT PARTNERS

Not owning the process entirely, and not being able to reengineer the process from the shared service operation, is no reason not to initiate reengineering of the process. However, it must be done in partnership with the business unit partners.

Sometimes, the desire to move to a shared service method of operation allows an organization to see a lot of the problems that have existed for a long time. When the shared service operation points out to a business unit management that shared services cannot really work until a problem is solved, it forces the issue of accountability onto the business unit. In effect, the desire to move to a shared service method of operation can work as a lightning rod for business problems.

For instance, one company's movement toward shared services highlighted the issue of bad debt in the company. The company had never effectively managed working capital, but the problem had been hidden within the entire credit and collections process and never made explicit. The problem was discovered through an attempt to move many of the credit-to-collection activities into the shared service organization and make them more efficient and effective. In effect, the shared service management said: "We can make the activities we have control over more efficient, but we can't make them more effective until you (the business unit) reengineer the process."

The company slowed down the move to shared services, and put its energy into fixing the process. This drove out literally billions of dollars on an annual basis. After the working capital management process was made more effective at the business unit level, the shared service organization was able to work on making the activities within that process more efficient.

THE BIG QUESTION: SHOULD A COMPANY START FROM SCRATCH IN A "GREENFIELD" OR CHANGE THE CONTEXT OF WORK FOR CURRENT EMPLOYEES

Answering the question calls for a lot of diplomacy.

Too many managers are inclined to take the easy way out and seek to operate a shared service operation from a green field. We believe that in most circumstances, this is a terrible waste of the talents that already exist within the company—talent that has often been unable to shine because of the operating model the company uses.

In any business big enough to be looking to shared services—at least $2 billion in revenues and multiple operating business units—there is at least one place where a support organization exists that can be used as the core of a shared service operation. It usually is worth a company's time to benchmark business units' support operations against one another, create a vision for what its ideal shared service operation would look like, and begin building around the group that comes closest.

However, on occasion, the pain of a massive culture change is so overwhelming that this is both politically and psychically untenable. In this circumstance, it is usually worthwhile to start from scratch in a green field.

The key is to create a vision for the company's future in which the corporate culture is stronger than the national culture, the division's culture, or the particular site's culture. The vision should be revolutionary, but in more cases than not, how the company gets from point A to point B should be evolutionary.

CHECKLIST

☐ Before reengineering, ask the following two questions to determine whether the process will be worthwhile:
  1. Has the process been reengineered before?
  2. Will the reengineering effort pay for itself in one year or less?

☐ Pick up incremental improvement through process redesign prior to moving a particular set of activities into the shared service environment or immediately after setting up the shared service organization.

☐ Reengineer *prior* to fully implementing shared services when:
  1. *Volumes* or *productivity* are out of control
     Benchmark and baseline three measures: cycle time, cost, and volume
  2. *System replacement*, especially if moving to an ERP system
  3. *Postmerger/acquisition*—integration of like activities

☐ Reengineer *after* implementing shared services when there exists a *need* to simply pull the disparate groups together as soon as possible in order to get the activities under control.

☐ Address corporate culture issues—design a new human-resource structure:
Figure out costs to: train; manage the change in terms of reduced productivity during period of change; counsel; retrain those who will stay; separate those who will not; seek out and hire those who will bring new and necessary skill sets.

☐ Consider reengineering opportunities upstream (toward the vendor) and downstream (toward the customer).

☐ Seek reengineering opportunities on an ongoing basis.

☐ Shared service operations should look to spark reengineering in their business unit partners.

☐ Decide if you should start from a green field or change the context of work for current employees.

☐ Benchmark, create a vision for the ideal shared service operation and build around that.

6

Shared Services and Its Relationship with Information Technology

- **Leverage technological innovation**
- **Enterprise resource planning (ERP)**
- **Eliminate 100 percent verification by management**
- **Paperless, streamlined process**
- **Rapid handling of high volume of transactional information**
- **Minimal human interference**
- **Cost savings**
- **Call centers**

One of the major implications of moving to a shared service environment is the need for enabling information technology (IT). The two enabling technologies with the greatest potential are enterprise resource planning (ERP) software and call centers.

Information technology systems must also be rationalized, so that all of the business units are feeding the necessary information into compatible IT systems. Systems are a critical infrastructure component to shared service success. The ultimate goal is to move from the current hodgepodge of transaction systems to a common system platform, as seen in Figure 6-1, although some companies may need to take an intermediate step and rationalize to a handful of IT platforms.

It is possible to implement shared services in a hybrid systems

Figure 6-1   Movement from Multiple Systems to One Common System

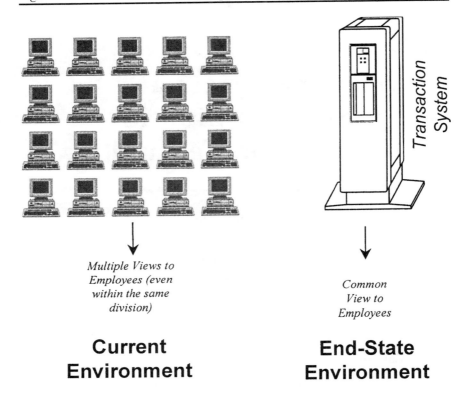

Multiple Views to
Employees (even
within the same
division)

**Current
Environment**

Common
View to
Employees

**End-State
Environment**

environment, as long as the number of systems is limited, but there should be absolutely no more than five systems with which the shared service organization must work.

Shared services also mandates some level of process change, in order to take what are often considered to be "non-value-added" activities out of the business unit and consolidate them into a shared service operation, where they become value-added activities and part of the shared service operation's core business processes.

In Chapter 5 the question was asked, which comes first, process reengineering/redesign or shared services. A similar question exists in the realm of IT: Which comes first, IT enhancement or shared services? The answer is the same as it is for the question of process reengineering/redesign: It depends.

The key in answering these questions lies in the company's overall strategy. The company needs an IT strategy, and the move to a shared service environment must be undertaken with a full understanding of the company's IT strategy. In order to get the biggest bang for the buck out of shared services, executives must determine what technologies exist today or will exist in the time frame of the new shared service processes. Shared services must capitalize on and match the available enabling technology.

The organization's technological maturity should not be the sole consideration in determining the shared service strategy. A number of system factors must be taken into account, they are seen in Figure 6-2.

Shared service operations are now serving as "hothouses" for technological innovation throughout entire companies. Shared service structures and processes are being designed to take advantage of technological innovation. Activities are expedited utilizing technology. The shared service organization can be the focus for implementing new technology to reduce costs and enhance performance. Proper utilization of technology can lead to major cost savings.

Figure 6-2   Influencing Factors

- **Existing systems profile/direction: "Best-of-Breed" of "Enterprise-Wide"**
- **Architecture direction: distributed processing or mainframe**
- **Likely utilization of outsourcing**
- **Degree of process orientation vs. functional**
- **Levels of standardization of policy, procedures, and practices**
- **Previous systems strategy achievement: on time, on budget**
- **Connectivity and geographical spread of the organization**

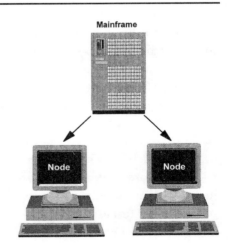

Remember, process is the driver, but technology is where the opportunity really exists. Taking full advantage of technology allows the company to leverage the new shared service processes.

ERP IS THE PRIMARY VEHICLE FOR TECHNOLOGICAL INNOVATION

We have all had to perform tedious transactional tasks. Many of these no longer have to be done when the appropriate technological backbone is brought to bear. Enterprise resource planning software allows companies to collapse both the breadth and scope of transaction and reporting systems.

A number of companies are producing ERP software, but four dominate the marketplace for the most comprehensive: SAP, Baan, PeopleSoft, and Oracle. Between them, they control well over 80 percent of the global market for companies that have installed ERP systems and have created shared service operations.

Using sophisticated ERP software, a transaction is entered only once. The software then records this transaction on all of the appropriate modules, such as accounts payable (A/P), procurement, general ledger, and materials management. This allows for a comprehensive, integrated support system that can cut across different business units. A business unit enters information itself and the system transmits appropriate information both within the business unit and to the shared service operation. This common language allows for true business support.

A number of large companies have combined successful implementation of ERP software with the creation of a shared service operation to garner major cost savings. Examples include Bristol Myers Squibb, Microsoft, Chevron, and Hewlett Packard.

At Hewlett Packard, the company enters orders into its ERP software for specifically configured computers. The software sends the appropriate information to procurement, which ensures the proper items are purchased, and to materials management so that when the necessary materials are procured, they are there for the specifically configured computer to be built. It also assembles the information necessary for production planning. At the same time, the ERP software sends the appropriate information to the shared service operation to do financials such as A/P and general ledger.

Other Technological Advances

There are a host of other technological tools that can be used to enhance the ERP system and its abilities to enable the shared service operation. These include imaging technology, automatic faxing, Internet requisitioning, automated messaging, and work-flow management software.

Work-flow management is a way to group work into packets and send these packets to individuals to work on. Automated messaging has a number of applications, among them internal auditing of quality. The system can be set to send messages to supervisors, managers, or inspectors when product is outside preset tolerances or is "irregular." Imaging technology can be used to solve the need for "seeing" documents without shipping them; this can satisfy both company needs and country regulations that documents not leave the country.

An example of how this technology works might be the following: Someone wants to order something. A purchase order is entered into the ERP software. Internet requisitions are sent to a vendor for the necessary materials. The vendor sends an invoice, which is image scanned into the system. An A/P supervisor queues the work into the work-flow stream using work-flow management software. The receiving dock receives the material and enters this into the system. The software does an automatic three-way match, matching the purchase order, invoice, and receiving dock acknowledgment. If a discrepancy is found among the three documents, an exception notice is sent to the person who authorized the transaction.

Advantages of such a system include the following:

- There is no need for 100 percent verification by management—verifications are done on an exception basis.
- The process is paperless and streamlined.
- There are major cost savings.

Such a system permits the handling of massive amounts of transactional information rapidly and with minimal human interference. Building such a process to take advantage of the latest technology not only leads to major cost savings, but creates an easier transaction for the end user.

The key is linkage, an understanding at both the shared service operation and the business unit of how the software works and what each party's obligations are to the other party. If a company does not have ERP software, a number of different systems must be gerry-rigged to create such an environment.[1]

YEAR 2000 ISSUES

A number of companies have been putting enormous resources—both financial and human—into correcting their computers systems' Year 2000 (Y2K) problems. It is simply ludicrous to stop there.

With all of the organizational pain and financial cost entailed in that effort, companies should also seek improvements in process execution and management information reporting that can come only through an ERP solution. They should also seek the improvements in transaction processing and cost reductions that come about from shared services.

CALL CENTERS

Call centers are a rapidly emerging method for providing services for either customers or internal partners. They can be built as standalone operations or within a shared service operation. The best of them link voice, video, and data into a comprehensive system to provide cutting-edge customer contacts or to provide services for employees. These call centers are often called "customer care" or "employee care" centers.

Any call center system and process must be constructed with the customer, or the employee whom it is servicing, in mind. The discussion here focuses on call centers set up within corporate shared service operations. Call centers are best used to support employee benefits and travel; accounts receivable (A/R) management (credit and collection), and customer care for external customers.

For instance, Dell Computers does over $1 billion of sales via its web site and a call center located in Bracknell in southwest England, near Heathrow airport. All of the transactional processing for these sales is done in Bracknell. In addition, finance operations for 15 European countries are located in shared service centers in Dublin, Ireland and Bracknell.

Polaroid runs a successful call center in Glasgow, Scotland, for after-sales service. Customers across the U.K. and continental Europe call a local or national toll-free telephone number. The computer software at the call center identifies the country the call is coming from and automatically routes the call to a customer service agent who speaks that country's language.

Before creating a call center to support business units, it is important to determine the boundaries of the shared service operation both today and in the future. Customer contact and the sales point should always remain with the business unit. Receivables management can be in the shared service operation from the beginning. Between these two points, there are activities that may start in the business unit and "leak" into the shared service operation over time, as the business units become more comfortable with the service level provided by the shared service operation. Such an activity might be billing.

Call centers should have a three-tier environment:

1. Technological screening
2. Service representatives
3. Specialists or case managers

This three-tiered environment drives speed and consistency, facilitates self-service, optimizes resource utilization, and provides the necessary level of expertise when it is needed.

In the case of an employee care call center, the goal is for a broad scope, which provides transactions, general information, and employee-specific information in such areas as 401(k), life and disability insurance, and health insurance. There should be a heavy emphasis on case management.

Call centers must have a number of attributes. At all levels, there must be *informational attributes*, including:

- Accuracy
- Confidentiality
- Accessibility
- Reliability

At the first-tier level, there must be *technological attributes*, including:

- Intelligence
- Efficiency
- Controllability
- Human interface

At the second and third tiers, there must be *personal attributes*, including:

- Helpfulness
- Knowledge
- Responsibility
- Comprehensiveness

Call Center Technologies. A number of important technologies go into a state-of-the-art call center. These include sophisticated workstations for customer or employee support representatives, as well as a host of hardware and software systems to feed into these front ends. Workforce management and case management software are integral to an effective call center. Figure 6-3 shows a "best-practice" call center architecture.

Figure 6-3 Best-Practice Call Center

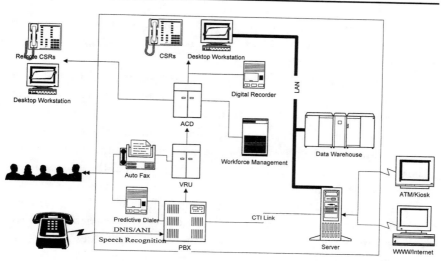

Service Options. It is important to provide customers or employees with a number of service options, such as general information, account-specific information, and most-preferred transactions. There also should be a language options, especially for a global operation, as well as access to the system for hearing-impaired individuals. Of course, this needs to be up and running for the most time possible—24 hours × 7 days if possible.

Key Performance Metrics. There are a few common metrics for call center performance, including the following:

- Average speed to answer (the average should be 20 seconds, and the service level should be that over 80 percent of calls are answered in under 30 seconds).
- Ninety-five percent of callers should receive one-call service.
- Seventy-five percent of customers surveyed for satisfaction should consider service excellent; 95 percent should consider service good or excellent.

Key Issues in Call Centers. There are two major issues in call centers: load leveling and cross-training.

Load leveling is the ability to make sure each customer service representative or case manager/specialist is handling approximately the same volume of work.

The best way to attain a level load is to cross-train both customer service representatives and case managers to handle calls from more than one interest area with which the call center works. In this way, illness, vacation, and other absences do not load work on a few people.

In addition to helping level the load, cross-training also helps alleviate the feeling on the part of call center employees that they are doing the same thing all the time.

Organizational design considerations include integrating call and case work. This is done by building in flexibility to meet peak demand, creating some level of specialization within work teams, establishing career paths for individuals in the call center, and focusing supervisory attention. There is also the need to have a point person in the management information systems (MIS) group. This person manages boundary issues and ensures overall ownership of service levels.

A FINAL WORD

It behooves any company undertaking a shared service implementation to work closely with those undertaking movement to an ERP software environment. If ERP is not being or has not been implemented, executives need to consider carefully the compound benefits available from moving to ERP and a shared service environment.

The same can be said for call centers; they are critically important in order to attain maximum benefit from a shared service implementation, especially if human resource activities are being consolidated into the shared service organization.

NOTE

1. A complete text on ERP software and its benefits can be found in our PWC colleagues' book, *SAP: An Executive's Comprehensive Guide,* John Wiley & Sons, 1998.

CHECKLIST

☐   Take advantage of technological innovation.

☐   Use ERP software to collapse both the breadth and scope of transaction and reporting systems.

☐   Use other technological advances to enhance ERP system and its abilities to enable the shared services operation:
- Imaging technology
- Automatic faxing
- Internet requisitioning
- Automated messaging
- Work-flow management software

☐   Set up call centers to:
- Support employee benefits
- Support travel for employees
- Support A/R management (credit and collection)
- Provide customer care for external customers

☐   Call centers should have a three-tiered environment:
1. Technological screening
2. Service representatives
3. Specialists, case managers

☐   Choose among the numerous call center technologies:
- Automatic number identification (ANI)
- Speech recognition
- Workforce management
- Advanced private branch exchange (PBX) support
- Desktop workstations
- Predictive dialers
- Internet connections
- Computer–telephone integration; also fax, e-mail, and imaging capabilities
- Case management and all tracking tools
- Digital recording of all calls (for quality and training)

☐   All in support of customer service representatives (CSRs)

- ☐ Must provide service options:
  - ◦ General information
  - ◦ Account-specific information
  - ◦ Most-preferred transactions
  - ◦ Language options
- ☐ Use key performance measures for call center performance such as:
  - ◦ Average speed to answer
  - ◦ One-call service
  - ◦ Customer satisfaction
- ☐ Address two key issues:
  1. Load leveling: Make sure each CSR or case manager/specialist is handling approximately the same volume of work.
  2. Cross-train both CSRs and case managers to handle calls from more than one interest area the call center works with.
- ☐ Facilitate use by building both functions and features into the system.

7

Considering Outsourcing

- **Strategic relevance**
- **Current performance level**
- **Future required performance level**
- **Creating a service operation that is good enough to sell**

In any discussion of creating a shared service operation, the question arises: Why not outsource these activities that are being collected and save the costs associated with running the shared service operation? In fact, many companies do decide to outsource the activities.

Shared services and outsourced services are flip sides of the same analytical coin. Whether to outsource or "insource" into a shared service operation is the final question to ask after all of the data has been collected and analyzed.

In the past, many companies ran into two major problems when they decided to outsource finance activities. These problems have led many companies to the determination that the challenge of building a shared service organization is worth the effort. The experience of Lucent Technologies, in which the company ran up against both of the major problems in outsourcing, is illustrative. They are:

- Companies that sell outsourced services often "back load" the costs, meaning that it is cheap to get into the arrangement but often expensive to maintain it over time.
- Many of these companies do not really have a "value proposition" on which to sell their services. Their sole selling point is often merely lower transactional cost, without the benefit of the

changes in the process that can be made through in-house shared services with the necessary process redesign or reengineering and the appropriate new systems put in place.

This is less of a problem today. The universe of vendors of outsourced financial management is segmenting into those who focus on transaction item processors (where these problems are still common) and those who focus on managing financial and accounting processes, of which PricewaterhouseCoopers is the leading provider.

A company seeking to contract with a provider of outsourced services needs to make sure that the company offers long-term flexible contractual arrangements that strive to be at least as effective as the internal relationship between the company's shared service center, if one exists, and its business units.

As an example of how many of yesterday's problems with outsourcing relationships have been solved, the 1998 Outsourcing World Summit reported that 70 percent of all outsourcing initiatives have met or exceeded expectations.

Outsourcing is an increasingly viable option, for both customers and providers of these services. However, in order for outsourcing to be successful, the relationship between the provider and the customer must be the same as the relationship between a shared service organization and a company's business units—one of partnership rather than simply customer/vendor. Simply lowering transactional costs on a one-time basis is not where the power of shared services or outsourcing lies. The power of both of these methodologies comes from continuously improving the processes in a partnership mode to continually provide better service at lower cost.

One can think about the possibilities for outsourcing as three-tiered.

On the lowest tier are transactional or routine processing activities. These are operational activities and can always be fully outsourced. Examples of such activities are accounts payable, accounts receivable, travel and entertainment, cost and inventory accounting, and billings and collections.

On the middle tier are reporting and controls. These are tactical activities; they can be partially or fully outsourced. Examples of such activities are tax compliance, budgets and forecasts, financial systems, and treasury.

On the top tier are business-decision making issues. These are strategic and should always be maintained by the company's CFO organization. Examples of these activities include strategic analysis, mergers, acquisitions and divestitures, tax planning, investor relations, and risk management.

Market research forecasts robust growth for outsourcing as we approach the 21st century, as shown in Figure 7-1.

As seen in Figure 7-2, most of the opportunities for outsourcing vendors lie in a handful of companies: manufacturing, government, banking, insurance and other financial services, and communications, which together are projected to account for 75 percent of outsourcing revenues in the year 2000, according to International Data Corporation (IDC), a research firm.

Figure 7-1   Outsourcing Forecast

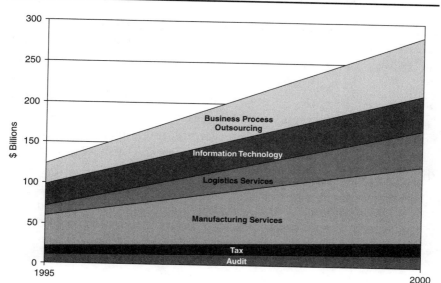

Figure 7-2   Worldwide 2000 Outsourcing Revenues by Industry (IDC, 1996)

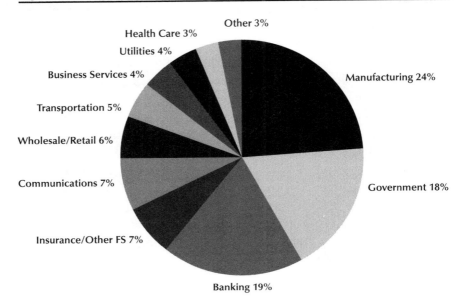

THE PROCESS FAMILY

Both outsourcing and shared services are logical by-products of what is called a *process mindset* within a company. This process mind-set stresses end-to-end business processes rather than corporate functions. The authors of *Business Process Reengineering: Breakpoint Strategies for Market Dominance,* outlined what they called the "process-orientation family" of management concepts.[1] This family contains just-in-time (JIT) manufacturing, total quality management (TQM), and business process reengineering (BPR). They argued that:

> BPR pushes the JIT and TQM philosophies both upstream and downstream to the customer and the supplier in order to mag-nify their impact and take them outside the company's four walls, in order either to control the supply chain more effec-tively or to reach the market more effectively.

102

Since 1993, the process-orientation family has been expanded to include the concepts of supply-chain management and value-chain management.

In this process-orientation mindset, a company has a small list of core business processes, which are the strategic keys to its success in the marketplace. These core processes are drawn from the list of potential core processes shown in Figure 7-3.

The processes from the list that are not core to the company's success are seen as secondary. Regardless of which processes are core and which are secondary, certain processes are always supporting. These supporting processes are the processes that are ripe for coalescing into a shared service operation or outsourcing.

Outsourcing was a hot button in the early 1990s, with many companies rushing into contracts to farm out services ranging from security, food services, and maintenance to computer data center management, product help lines and service, and accounting.

At the end of the decade, it is increasingly clear that, to some degree, outsourcing did not serve many of these companies well. In a decade of experience, many companies have learned that entering into an outsourcing relationship must be done very carefully. Having a contractor outside the company perform important (though not core) processes brings in a huge issue of trust and can muddy the waters of accountability and responsibility.

Any company management that enters into an outsourcing agreement must do so with open eyes, and must realize that it still has ultimate management responsibilities to its employees, vendors, customers, and shareholders. A botched paycheck cannot simply be blamed on the contractor. It must be dealt with by management. A company can only

Figure 7-3   Typical Core Processes

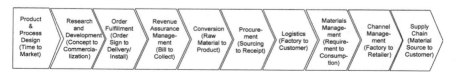

outsource for the execution of transactions and processes. The company always retains responsibility for policy and decision making.

In information technology (IT), companies that provide outsourcing services include the large computer services firms EDS and Computer Associates, as well as the service organization of IBM; the Big Five accounting/consulting firms in such areas as internal audit, accounts receivable (A/R), accounts payable (A/P), and general accounting; American Express for purchasing; and Ryder for logistics. In some instances, these providers create joint ventures, such as the one described later in this chapter in our case study. PricewaterhouseCoopers has determined that as one of its strategic initiatives in the 21st century, it will become one of the largest providers, if not the largest provider, of outsourced services in a number of areas.

Some companies have taken outsourcing one step further, outsourcing all noncore processes. Athletic shoe manufacturers have led the way in this regard, contracting out everything but design and marketing, including manufacturing and distribution. Car manufacturers have been moving in this direction since the early 1990s, focusing on marketing and design of overall vehicles, and contracting out design and manufacture of major subassemblies to first-tier component suppliers rather than simply procuring individual parts and doing all assembly in house.

The focus in this book is processes that are clearly support processes and the activities that fall within them. A list of support processes that are candidates for potential outsourcing (or coalescing into a shared service organization) is shown in Figure 7-4.

KEY CONSIDERATIONS

After the activities within support processes that are to be collected have been determined, the decision of whether to outsource those activities/processes or maintain them inside and collect them in a shared service operation is based on three key considerations:

1. What is the strategic relevance of the service to the company?
2. What is the current performance level of the service within the company?

Figure 7-4   Outsource Possibilities

Finance Function:

- Transaction Processing: e.g. A/P, T&E, G/L, Billing
- Full Finance Function: e.g. BBC (UK)
- Center of Expertise: Credit & Collections; Vendor/Customer Inquiries

Technical Services:

- Fixed Asset Registers
- Freight Invoice Audit
- Archiving & Electronic Storage
- Scanning/Imaging
- Reprographics

Professional Services

- Tax Planning and Compliance
- Internal Audit
- Insurance
- Stocks, Dividends, Unclaimed Property
- Treasury Management, e.g. Hedging, Check Preparation
- Loan Securitization

Human Resources:

- Payroll, Pensions, Government Reporting
- All Employee Services - Personnel Files + Travel Expense Reimbursement
- HR Planning and Execution
- SEA - Services to Expatriates Abroad
- Benefits Processing and Reporting
- Recruitment
- Relocation Services

Facility Services:

- Building and Site Maintenance
- Fleet Administration
- Facility/Mailroom Services

IT Services:

- Data Centers
- Desk-Top Support
- Full Functional Responsibility - Maintenance and Support
- Voice/Video Management

3. What will the future required performance level of the service be?

Think about these three questions as matrices, as shown in Figure 7-5.

These decision-support matrices do not take into account any bias for or against outsourcing in management philosophy. Many companies have a philosophical commitment to perform all tasks in house; for them, the benefits of outsourcing would need to be clearly compelling. Other companies have a bias toward outsourcing; for them, the decision to maintain activities inside the company in a shared service operation would need to be equally compelling.

Strategic Relevance

Along the horizontal axis of this matrix is available capabilities. This asks: Do we have the capabilities in house to perform the activities in a "best-of-class" mode?

Figure 7-5 Key Considerations When Deciding Whether to Outsource

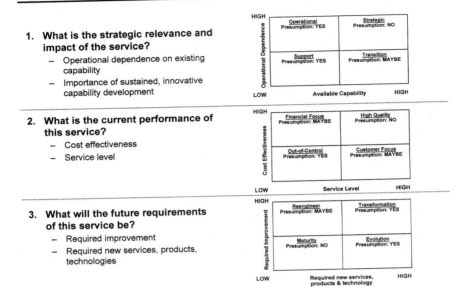

1. **What is the strategic relevance and impact of the service?**
   - Operational dependence on existing capability
   - Importance of sustained, innovative capability development

2. **What is the current performance of this service?**
   - Cost effectiveness
   - Service level

3. **What will the future requirements of this service be?**
   - Required improvement
   - Required new services, products, technologies

The vertical axis asks the question: To what level do our operations activities depend on these support services?

If capabilities are low, the presumption is always to outsource rather than insource, regardless of the degree to which the company's operations are dependent on the activities. If in-house capabilities are high, and there is a high level of operational dependence on the activities, the activities should never be contracted out. If capabilities are high and the operational dependence is low, it is a judgment call.

Current Performance Level

The horizontal axis in part of Figure 7-5 asks the question: What is the current service level at which these activities are performed?

The vertical axis asks the question: How cost effectively are these activities performed?

If the activities are performed with a high service level and in a cost-effective manner, they belong in house in a shared service environment (upper right box). If the service level is currently poor and the activities are not being performed in a cost-effective manner, the decision to outsource is clear (lower left box).

If the activities are currently being performed in a cost-effective manner, but with poor service, or with good service but high costs, one must decide if it is worth the effort to reengineer the processes (either before or after pulling them together in a shared service environment, as discussed in Chapter 5) or simply cut losses and contract the activities out.

Future Required Performance Level

In the matrix in part 3 of Figure 7-5 the horizontal axis asks: What do we anticipate future requirements to be for this support process in terms of services, products, or technology?

The vertical axis asks: Will performance improvements be required over time?

If expectations are that there will be many "new" activities within the process over time (right boxes), it might be wise to let a dedicated provider of those services handle them for the company, whether or not a great deal of improvement will be necessary.

Even if there is not a need for a lot of "new" activities, but a high need for improvement over time (upper left box), it might be wise to contract out. Only when there will be little need for new activities and only a need for natural, evolutionary improvement over time is the choice clear to keep the activities inside the company.

IT HAS MOST EXPERIENCE WITH OUTSOURCING

Information technology organizations within companies have the most experience with outsourcing. The trend started in the 1980s with the outsourcing of data center operations—the IT engines. In the 1990s, IT outsourcing expanded to the management of the networks and maintenance of the desktop units tied to those networks.

As we enter the 21st century, many companies are moving to enterprise resource planning (ERP) software that links the entire company's IT operations through distributed processors and a network.

After this is installed—almost always with help from an outside contractor—development of new applications or modifications of canned applications software is handled by inside personnel, while maintenance of those legacy systems that were not decommissioned as a result of the switch to ERP is often turned over to an outside contractor. Over time, as new applications come on line, it may be possible to reduce the dependence on legacy systems, and hence on outside service contracting.

BBC CASE STUDY: OUTSOURCING AN ENTIRE FINANCE OPERATION

In March 1997, the British Broadcasting Company (BBC) transferred 90 IT personnel to a new company, Media Accounting Services Ltd. (MedAS). MedAS was set up as a joint venture established by Coopers & Lybrand (now PricewaterhouseCoopers) and EDS, the large systems outsourcing company. The new venture was established to be the repository of the BBC's shared service center for finance (SSC), and signed a contract to provide those services to the BBC for an initial period of three years, with the BBC having an option to extend to 10 years.

The goal of establishing the new company, according to the BBC and MedAS, was to redesign the BBC's finance processes, seeking standardization of processes, and to create a single shared financial system and service. Through its relationship with MedAS, the BBC hopes to achieve greater business efficiencies and improvements in financial information, and intends to plow back savings into programming and services for viewers.

The BBC's reason for seeking an outside vendor rather than creating an SSC inside the company were twofold:

1. Executives did not believe the company was big enough to justify such an effort.

2. The creation of such a center would have entailed hiring experts in IT transformation, BPR, and shared service management. Much of this talent (in IT projects and BPR) would have been super-

fluous once the center was set up. Redundancy costs in the United Kingdom make this a key issue.

Rodney Baker-Bates, director of finance and IT for the BBC, laid out clearly the many issues involved in creating such an arrangement in an interview he gave to the *Financial Times* in July 1997:

> You are not buying water. You are buying a complex interaction. In the end, if any relationship like this is to survive, it requires sophisticated management. The buyer–supplier relationship has to be right. It has to be transparent. You can't have one partner feeling aggrieved. (You don't want to) get cornered . . . boxed in after three years. We worked out what our costs would have been if we had set up the SSC—we got an internal benchmark."

The initial contract between the BBC and MedAs was for three years. By the end of the first year, the BBC Board of Governors needed to affirm the vision for the BPR and IT transformation and extend the contract to its full 10 years, or make a decision to terminate after three years.

In October 1997, the Board of Governors did affirm the vision and extended the contract. On March 1, 1998, an additional 350 BBC staff—260 from group financial services and 90 more from IT—transferred to MedAS.

MedAS's contract with the BBC is not exclusive. In fact, the goal of creating the joint venture company is to create a business that can attract other clients. The BBC, in effect, becomes a pilot program that proves the concept of outsourcing finance and related IT. The personnel who transferred from the BBC are to become the core of the MedAS team, along with managers who moved to the new venture and who continue to do so from both PricewaterhouseCoopers and EDS.

ANOTHER CASE: BP MOBIL

BP Mobil in Europe decided in the mid 1990s to outsource many of its finance and accounting activities. However, the company was not fully confident with the state of outsourcing services, and decided to create some market competition. The way it did this was to create relationships with two different vendors of outsourcing services, Price Waterhouse (now PricewaterhouseCoopers, PwC) and Anderson Consulting. While both companies consolidated finance activities into a shared service style of operation, each company uses a completely different model.

In the case of Anderson, which was given the contract to run the finance and accounting activities in the southern part of Europe, the company set up one shared service center in each country; one for France, one for Spain, one for Italy, etc. PwC, on the other hand, set up one shared service center for all of the northern European countries in the Netherlands.

Both Anderson and PwC own the shared service centers, have Mobil as their first client for the center, and are using their centers as the core from which they are attempting to build finance outsourcing businesses for European clients. This use of two different models by companies competing for business should provide, over time, a wonderful laboratory through which companies can explore outcomes for both the shared service concept and the outsourcing relationship.

It is instructive to compare and contrast the benefits of these two approaches.

The PwC shared service center for BP Mobil employs about 150 people in the Netherlands. Only a handful of individuals had previously worked for BP Mobil in any of their previously far-flung finance operations in Germany, Belgium, Switzerland or any other country covered under the contract. It was, in essence, a "green field" operation, starting up fresh. At Anderson, each of the single-country shared service centers are staffed mostly by former BP Mobil employees.

Anderson's model clearly reduces social costs. There is very little need to lay off employees. The PwC model encounters high social cost, because the financial ramifications of laying off employees is very high in many European countries.

However, PwC believes that these downside social costs, while very real and clearly important to those individuals let go, are more than made up for by the green field site's abilities to:

- Capture lower employment costs immediately; in the case of this center in the Netherlands, a 30-40 percent employment cost reduction from the cost of BP Mobil employees in Germany, Switzerland, and other countries.

- Capture economies of scale immediately. Volumes in a green field site are known from the start, and work flow can be designed from the start.

- Engineer one process rather than reengineer multiple processes. When setting up single-country centers that collapse activities from many offices located in that country, you need to go through all of the reengineering questions asked in Chapter 5.

Taking into account the high up-front costs of work-force reduction in many locations, and recruiting, hiring, and training in one location; then the relatively low secondary costs of engineering one process, the PwC model achieved financial payback in 18 months. While PwC is not privy to Anderson's results, it can be assumed that the high costs of the process reengineering necessary in Anderson's model could have delayed payback significantly beyond that.

A FOURTH POSSIBILITY: GOOD ENOUGH TO SELL

If a company is to create a shared service operation in house, the end product of that effort should be an organization that is good enough to sell its services to other companies that wish to outsource.

Whether or not the company ultimately does become a provider of outsourced services is a decision that hinges on the following:

- Does the parent corporation want to create a business unit with such core competencies, and will it allow the unit to charge sister business units at a market rate in order to earn a profit?

- Does the parent company want to spin off the unit and then outsource to a provider it already knows and trusts?

111

Even if company executives have an inkling that they might want to create either of these two options, it is important that they not move in that direction too fast. By not building the shared service organization with the time and care necessary, but rather hoping to imitate the big outsourcing providers too early, one can drop the ball and end up with an organization that not only cannot compete in the marketplace, but does not even accomplish what a shared service operation should for its internal business partners.

CHECKLIST

- ☐ Manage outsourcing relationship the same way as shared services—as a partnership.
- ☐ Determine which activities within support processes are to be collected and considered for outsourcing or shared service "insourcing."
    1. What is the *strategic relevance* of the service to the company?
    Available capabilities
    Operational dependence
    2. What is the *current performance level* of the service within the company?
    Current service level
    Cost effective
    3. What will the *future required performance level* of the service be?
    Future requirements in terms of services, products, or technology
    Required performance improvements
- ☐ Set the goal of your shared service center to "be good enough to sell."

Part Three

———

Design

In Chapters 8 through 13, the reader is asked to go through the planning and program design steps in preparation for implementing shared services. These steps include determining which support processes to consolidate into shared services and how to set up the shared service organization—by organizational unit, by country, by region, by center of excellence for each particular process, or globally.

Another major step is the selection of a location for each of the company's shared service processing centers, an often difficult decision that requires a detailed analysis of many variables. Again, while this is difficult for a company working in one country or one region, for companies pursuing shared services on a multiregional or truly global level, the complexities of choosing a location or series of regional locations are increased by differing business cultures.

The creation of the business infrastructure is equally as complex for multiregional or global companies, due to the myriad of tax, legal, and regulatory requirements of different countries.

This part also tackles the issue of service-level agreements between the shared service unit and its business unit partners throughout the corporation. The creating of a service-level agreement is integral to the type of pricing arrangement that can be created.

All of this leads to creation of a final business case, which documents the costs—organizational and financial—of creating the shared service organization, and enumerates the benefits—both tangible and intangible—of moving to a shared service method of organization.

8

Getting Started

- **Develop a business case**
- **Develop support for the initiative**
- **Organize the initiative**
- **Communicate intent and plan**
- **Identify desired skill set**

At this point, we will assume that you have decided to move to a shared service environment and that if outsourcing is to become a part of your solution, it will not occur until sometime in the future. The question now becomes: How do you get started on shared services?

There are three key issues to keep in the back of your mind as you organize to move to a shared service environment: *challenge, rationale,* and *like initiatives*:

1. Do not underestimate how much effort will need to be put into moving to a shared service environment. It is truly a major effort that entails a lot of work.
2. The rationale for moving to shared services must fit with the company's overall direction and strategy.
3. Be mindful of initiatives, organizations, or processes currently underway in your organization that resemble shared services.

Moving to a shared service environment will entail challenge for a number of reasons. To be sure, the effort will appear to some in the company to be just another attempt to centralize, with all of the fears that centralization brings to bear. Even if there is not much real fear about centralization, the effort is a change in the status quo, which is always frightening to many people.

In many instances, the effort means taking control away from the strategic business unit heads. These people are asking an important question of their partners in the shared services organization implicitly, even if they are not articulating it: "Are you really going to focus on service and quality to me so I can do my job, or are you going to be a central, bureaucratic anchor around my neck?" The relationship must be laid out clearly in the service-level agreement, which is discussed in detail in Chapter 12.

The shared service organization must be able to honestly answer that it will work to solve strategic business unit (SBU) problems. Although the shared service operation cannot actually solve the SBU's business problems, removal of day-to-day control over the activities being moved into shared services will do this by freeing up the SBU head's time and effort to focus on those business problems.

Because of this, it is imperative that you have a clear rationale for moving to a shared service environment, one that meshes closely with the company's overall strategy. Some strategic underpinnings for a shared service undertaking include the following:

- Moving to a global organization
- Moving to an enterprise resource planning (ERP) information system
- Changing the paradigm from manufacturing and selling product to creating solutions for customer needs (the IBM shift)
- Moving away from a holding company environment with completely autonomous businesses to one of business units in which common activities can be consolidated
- A deliberate attempt to reduce the power of currently "all-powerful" business unit heads
- A significant effort to gain or regain control of general and administrative (G&A) expenses

As you explore the reason for undertaking the effort and create a rationale, you may find that you already have like initiatives underway.

These may include common process initiatives, in which the thinking logically leads from creating a common process to consolidating the activities within those common processes. Common process initiatives can be as disparate as creating one general ledger within an ERP system to standardizing the methodology for employee review and evaluation.

They may include consolidation efforts underway in anything from materials management to travel and expense reporting, or they may entail the creation of centers of excellence for particular activities.

All of these efforts are one-off, but logical, precursors to a full-blown shared service organization. It is important to take advantage of them, build off them, and use them when arguing that shared services is not as scary a notion as some people find it.

The actual organizational effort entails four distinct parts:

1. Development of a business case
2. Development of support for the initiative
3. Effectively organizing the initiative
4. Communication of the intent and the plan

THE BUSINESS CASE

The development of the business case will be discussed in much more detail in Chapter 13. For now, it is important to merely identify the pieces of a business case. Throughout your business case analysis, the effort must be self-funding, and payback of implementation costs should occur within a few years. But cost reduction cannot be the only reason for engaging in shared services. The business case should be used to clarify reasoning for implementing shared services in terms of increased service to business unit partners.

It is important to note that in Europe, on average the first year's labor cost savings are used up by severance costs. This pushes payback for implementation into a 30-60 month time frame, while most American companies wish to see payback for implementation at two to three years. That means that in Europe the strategic reasons for entering into shared services must be even stronger than in the U.S. Such rea-

117

sons usually include "one company" visibility to cross-border customers and suppliers, as well as reducing the cost of multiple-country information technology rollouts.

The first step in creating the business case is identification of what business areas can potentially be included in the shared service organization. This identification is done both by function and by process. For instance, it is not enough to say that "finance" can be put into a shared service environment; one must determine which activities within the finance function, as well as which activities from related functions like purchasing, are necessary to properly address processes such as purchase-to-pay or credit-to-collection (revenue management) that are to be put into the shared service organization.

It is imperative to measure the baseline performance on the value metrics (cost, cycle time, error rate) of performing the process (not the costs of maintaining the function), and to compare those baseline results against industry norms. This is called *benchmarking*, and it is performed against an objective external database. Such databases are maintained by a number of firms that specialize in doing baselining and benchmarking projects (see Figure 8-1).

Rather than doing a detailed analysis of the as-is state of the process, which is recommended for business process reengineering (BPR) efforts, you merely create a straw-man of the environment you envision as the end state, the so-called to-be state. This allows the gap between the performance in the as-is state and the desired performance of the to-be state to be measured, a so-called *gap analysis*.

Next, identify the benefits that will accrue in the as-is state, in terms of reduction in cycle time and cost, and finally the costs of actually carrying out the implementation.

BUILDING SUPPORT

As with any business change effort, support for the undertaking must come from the top of the organization. The effort must have as its champion someone from within the executive suite, or it will stumble.

Important stakeholders throughout the management ranks must be identified and invited to participate on a steering committee. These

Figure 8-1 Baselining and Benchmarking Tools

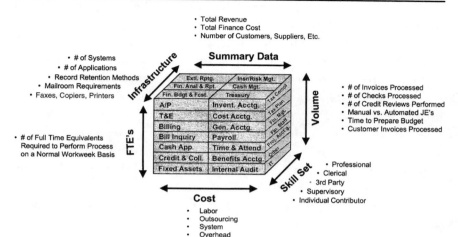

stakeholders are executives and senior management from the areas of the business directly affected by the change. The key to building support in this group is to assure them that they will not lose control over activities that they are currently held accountable for, and that the development of a shared service organization will actually free up more of their time to concentrate on revenue enhancement through their core processes.

Line managers and supervisors must be brought on board. The key to bringing them on board is the assurance that the shared service environment will unburden them from some of the issues that have been dropped into their lap as middle management ranks have been thinned since the late 1980s.

At all times during the phase of building support, listen closely to the concerns of these individuals and groups, understand the barriers they perceive to successful implementation, and address them one at a time.

EFFECTIVE ORGANIZATION

The implementation organization is composed of three pieces. What these pieces are called depends on the formality or informality with which the company operates. Regardless of what terminology is used, some model of governance is needed, such as the governance model in Figure 8-2.

As you can see from the figure, this is not a hierarchical model, but rather one that is set up against the time commitment necessary and each group's position on an operational–strategic continuum.

A *program office* is a small group of individuals who work full time on the efforts and are accountable for the initiative. These people need to be top-notch individuals; it has to hurt for their managers to let them go from their usual organizations and routing duties. If the core team becomes a dumping ground for poor performers who managers are anxious to get "off line," the effort will fail.

These are people with project skills, who can be taken from anywhere in the organization that they can be found. They need good knowledge of the business in general but do not need to be functional experts, since they will be able to call on a large number of functional experts on the project team.

Process/project teams are cross-functional groups drawn from ex-

Figure 8-2   Governance Model

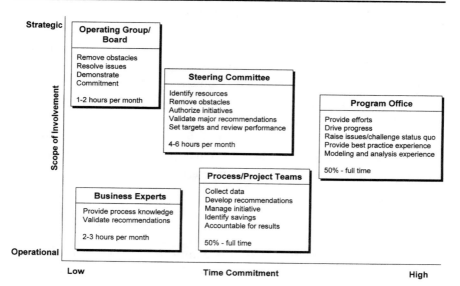

perts in particular areas of the company who have line responsibility for the activities in question. Throughout the effort, they must maintain these responsibilities. Project team members are responsible for data collection and analysis, identification of projected savings from the effort, and recommendations for changes. This group also manages the initiative and is accountable for results.

A *steering committee* is made up of senior-level stakeholders who have vested interest in the activities that will be consolidated into the shared service operation. They must have access to the executive group. These people maintain contact with the executive suite. The steering committee must focus not on bureacratic details, but rather on the business problems to be solved and on getting things done.

In some organizations, such as Lucent Technologies, the steering committee is the same group as the shared services board. However, in many organizations, the steering committee is a buffer between the board and the actual project work, and the board is responsible for demonstrating commitment throughout the organization.

Business experts attend some all-team meetings, but they also come into the core team on an as-needed basis, usually for a half day or one day at a time, in order to help the core team determine which pieces to pursue, and to give feedback to the core and process/project teams on work that has been done. These people maintain contact with the rank and file.

CONTINUOUS COMMUNICATION

All three groups within the program organization must communicate continuously with each other, as well as with the various constituencies they represent.

Project committee and steering committee meetings must be frequent enough to communicate program status and identify barriers, but short enough to not be disruptive to team members who are maintaining all of their line responsibility. The same holds true for steering committee members.

Communication among the various program groups must be honest, pointing out deficiencies in the effort as it moves along. However, after issues are resolved within meetings of the various program groups, communication with constituencies must remain positive. If members of the project team or the steering committee begin to voice disagreements publicly, rank-and-file employees or executives will begin to put up additional barriers to the effort.

It is important to communicate with all of the various populations early and often. There is no such thing as too much communication.

NEW SKILL SETS NEEDED

Adoption of the shared service methodology forces companies to rethink the skill set they are looking for in employee selection, as well as the skills they need to be developing in company education and training. The skill set needed for successful shared services is robust and does not focus on narrow technical expertise in transaction processing. The skills needed are broader service partnership skills used to focus on solving business problems through understanding the four components of value: cost, time, quality, and service.

Figure 8-3 shows the kinds of individuals who fit into a matrix which has internal versus external thinking as a horizontal axis; and flexibility versus control as a vertical axis.

Again, the kinds of people who will flourish in a decentralized organization are on the external end of the horizontal axis; the tension comes between those who are growth oriented in their management philosophy and practice and those who are more command-and-control and task focused in their management philosophy and practice.

A shared service organization demands visionary and growth- oriented management, as shown in the following section on how Lucent Technologies went about getting started.

THE LUCENT STORY (TOLD BY JIM LUSK)

It began as we talked about the value that we as a chief financial officer (CFO) team bring to the company. We decided we needed to focus more resources on being strategic partners with business units. As we did that, others were thinking about shared services throughout the company, and the two lined up perfectly in time.

Figure 8-3   Management Philosophy for a Shared Service Organization

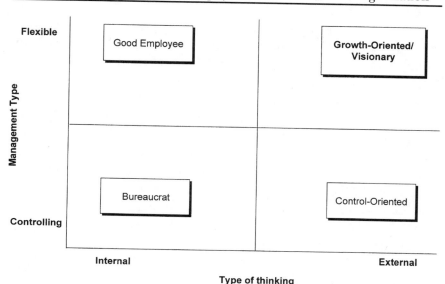

Once we in the CFO organization decided we wanted to focus more people on strategic partnership, it was very logical to go to a shared service model. Once we decided we wanted to go to a shared service operation, we brainstormed a vision for shared services and came up with the vision of "incredibly awesome partner service powered by incredibly awesome people." It was also at this point that we started articulating the "it's a business" mindset.

We did all this without really knowing exactly how we were going to get it done. We wanted most importantly to create a future in which to put all of these people who were moving into the shared service organization. As we got into it, we put more tactical flesh on the bone, and that is when we decided that one of the things the business would need to have is a strategic plan.

A strategic plan made us feel more like a business. The biggest step was to begin thinking of shared services as a business so that we could run it as a business. A business plan helped us come to the realization that "this is a bigger project than we originally thought." It needed program management, getting the right people on the job, and setting some aggressive goals for ourselves, even in the context of a big future vision.

A strategic plan also helped us realize that we had to set some very aggressive interim milestones and time frames and make them. Things had to be implemented fast. We could not wait for SAP (our ERP software) to change a lot of the processes; we had to change processes and make them much more efficient.

The reason we started in finance was somewhat serendipitous, although it was the product of much conscious thinking. At Lucent, and at AT&T before Lucent was spun off, finance had a strong tradition of being centralized. Although a centralized group and a shared service organization are quite different, in many ways moving from centralization to shared services was a natural evolution for a CFO who had decided that the CFO organization needed to add more value to the company. At the same time those running the corporation were thinking about how to releverage a host of back-office operations. These two things coming together was really the birth of the shared service organization.

Benchmarking has always been used as a key driver of business decisions at Lucent. When Lucent was formed, the CFO organization carried a cost of about 2 percent of the company's revenue. In fact, the company's cost structures in general were high.

Now, you can either study costs to death or you can agree that they are too high, and you have to cut them substantially and begin working on solutions. We did the latter.

Within the CFO organization, the goal was to reduce costs to less than 1 percent of revenue. Other areas of the company set other targets.

We went at it with a package of innovations, of which shared services is just one. Others are the installation of SAP software and use of materials-only costing to revamp the entire costing process in the company. We are also looking at enhancing the revenue management process and other areas.

It is impossible to stress enough the importance of identifying stakeholders up front. To do this, we did not create an elaborate interview process. What we did was force ourselves to think about the value that we bring to the company and to put ourselves in our strategic partners' shoes. We asked ourselves: "If we were our strategic partners in the business units, how would we want this place to look and be different?" We committed ourselves to a future we both wanted.

In all honesty, it does not take a lot of detailed analysis to figure out what those improvements are. They are painfully obvious when you step back and really look at them. Our vision for partner service really coalesced when we visited the Hilton Hotel in Short Hills, New Jersey, one of the finest hotels in the state. It was amazing to feel as a customer that you really mattered.

In addition to those who would enjoy the output of our efforts, the other key stakeholders are, of course, those who are going to create new processes, or fix old processes, and own the new processes. One cannot spend enough time with these associates, encouraging them, sometimes prodding them, and seriously applauding their efforts.

The bottom line is that in retrospect, the time was perfect to do this—a new company being born from a large organization, a company that had as its backbone a long tradition of innovation in Bell Laboratories. Whatever your circumstances, whatever the original reasons for getting into shared services, whether it is cost reduction or better service or rationalizing a number of acquisitions, it does not take long before you really realize the business value of doing it. You really do not quite see it up front because you have never been in that mode. It is a case of "you just don't know what you don't know." Once you begin to get your arms around it, you can really feel the power of it as a business model.

CHECKLIST

☐ Develop a business case:
  ○ Selection—Identify (by function and by process) the business areas to be potentially included.
  ○ Benchmarking—Measure baseline performance on the value metrics against industry norms.
  ○ Gap analysis—Create a straw-man of the ideal end-state environment to measure the gap between the performance in

---

the as-is state and the desired performance of the to-be state.

☐ Develop support for the initiative:
- ○ Identify important stakeholders.
- ○ Create steering committee of the stakeholders.
- ○ Assure the stakeholders that shared services will enable them to focus their time on revenue enhancement.
- ○ Dispel the myth about stakeholders' loss of control due to shared services.
- ○ Recruit line managers and supervisors.
- ○ Listen to the concerns of the recruited individuals and address them.

☐ Organize the initiative:
- ○ Core team—Top-notch individuals who will work full time on the efforts.
- ○ Process/project team—Larger, cross-functional group drawn from experts in particular areas of the company who have line responsibility for the activities in question. Come into core team on an as-needed basis. Maintain contact with all employees.
- ○ Steering committee—Senior-level stakeholders who have a vested interest in the activities that will be consolidated into the shared services operation. Must have access to the executive group.
- ○ Business experts—Help core team determine which pieces to pursue. Maintain contact with all employees.

☐ Communicate intent and plan:
- ○ Continuously
- ○ Honestly, pointing out deficiencies
- ○ Positively

☐ Identify desired skill set.

9

Planning and Approach

- **"Burning platform"**
- **Appropriate model**
- **Path of least resistance**
- **Decision-making process**
- **Influential factors**

Having achieved buy-in throughout various levels of the organization, it is now time to design how the shared service organization will operate as well as how the implementation program of moving to a shared service environment will be carried out.

This chapter will discuss the concepts behind the five geographic models for a possible shared service organization and the questions arising around what aspects of business will be placed into the shared service operation. Looking at the shared service organization in terms of geography is just one way to conceptualize a shared service organization; but it is both useful in general and instructive.

It is critically important that throughout this period of planning, focus be maintained on the business problem. After the business problem is clearly defined, solutions can be sought through the use of process enhancement. This determination is called the *burning platform*. Only when you agree that you are standing on a burning platform—by defining a business problem as so severe that it hinders business growth—are you willing to jump into the icy waters of major organizational change.

The natural answer to the question "what is the business problem?" is often "cost!" We urge you to throw that answer aside; cost is really more of a symptom than it is the underlying problem. Creating processes that are cheaper but still not effective is no solution; it does not add value.

The real reasons companies should be moving toward a shared service environment are:

- To present one face to the business unit partner or customer.
- To create a one-company approach among many disparate business units; and often among a number of acquisitions (this was Lucent's main reason).
- To free up the sales force from supporting tasks.
- To globalize from a group of regional or national organizations.

Once everyone throughout the organization is aligned on the business problem that needs to be solved, then potential solutions can be explored and agreement can be reached on the most appropriate way to pursue a solution.

NO COOKIE CUTTERS HERE

Figure 9-1 shows three of the five possible geographic models for a shared service organization: by organizational unit, by country, and by center of excellence.

Organizational Unit

One shared service center for each line of business or product line encompasses all of the activities that are brought together in the shared service organization. For instance, there is a global corporation with a division that manufactures automotive after-market parts in seven factories in five different countries, sells to auto manufacturers around the world, and is headquartered in the United States.

The company decides to establish a shared service center for global finance processes to handle all purchase-to-pay and credit-to-collection activities for all of the factories and marketing organizations.

Figure 9-1   Possible Geographic Models for a Shared Service Organization

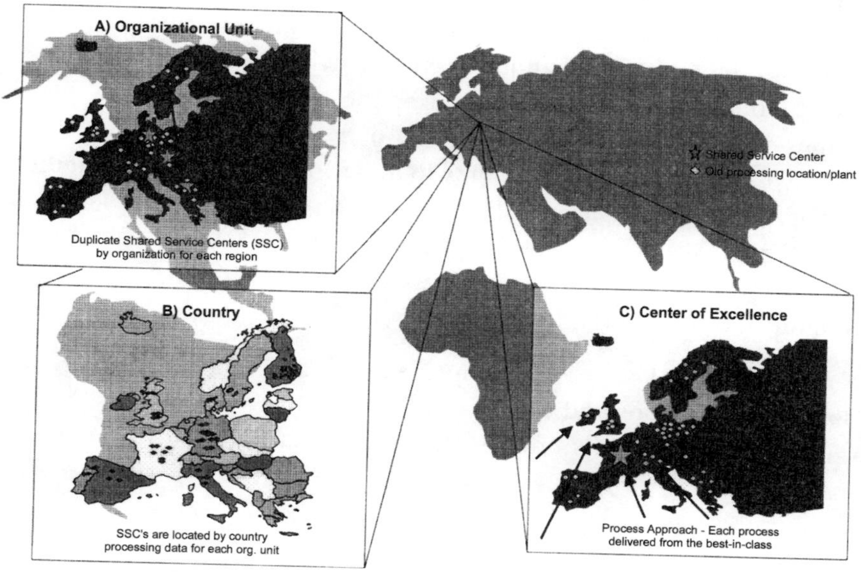

The key here is that the industry or product line is common, enabling the company to obtain maximum efficiency.

Country

In this model, all shared service activities for all operations, from manufacturing through sales, are done on a country-wide basis, with a center in each country in which the company has operations. Shared service organization management is global.

The philosophy here is that the requirements are unique in each country, and most of the savings can be achieved by this first step, while minimizing risk.

Center of Excellence

In this model, a shared service organization, under one management, sets up centers to concentrate on one particular set of common activities for the company as a whole. For instance, in a global corporation with seven business units, a shared service organization is created, headquartered in Atlanta. All human resource activities are carried out at a center in Phoenix; credit and collection activities are handled at a center in Greensboro, North Carolina for the United States and Amsterdam for European operations, and so on.

This option allows a company to move to a shared service method of operation with the least dislocation of existing staff.

Figure 9-2 shows the regional geographic model.

Region

A regional model coalesces the operations of a number of different national organizations and carries out the shared service activities at one regional center, usually one for the United States, one for the rest of

Figure 9-2   Possible Models for a Shared Service Organization: Regional

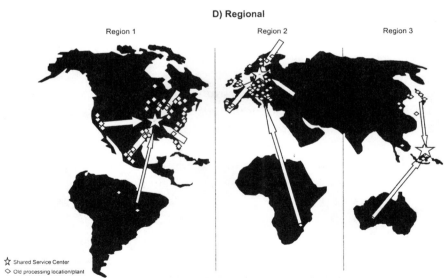

D) Regional

Region 1   Region 2   Region 3

☆ Shared Service Center
◇ Old processing location/plant

SSC processes all BU's across a given geographical region.
Regional can, of course, incorporate the Organizational, the Center of Excellence, and the Country models.

the Americas, one for Europe (often including Africa and the Middle East), and one for Australia/Asia and/or China/Pacific Rim.

This model delivers significant savings, but is without a doubt more challenging than any of the preceding three geographic models.

Global

In this instance, shared service operations are carried out at one center for operations around the world. It is important to acknowledge that no one solution is right for all companies, and at times one solution does not fit the needs of an entire global corporation. A company may be at different levels of maturity or sophistication in different regions, which may necessitate a mixed approach. Figure 9-3 shows the global geographic model.

There is often a need to tailor a particular approach to a company's philosophy. For instance, a company might need to work nationally in

Figure 9-3   Possible Models for a Shared Service Organization: Global

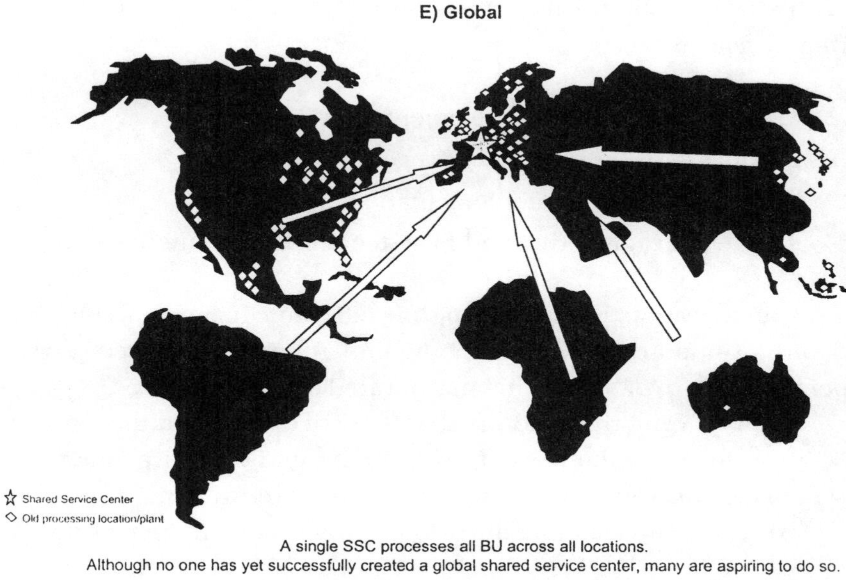

E) Global

☆ Shared Service Center
◇ Old processing location/plant

A single SSC processes all BU across all locations.
Although no one has yet successfully created a global shared service center, many are aspiring to do so.

Europe because of regulations (discussed in detail in Chapter 11) or because of local corporate politics. In the rest of the world, a regional approach, or a center of excellence approach may work. The right choice is a combination of the particular corporation's profile, as well as where the best business opportunities lie.

LINING UP THE VARIABLES

Whatever geographic model is chosen, there are a number of up-front decisions that need to be made at the planning stage in order to get the implementation off on the right foot.

First, on which processes will the shared service organization focus? If the company will take a staged approach, bringing different functions into the shared service organization over time, which function(s) will be first in?

Second, which activities from each of those processes will actually be part of the shared service operation?

Third, when will these activity sets be brought into the shared service operation? Here, the issues of timing relative to reengineering and information technology (IT) system implementation must be resolved (discussed in detail in Chapters 5 and 6). There are four options for bringing activity sets in:

1. At the outset of the implementation
2. During reengineering of processes
3. During IT system implementation
4. After reengineering and IT system implementation

Fourth, will activities running on different financial accounting systems (as opposed to IT systems) be brought into the shared service operation before or after being harmonized and standardized?

Fifth, do you bring into the shared service operation the employees currently doing the work at disparate locations for disparate organizations, or do you hire a new team? If you are bringing in current employees, how do you time this? Do you train them in the new operations on their own work, or bring their work in for the previous group of employees to do, then bring them in and train them on the next set of work you bring in?

A corollary to this question is whether to bring people in only when they can be physically located at the shared service operations center or whether to use the "early adoption" methodology of bringing people into the shared service operation's systems and standards even while leaving them physically in their former locations, setting up a virtual or distributed shared service center (discussed in greater detail in Chapter 5 on the question of reengineering and shared services).

Sixth, there is a question of legal entity, which is discussed in detail in Chapter 11.

Seventh and finally, where do you start the implementation regionally? Even if you go to one global shared service operation, it is impossible to simply bring in all activities from around the world all at once. From which part of the world do you bring in the first batch of work, or, if using the regional model, which regional center do you set up first?

TAKE THE OPPORTUNISTIC PATH

The answers to all of these questions must take into account how your company operates today, which methodology would cause the least disruption and entail the least cost (financial and social), and what the ultimate strategic goals are of moving to a shared service organization.

Although cost reduction is an important outcome of moving to a shared service environment, cost reduction cannot be the reason for pursuing shared services. The reasons for pursuing shared services must be strategic in nature.

For instance, if one of the reasons for pursuing shared services is to move away from a country-centered operational model in Europe and to defuse power struggles between country business unit leaders—to create more of a "one-company approach" throughout the European economic community—you might feel that it is imperative to regionalize quickly, despite the disruption and social cost of such a move. Disruption is, in fact, your strategy.

HOW DO YOU MAKE THE DECISIONS?

These decisions can be made only in the context of a process of decision making. This process uses objective criteria for success, the strategy of the business as defined by executive leadership, the creation of a vision for the business and how a shared service organization can help attain that vision, and thorough communication across the entire business so that all constituencies understand the vision, the urgency of making the change, and the impact that change will have on their life and the work they do.

The decision-making process has seven steps:

1. Use baselining of your current processes and measure them against benchmarks and other external data points to determine where the greatest opportunities lie.

2. Establish a set of kick-off workshops with a wide array of business management to build a consensus on the focus of initial opportunities.

3. Ensure that business leadership articulates the necessity for change—the burning platform—and the vision for what the end state of that change will look like—the safe harbor.

4. Talk to individuals at organizations that have successfully moved to a shared service environment. Have them address management about the real change management issues involved in the effort.

5. Build support within key influential pockets of the organization (create champions).

6. Leverage external advice (from those who have been successful and from professional advisors) to gain "distance" from personal bias and attain objectivity around decisions.

7. "Socialize" the proposed approach with key decision makers and build understanding and support.

A number of key factors will influence the success of the decision-making process, including the significance of the opportunity you wish to capture; the maturity of IT systems; the receptivity to the proposal by business unit management who, after all, will need to be participatory partners; the concentration of senior influencing agents (critical mass of executive interest in the program); and the overall credibility of the approach you propose.

Without a doubt, the most successful implementations have occurred around consolidating on common systems solutions, bringing in standard processes, with support by senior management who have confidence in the plan and the team implementing it. Even in the best of circumstances, however, these implementations are difficult, and outside assistance should almost invariably be utilized. After all, why make the mistakes that others have made before you if, with some professional advice, you can learn from the mistakes of others and attain a distilled best-practice approach to the implementation.

THE LUCENT STORY (TOLD BY JIM LUSK)

We chose our model by considering the model used by a number of other companies, based on our benchmarking efforts.

Organizations that we looked at included Cummins Engine, AlliedSignal, Hewlett Packard, and Johnson & Johnson. Everyone was very helpful.

I was really impressed with how willing people at other companies were to give me their time. Everyone I called would spend time with me. There is actually a sense of pride people have in inventing something. People are very excited about it. Also, they are clearly engaging this challenge and are very interested to speak with people and debate with people who are also involved in similar work.

In terms of thinking about which activities from which processes we wanted in the shared service organization, the first thing we did was concentrate on our vision and the results we wanted to produce—what we call the four conditions of satisfaction that we in the CFO organization wanted to deliver to our business partners and be measured by. From there, we looked at what activities we should move into shared services that would give us the greatest chance of achieving our objectives.

Some things were easy, while others sat on the fence. For instance, factory accounting was a challenge. Where does that go? Is it part of operations? When we really got down to it, in discussions with our strategic partners, we decided: "Let's not take anything away from our strategic partners now where we cannot really add a lot of value; let's go after the ones we can really attack the most and deliver the most value added, and we will grab the rest later on."

We also did not want to take on more than we could handle. For instance, we did not pick up billing all around the world; we just picked up billing for two divisions.

We wanted to get it right. Our goal was really to have business units coming to us because we were the best in class. That is when you really know you are ready. We have had one or two groups just starting to come to us. But that is where we hope it is going, to a sort of demand-pull notion. This speaks to the notion laid out in Chapter 7 about having a shared service operation that is "good enough to sell" on the open market. We are not looking to sell our services on the open market, but we want our strategic business unit partners to want to come to us rather than to go to a provider of outsourced services.

We did not have as much work to do reconciling computer systems as we did reconciling business practices. Getting the practices as common as possible is really the key (eliminating customization), getting them all ready to move to an SAP platform. A good CIO organization can handle multiple software systems and hardware platforms; where the shared service operating head has to focus is on reconciling all of the processes so that they are handled in a similar manner.

In terms of staffing the shared service organization, we did not bring in a lot of new people. Aside from Don Peterson, our CFO, and a few other people hired from outside, the people within Lucent did this. What was different was that they had a different vision, a different future to create. Just as Lucent Technologies itself was not about new people, but rather a new context for what had been part of AT&T, our shared service effort was about a new vision for what had been a centralized finance organization.

Regionally, we actually started in the Far East. In fact, China was the first hub, because all of the people and activities were pretty well contained and were running well. Asia-Pacific and North America followed pretty quickly. Europe, the Middle East, and Africa will be last, because in that region you have to pull together people and activities from so many different countries with so many disparate business cultures. Everyone told us that Europe would be the most challenging region, and it has shown itself to be so.

There were a few major factors for our success. One was a philosophy that the whole CFO leadership team was responsible, not just a few people. Number two was getting people focused on producing results, not just on actions. The flip side of that is keeping people accountable for those results.

Another major success factor was communicating. This means more than just keeping people informed. A lot of times we in senior management thought we were communicating a lot, and people said, "Yeah, but you're not communicating with me." To me, that means that that person may have a piece of paper and may have been to a briefing, but we have not communicated clearly and effectively. We need to show how that individual's life and work is a living, breathing part of the vision and the plan for how to reach the vision. People have to see the business value coming out of the change before they can fully understand how they, individually, fit in. I cannot stress enough how much, at every step of the way, people need to feel not just informed but connected to the vision, the action plan, and the actions themselves. The truth and nothing but the truth.

CHECKLIST

☐ Determine the "burning platform"—define a business problem that hinders business growth.
Remember, cost is a *symptom*, not the problem
Common business problems/burning platforms:
  ○ To present one face to the customer

- To create a one-company approach among many disparate business units; and often among a number of acquisitions
- To free up the sales force from supporting tasks
- To globalize from a group of regional organizations

☐ Choose the appropriate model for the shared service organization by answering the following questions:

1. Which *processes* will the shared service organization focus on?
2. Which *activities* from each of those processes will actually be part of the shared service operation?
3. *When* will these activity sets be brought into the shared service operation? (need to have already resolved issues of timing relative to reengineering and IT systems implementation)
   a. At outset of implementation?
   b. During reengineering of processes?
   c. During IT system implementation?
   d. After reengineering and IT system implementation?
4. Will activities running on different *financial accounting systems* (as opposed to IT systems) be brought into the shared service operation before or after being harmonized and standardized?
5. Do you bring into the shared service operation the *employees* currently doing the work at disparate locations for disparate organizations, or do you hire a new team?
6. Should you create a separate *legal entity*?
7. *Where* do you begin the implementation regionally?
   Choose the path of least resistance:
   - Ultimate strategic goals
   - Least disruption
   - Least cost (financial and social)

☐ Decision-making process
   - Benchmark.
   - Build consensus.

- o Articulate the necessity for change and the vision for the end state.
- o Address real change management issues from outsiders who have experienced the process.
- o Create champions.
- o Attain objectivity.
- o Build understanding and support.
- ☐ Influential factors should be:
  - o Significance of opportunity you wish to capture
  - o Maturity of IT systems
  - o Receptivity to proposal by business unit management who will need to be participatory partners
  - o Concentration of senior influential agents
  - o Credibility of approach

10

Selecting the Location

- **Quality/skill of workforce**
- **Availability of IT skills**
- **Cost/flexibility of workforce**
- **Influential factors of cost/flexibility of workforce**
- **Workforce flexibility/openness to new ideas**
- **Availability of government grants**
- **Tax considerations**
- **Cost of communication**
- **Communications infrastructure**
- **Real estate cost**
- **Statutory/legal requirements**
- **External infrastructure**
- **Travel accessibility**
- **Political stability**
- **Language suitability**
- **Company infrastructure**

One of the key variables in setting up a shared service organization is the choice of physical location, both for the management team of the shared service organization and for the personnel who will conduct the business.

For U.S. domestic businesses, the decision sometimes comes down to locating the shared service organization at the same location as the business unit around which it is constructed. For instance, a company that has six business units and decides to create a shared service unit for its information systems (IS) might benchmark which of the IS organizations within the six business units is most effective, set up the IS shared service organization at that location, then fold the other IS units into the one that has been determined to be the best. With only three time zones (excluding Alaska and Hawaii), the IS help desk for national operations could be run from anywhere.

In the case of a transaction-processing shared service operation (e.g., finance operations), a U.S. domestic company might look for a location in a state that offers an abundance of relatively well-educated workers, a moderate wage base, room for expansion, and low business taxes.

For global companies, creating shared service operations is much more difficult, and so is the decision of where to locate the operations. Typically, companies choose some kind of a "hub" strategy, with one hub for Europe, the Middle East, and Africa; another for Asia; a third for Central and South America; and a fourth for North America (the United States, Canada, and Mexico).

A few difficulties arise, in Europe more than anywhere else. Throughout Europe, different countries have completely different working styles, different currencies (despite the advent of the Euro in January 1999, over half of European countries will have their own currencies at least until 2002), different languages, different regulations regarding working conditions; even different accounting standards; as well as a sense among many that only people from that country can truly understand how to do business there.

This is complicated even further in Asia because of the differences in level of development from one country to the next.

Before getting into the specific variables that one must consider when exploring where to set up a shared service operation, it is important to reiterate that the focus of the decision should be on the key question: Is this the right place from which to work in order to solve the basic business problem we are setting out to solve?

COST/SKILLS PARADOX

A key principle in moving to a shared service environment is to set up operations within a low-cost environment, with cost reduction being a major concern, along with process standardization.

However, many of the pioneers in pan-European shared services have initially located their operations in such high-wage cities as Geneva, Milan, Paris, and Amsterdam.

The paradox is that, in order to get the kind of highly developed technical and program management skills necessary to manage such an operation, these companies have had to stay close to capital cities. As telecommunications continues to advance, however, and as more management personnel are willing and even anxious to live outside crowded cities, it is becoming increasingly possible to move these operations to suburban or exurban areas where companies can take advantage of the lower cost of living to keep wages for less-skilled jobs lower than in capital city areas.

The challenge continues to be balancing the lifestyle needs of more highly skilled, educated, and compensated managers with the corporate needs of recruiting, training, and retaining lower-skilled employees at reasonable costs. This kind of balance *can* be maintained.

KEY CONSIDERATIONS

The rest of this chapter will discuss the key considerations one should consider when determining a location in which to place a shared service operation. Many of these considerations can be measured objectively, such as wage levels. Others need a subjective evaluation, such as the significance of your business presence in a particular country. Everything else being equal, where you have business operations will likely be a key driver of where you locate a shared service operation.

At the end of the chapter, after a brief discussion of these variables, how Lucent Technologies went about making its location decisions will be analyzed. It is important to remember that you need to create a weighting factor for your own evaluation, and that you will weigh the variables differently depending on the process you are looking to move to a shared service environment.

For instance, if you are looking to create a shared service operation for accounts payable, you should be looking to establish a low-cost center; if you are looking to create a shared service operation for treasury functions, you need a higher-skill-level employee, with more language capabilities. It is often this conflicting set of requirements that drive decisions to *not* co-locate all shared services operations in one physical location.

Figure 10-1 shows our analysis of four different location possibilities in Europe, across 15 key variables. (Appendix B is a more complete location decision matrix, giving four locations for Europe, the United States, South America, and Australasia. These variables are as follows.

1. Quality/Skill of the Workforce

A number of countries have increasingly skilled workforces with limited domestically driven employment opportunities. While many of these people emigrate for economic opportunity, others stay home for a variety of reasons, from family to quality of life to immigration policies in countries into which they would be willing to move.

Figure 10-1   Greenfield Site—Decision Matrix/Europe

SSC Location Criteria*	Weighting Factor%	Europe			
		Belgium	Holland	Rep. of Ireland	UK (N. England)
Quality/Skill of Workforce		●	●	●	●
Availability of IT Skills		◑	●	●	●
Cost of Workforce		○	◑	●	◑
Workforce Flexibility		◑	●	●	●
Availability of Govt. Grants		○	○	●	●
Tax Considerations		●	○	●	○
Cost of Communications		○	○	●	●
Communication Infrastructure		◑	◑	●	◑
Real Estate Cost		○	◑	●	●
Statutory/Legal Requirements		○	◑	●	●
External Infrastructure		●	●	◑	●
Travel Accessibility		●	●	●	●
Political Stability		●	●	●	●
Linguistic Ability		◑	●	◑	○
Company Infrastructure**	To be completed according to each organization's profile				

* Assessment of comparison is within region, not between regions
** Concentration of organizational presence

Key

● Recommended   ◑ Neutral   ○ Unfavorable

2. Availability of IT Skills

Because the central nervous system of a shared service operation is its information technology (IT), there is no room in a shared service organization for technophobes. Everyone in the organization must be conversant with a computer keyboard and willing to talk to the "techies" on the help desk if they need assistance.

It is also helpful if there is an IT-skilled workforce available for the organization to resolve local system problems, so one does not have to be transplanted from somewhere else. (Recall from the discussion of the BBC in Chapter 7 that 90 IT personnel moved over to MedAS one year before any finance personnel made the jump.)

3. Cost/Flexibility of Workforce

Elements of workforce costs include the hourly or daily rate, amount of paid holiday and sick time, social security and other social welfare payments, training costs, benefits in kind, and redundancy payments (costs of laying off an individual, which in some countries amount to a year's pay or more).

Labor flexibility is a combination of government policies regarding social welfare payments, costs of layoffs and other factors, as well as the work culture and work ethic. "Is the country heavily unionized?" and "Do the unions bargain by business or by trade?" are important questions when looking at labor flexibility. It is also important to look at working hour and holiday norms.

4. Workforce Flexibility/Openness to New Ideas

An ability to innovate and not be bound to old parameters is critical to implementation of a shared service operation. Some countries may be more amenable to change than others as part of their national culture. Another consideration is whether a company has a large operation in a particular country.

5. Availability of Government Grants

Governments often offer grants to foster public policy benefits that they consider important. Economic development is clearly one such policy. Such grants may take the form of area grants to bolster employment in a particular region; training grants to pay for improvement of workforce skills for the purpose of placing people in higher-skilled private jobs, or transportation or infrastructure grants. In the United States, local utilities often offer reduced rates for water, electricity, or natural gas for a period of time to new industrial clients who increase the economic base of a city, region, or state.

6. Tax Considerations

The basic business tax rate is an important consideration. Some countries, regions, or states offer low business taxes to companies that will locate there and hire some of the surplus labor, especially the more skilled labor. Some countries also offer lower tax rates for a period of time for new investments. Benefits can also be obtained by using European economic interest groups and commissionaire tax structures.

Hand in hand with the basic business tax, some countries (or states, counties, cities, and towns within the United States) offer tax breaks for companies that locate there. These often are reduced property taxes for a period of time, if the company remains in the location for two times the length of the tax holiday. If the company leaves early, it repays part or all of the tax holiday.

7. Cost of Communication

For decades, the cost of international communications was enormous. Today, with deregulation, costs are falling rapidly in much of the world. Costs still differ considerably, however, especially for calls within the country. A company must determine how much telephonic communication will be in-country and how much cross-border.

8. Communications Infrastructure

How is the phone system? It is okay for individuals to go cellular to get around the fact that it still takes the government-run Post, Telegraph and Telephone two years to install a line. However, that will not work for a company that needs to receive 2,000 faxes and 5,000 electronic data interchange (EDI) messages each day to transact its purchasing and payments for five operating units. If you cannot get on-line, you cannot run a proper shared service operation.

9. Real Estate Cost

You should consider whether locating in a central business district, which usually entails higher real estate costs, is necessary to the proper functioning of the shared service center. Many U.S. companies have located their shared service centers in suburban or exurban areas in faster-growing parts of the country, such as the South, Southwest, and lower Midwest.

10. Statutory/Legal Requirements

Some government regulations can be onerous to business (e.g., the stamp requirement in Italy, where a government official physically stamps each page of a company's books). In Europe, each country has different reporting requirements for business recordkeeping and reporting. Wherever the shared service center is located, it must comply with the tax and statutory requirements of each country it is servicing.

11. External Infrastructure

This item deals with issues such as roads and utilities. This can be especially important if a company chooses to accept special development tax advantages from countries looking to move industry to more remote areas. How far off the path of effective and efficient infrastructure are you willing to be?

12. Travel Accessibility

It is important for shared service executives to visit sites, whether they are located there or not. For global companies, shared service center managers will need to travel to meetings of worldwide shared service teams, and shared service organization executives will need to visit each site.

Also, if you are doing things well, the shared service executives will want to show off the organization and its service centers to corporate executives, business unit partners, and other companies who might be looking to you for tips on how to create a shared service organization in their own company.

Typically, busy international airports have many more flights available and much more competitive fares than those in less busy regions, reducing travel costs for the global corporation.

13. Political Stability

Whether democracy is a precursor to capitalism or capitalism is a precursor to democracy is a question for philosophers. For businesspeople, however, the question is whether there is governmental/political stability in the country in which they do business, and a tradition of peaceful transfer of power, with no radical shift from one leader to the next in terms of its stand on business.

As we enter the 21st century, we are probably beyond the point of anyone's being elected who advocates state expropriation of foreign-owned companies. Until there are clearer indications from such countries as China as to what position foreigners actually hold in the country, investment will remain tepid and companies will be loath to locate critical shared service operations there.

The same can be said for economic stability. Although being foreign can shield a company to some degree, it can still be unnerving to be located in a country where the economy is going down the drain.

At the dawn of a new millennium, this is a critical issue for companies looking to set up shared services in an Asian country, as many of the former high flyers have been caught since mid-1997 in round after round of currency devaluations. Of course, this reduces the cost of labor on a dollar or European-currency basis. However, it plays into economic and political instability.

Currency stability is also a part of political stability. On the European scene, the advent of the Euro in 1999 reduces the issue of currency stability, eliminating it completely for those countries who join the Euro in 1999 and presumably reducing it for those who aim to join in 2002 as they seek to stabilize their currency against the Euro prior to their admission. In Asia, currency destabilization in 1997 and 1998 has led to economic and some political destabilization as well.

14. Language Suitability (Capabilities of Workforce)

When setting up a pan-European shared service operation, it is important that the workforce be able to speak at least three languages: English; German; and either French, Italian, or Spanish, in addition to their native language if not one of those five.

Asia represents a similar challenge, with a typical Asian shared service center in Hong Kong or Singapore having to cover operations where the language is Thai, Malay, Japanese, or one of a host of Indian or Chinese dialects.

Increasingly, this is even an issue in the United States, with its growing Spanish-speaking population.

15. Company Infrastructure (Significance of Business Presence in Country)

This can be a game breaker for any organization. You must weigh very carefully the presence your company has in any country before deciding where to establish your shared service organization.

For instance, AlliedSignal seriously considered setting up a greenfield operation for its European shared service operation. The company looked closely at Ireland and Manchester, England—both locations with relatively low wage rates and a skilled workforce. But with 60 percent of the company's European management and 40 percent of its business in France, the costs of leaving were simply too high. It would have cost the company somewhere in the vicinity of $50,000 to let go each employee.

How these company infrastructure issues play out will be examined at the end of the chapter when Lucent's decision-making process is discussed.

THE FINAL DECISION

When all is said and done, a few key variables will be the deciding factors and will have to be weighed against each other:

- Both company and governmental politics will come into play at the end, despite all the objective analysis you do.
- For most companies, especially in Europe with its many disparate cultures, a greenfield solution may do the most toward producing the required timely changes.
- Workforce availability will play a larger role than one might initially think. All companies today seek growth, and a country or region can quickly go from having a large, untapped labor pool to a labor pool that is tapped out. All it takes is two or three big operations to soak up excess labor.
- Today's tax haven does not always equate to tomorrow's long-term tax savings.

Through all of this, the best advice is probably to make decisions relatively quickly. Do not get caught in analysis paralysis. The situation is fluid, which makes it harder, but on a worldwide scale, labor is becoming increasingly mobile.

THE LUCENT DECISION PROCESS (TOLD BY JIM LUSK)

We really focused on seven or eight of the key criteria in the bubble chart (Fig. 10-1), including tax issues, infrastructure issues, and availability of a skilled workforce at a reasonable wage. At the end of the day, that is what put us in Ireland, even though it meant moving a number of key people from their former locations.

The key issue to me is really whether you can refocus everyone with the new vision and therefore get very different value out of them in the time required, or whether you have to change the people. Most companies will find that it is a lot easier to change around the vision and get people to think about their jobs differently. Of course, you will always have to have some changes in personnel.

150

CHECKLIST

☐ Suggested location choices:
- For a *U.S. Domestic* shared service center, choose either: the same location as the business unit around which the shared service center is constructed or choose by benchmarking the most effective organization and build the shared service center around that.
- For *transaction processing*, choose a location based on abundance of well-educated workers, moderate wage base, room for expansion, and low business taxes.
- *Global* companies often choose a hub in each region: Europe; Middle East, and Africa; Asia; Latin America; and North America.
- In *Europe*, people have different working styles, currencies, languages, regulations regarding working conditions, and accounting standards, so choosing a location must take into account all those factors.

☐ Some *key considerations* that should be weighed differently depending on the process you are looking to move into the shared service environment
- Quality/skill of workforce
- Availability of IT skills
- Cost/flexibility of work force include
  Hourly or daily rate
  Amount of paid holiday and sick time
  Social security and other social welfare payments
  Training costs
  Benefits in kind
  Redundancy payments (costs of layoffs)
- Cost/flexibility of workforce depends on
  Government policies
  Work culture and ethic
  Unionization
  Working hour and hourly norms

- ○ Workforce flexibility/openness to new ideas
- ○ Availability of government grants
  Area grants to bolster employment
  Training
  Transportation or infrastructure
- ○ Tax considerations
- ○ Cost of communication
- ○ Communications infrastructure
- ○ Real estate cost
- ○ Statutory/legal requirements
- ○ External infrastructure
  Roads
  Utilities
- ○ Travel accessibility
- ○ Political stability
  Economic
  Currency
- ○ Language suitability
- ○ Company infrastructure
- ☐ *Decide quickly.* Do not get caught in analysis paralysis.

11

Setting up the Infrastructure

- **Key principles**
- **Legal entity**
- **Billing shared service costs**
- **Funding the shared service organization**
- **Tax issues**
- **Physical infrastructure set up**

Deciding to create a shared service organization can be the easiest part of the exercise. True, the analysis leading up to the decision must be rigorous. Many people think that once the decision is made, the creation of a shared service center will occur naturally.

However, *setting up the organization* is often far more difficult than foreseen. The reason for this is that companies often do not stick to the following three principles:

1. Keep it simple.
2. Minimize bureaucracy.
3. Eliminate non-value-added activities whenever possible.

QUESTION OF LEGAL ENTITY

An early issue in the process of moving to a shared service environment is deciding which legal entity will house the organization. In most instances, it may be worthwhile to create a separate legal entity to house the shared service operation.

To American domestic companies, this is usually a nonissue;

internationally, however, tax and legal structures can make the decision fraught with complications. It is not unusual for global companies to operate with more than 200 legal entities in Europe alone. While this offers flexibility and supports pursuing whichever strategy makes sense, it does open itself to a number of issues, most notably the human resource dimension.

Whatever entity is chosen to house the shared service operation, if it entails transferring personnel in, there are numerous pension and benefits issues that need to be ironed out. These include seniority and continuous service credits, as well as accounting for pension and other government-driven benefits that are inconsistent across national boundaries. If you are operating with unions or work councils, there will be detailed discussions about continuity of benefits, representation, and equitable treatment of employees.

Another major issue will be wage rates as a component of cost. Although a major goal of operating in a shared service environment is finding low-cost opportunities, "sharing" a legal home may enforce unintended comparable/minimum wage rates, and/or across-the-board and consistent wage increases. In particular, as specific business fortunes climb and tumble, the consequent bonuses or belt tightening in incentives, benefits, and compensation might be legally enforced on the shared services staff as well.

There are also accountability issues. In many countries, the legal head of an entity may be ultimately responsible for any health, safety, and environment (HS&E) or other statutory violations, with personal consequences and risks. This can complicate decisions and actions the shared service center leadership may make. In addition, the legal entity chosen needs to be able to "legally support" the cash funding assets and investments that go with the shared service center. This can be a significant issue if the costs involved include a pan-regional information technology (IT) systems upgrade or implementation.

This means that, although you would like to minimize bureaucracy and costs in the implementation of a shared service operation and be a "team player" as well, your hands can be tied if you choose to cohabit in an existing legal entity within the corporate family. For this reason, whenever politically possible within the corporation, establish a separate legal entity by region and operate the "business" of shared services with the same autonomy and freedom that any strategic business unit and its leadership has.

This will not be the case, however, if the corporation has reengineered its fiscal and legal structure down to one corporation per country or even one entity per region.

For instance, in AlliedSignal Europe, the U.K. operating divisions are all "legally" owned or consolidated under the umbrella of one holding company. Operating management are measured and rewarded based on their divisions' profit before tax (PBT), and there is no incentive or reason for any single business management to be concerned with the "whole" legal entity together with its tax, reporting, and other statutory requirements. Only within the shared service operation is there any consideration or attention given to the consolidated operating results.

This situation, when established, created a void in identifying the board members (legal directors) of the holding company.

You might ask: Who cares?

The operating management in AlliedSignal Europe certainly cared. If they accept the title (albeit meaningless to their corporate careers), it carries consequences and risk. Why should they be liable for the risks taken by other businesses within the group that might have far greater HS&E implications?

Specifically, if you run an aerospace business, do you want to sign up for personal liability to a chemical plant with all the safety and environmental implications of its waste products? Equally, although it is a logical choice to appoint the leadership of the shared service operation as members of the board, it would have been grossly inappropriate to make them *solely* liable for the consequences of any operating business' actions or decisions.

The outcome was a compromise. The board of AlliedSignal in the United Kingdom was chaired by the European Director of the shared service organization. To ensure business-unit accountability, the board also included a representative from each of the significant business units represented in the consolidated financial results.

As you can see, in the United States the question of legal entity is usually simple—should we put the shared service organization within an existing legal entity or set it up as an independent entity—and the choice of location and operating structure is not affected, whereas outside the United States it is a complicated question.

Ultimately, every shared service organization should be a separate legal entity. Especially in Europe, however, this will in all likelihood be a two-step process. The first step will be simplifying where you can—moving toward one legal entity per country in Europe, with shared services within one country's entity. Next comes breaking off the shared service operation into its own legal entity. Finally, every company would move to one legal entity for all of Europe. In the short term, political and business practice realities will keep this from happening; but might by the second quarter of the 21st century, this will be possible.

However, it must be understood that one legal entity for all of Europe implies harmonization of tax and legal requirements, as well as a desire by companies to accept the business and legal risks of exposing all corporate assets to a claim in any country. Many believe this is unlikely to ever occur.

Having made the decision on legal entity, and hence the question of governance, everything else falls into place rather simply. The other issues are billing out costs, funding, and tax.

BILLING SHARED SERVICE COSTS

Billing out shared service operation costs is complicated by operating across entities and more so across national borders. At the simplest level, the question might be only whether costs should be billed out monthly, quarterly, or annually. However, as soon as you move across entities and borders, billing out shared service costs falls under the grouping of intercompany charges.

In Chapter 12, a unique model for billing shared services, known as *value management*, is developed. The key to successful value management, and to successful billing of shared services in general, is to create a system that drives behavior, on the part of both the shared service organization and the business unit partners.

This area always creates high sensitivity and risk from a tax jurisdiction perspective. The consequent impact on taxable profits and rates of tax cannot be ignored. Typically, tax considerations impose the need to make a markup on cost, so the shared service operation becomes a profit center.

This, however, is completely contrary to the intentions and desires of the shared service and corporate leadership. How can this be resolved?

You can make statutory-only adjustments and create permanent timing differences with the internal management books. Or you can risk the ire and negative perceptions from business unit partners by making a "profit." This opens further questions around how you will eventually distribute "profit," how you account for significant up-front set-up or systems implementation costs, particularly if you have a migration plan that spans many years. Again, this is discussed in more detail in Chapter 12.

It is not within the scope of this book to provide all the possible answers to these dilemmas. Rather, you need to work it out within your own organization and with assistance from outside legal and professional business advisors.

FUNDING THE SHARED SERVICE ORGANIZATION

Should the shared service operation have its own cash-flow targets, forecasts, and reporting? Or should it fold into one of the operating unit's results? If the latter, who should bear the consequences of over- or underperformance? If significant external funding is required, who should negotiate with external lenders, and who gives up credit lines to accommodate the shared service operation's needs? If hedging contracts and netting and discounting are extensively used, who carries the expense and risk? Which operating budget consolidates the cost of penalties or interest if mistakes, errors, or delays occur?

Some of these issues should be covered in the service agreements between the shared service operation and its business unit partners, discussed in more detail in Chapter 12.

Again, the purpose of this book is not to delve into a myriad of treasury questions and strategies, but rather to highlight that there are considerations to be thought through sooner rather than later.

TAX ISSUES

Equally, this book does not attempt to serve as an authoritative resource on tax planning, but instead aims to draw attention to tax considerations that need to be addressed. There are four key issues:

1. Grants and incentives. These include special investments, employment incentives, or the granting of "offshore financial center" status provided by some countries as diverse as Cyprus, Mauritius, Ireland, and the Cayman Islands.
2. Specific treasury or insurance center incentives offered in such countries as the Bahamas, Bermuda, and Dubai, as well as Belgian coordination centers.
3. Grants for investment and employment, and regional development assistance, in such areas as Wales, southern Italy, the Lorraine region of France, Indonesia, and Brazil.
4. Corporate tax holidays or extremely attractive tax rates, in areas such as Dublin and Andorra.

PHYSICAL INFRASTRUCTURE SETUP

In addition to all of the business infrastructure issues discussed above, there are physical infrastructure issues that need to be addressed. They fall into two areas: (1) the building and (2) equipment.

With regard to the building, you want to be able to set up the building's interior in a way most conducive to performing the work process in the most efficient and effective manner possible. You need to take into account work-flow layout, including the number and location of team stations, offices, and meeting rooms, as well as break and huddle rooms.

Access and security are important, both access to the work area and to records. Toilet facilities are mundane but often overlooked when considering design. How will the physical facility be supported during nonworking hours?

Equipment issues include cabling for voice, data, video and personal computers (PCs). Hardware and software standards need to be set for PCs, video conferencing, imaging, work-flow systems, faxing, and photocopying. Communication questions include phone types, number of phone lines, switch technology, and fax technology. Heating, ventilation, and air conditioning also must be dealt with.

Furniture can and should be used to help delineate activity and process flow and space. Workstation design and the use or nonuse of partitions say something about both the way work flows and the human relations atmosphere being created in the operation.

Typically, shared service operations start with a handful of people, ramp up rapidly in the initial phase, and then consolidate. Over time, as processes become more effective and efficient, headcount and thus space needs often fall incrementally. Proper layout can be critical to maintaining efficiency and effectiveness through this life cycle, and utilizing a design professional who has worked with corporations in designing flexible, fluid work spaces should be considered.

One other item that is incorporated in design issues is disaster recovery plans: Where are back-up tapes, files, software, and so forth to be stored? Who has access to them, and how they will be utilized? These are all questions that need to be addressed in the start-up phase.

SETTING UP LUCENT'S INFRASTRUCTURE (TOLD BY JIM LUSK)

We worked with three universal principles:

1. Keep the vision clear and as simple as possible.
2. Focus on shared services as a business. Think about where the roles and responsibilities are. Where is the marketing? Where is the manufacturing? Where is the research and development?
3. Anything we do has to increase the value for our strategic business partners, shareholders, and customers. In no way can we degrade the current value we bring.

159

In keeping with these principles, we did not create a new legal entity. In fact, at the same time we were moving to a shared service model, all of Lucent was working to simplify its legal entity situation. So we certainly did not want to create a new legal entity.

We have a very simple pricing formula, which will be discussed in Chapter 12.

Working in Ireland helps keep things simple. The tax structure is simple (and helpful.) The infrastructure in Dublin is good. In other instances, for simplicity, we kept our operations close to our strategic business partners in other Lucent operations.

CHECKLIST

☐ Key principles:
- Keep it simple.
- Minimize bureaucracy.
- Eliminate non-value-added activities.

☐ If you create a separate legal entity to house the shared service operation, you must consider:
- Pension and benefits issue
  Seniority and continuous service credits
  Accounting for pension and other government-driven benefits that are inconsistent across national boundaries
  Continuity of benefits
  Representation
  Equitable treatment of employees
- Wage rates as a component of cost
  Incentives—bonuses or belt tightening
- Accountability issues
  Legal head of an entity—health, safety, and environment or other statutory violations with personal consequences and risks
  Legal entity—needs to be able to "legally support" the cash funding assets and investments that go with the shared service center

---

- ☐ Billing shared service costs
- ☐ Funding the shared service organization
- ☐ Tax issues:
  - ○ Grants and incentives
  - ○ Special treasury or insurance center incentives
  - ○ Grants for investment and employment, and regional development assistance
  - ○ Corporate tax holidays or extremely attractive rates
- ☐ Physical infrastructure setup:
  - ○ Building

    Layout conducive to conducting the process in the most efficient and effective manner possible.

    Work-flow layout—number and locations of team stations, offices, meeting rooms, break and huddle rooms.

    Access

    Security
  - ○ Equipment:

    Cabling for voice, data, video, and PCs

    Hardware and software standards for PCs, video conferencing, imaging, work-flow systems, and photocopying

    Communication questions for phone types, number of phone lines, switch technology, and fax technology

    Heating, ventilation, and air conditioning

    Furniture

    Workstation design

    Disaster recovery plans

12

Service-Level Agreements and Pricing Issues

- **Breaking even**
- **Pricing strategies**
- **The effect of IT systems**
- **Performance tracking and continuous improvement**

In most competitive situations, companies are very focused on margin and cost management of their services or products. There is typically a large organization dedicated to analyzing this equation, in order to understand the impact of changes in the market, as well as changes in the company's cost structure. The sales, general and administrative (SG&A) cost structure is absorbed as part of margin and considered in the company's pricing strategy.

Within a shared service environment, however, a different model is needed. Shared service operations should be run with the goal of breaking even. For this reason, they do not have profitability goals, and because of this, the necessity (and capability) to do cost and margin analysis comes under question. However, shared service organizations still need to understand their cost structure in order to manage the relationships with their strategic business unit (SBU) partners.

ALTERNATIVE PRICING STRATEGIES

In short, the question is: "How do we set a price for providing various transactional services so our costs are met, but not so high as to artificially inflate the costs to our partners?"

We have created a model that does that, called value management. However, to fully understand value management, you need to first understand the five alternative pricing strategies:

1. Do nothing
2. Allocation
3. Transfer pricing
4. Market pricing
5. Value management

Do Nothing

In the *do nothing* methodology, there is no pricing formula. The shared service organization is treated as a pure cost center, with an annual budget, as if it were a centralized corporate function. The upside to this is that shared service management can focus on process enhancement without worrying about working out a pricing formula.

However, the downside outweighs the upside. The downside is that this methodology does not allow for a true capture of costing information and the ability to effectively benchmark. Also, it does not break the old paradigm, and this pseudocentralized function can have a difficult time convincing business unit partners that it truly is a "service" organization. While doing nothing is always a bad long-term choice, not charging immediately is a legitimate short-term option. In some instances, this option allows gathering good data for creating a pricing strategy and can enhance communication between the shared service center and its business unit partners.

Allocation

Allocation is the simplest form of pricing. In a pure allocation model, business unit partners are simply billed for the percentage of the total transaction volume they account for. If SBU-A is responsible for 20 percent of the volume, it pays 20 percent of the shared service operation's costs. The upside of this methodology is simplicity.

The downside is that it does not take into account any responsibility on the part of the SBU for providing the shared service operation with "clean" data on which to perform a transaction. In other words, the "input" from the SBU can be anything, and the "processing" that the shared service operation does can be easy or difficult, all for the same price. Allocation also does not take into account that some kinds of transactions are more complex than others, and more costly to process.

Transfer Pricing

Transfer pricing is a methodology by which one business unit sells goods or services to another, adding a markup for profit. The upside is that it allows a cost center to become a profit center, but the downsides are devastating. A business unit that uses transfer pricing has no incentive to reduce costs, because it is in essence working on a "cost-plus" model.

Market Pricing

Market pricing is the methodology of creating intracompany transfers of goods or services at the actual price at which a good or service is sold in the marketplace.

Market pricing is one of the two alternatives a shared service operation should use when determining a pricing relationship with its SBU partners.

Value Management

Value management is the pricing methodology by which the price of intracompany transfers of services is variable and dependent on both parties adhering to predetermined, agreed-upon criteria for value.

A number of our colleagues at PricewaterhouseCoopers have defined a formula for value in a number of previous books. Here, we simply extend that formula to make it useful in the context of shared services.

Our value equation derives from the shared service process, in which an SBU provides input to a shared service operation, which processes the input and provides an output back to the SBU. In graphic form, it looks like this:

SBU → SS op → SBU

Input → Process → Output

Within the processing of inputs, there is an efficiency element and an effectiveness element. Arithmetically, that looks like this:

Speed + Resources = Efficiency

Cycle time + Quality = Effectiveness

Efficiency + Effectiveness = Value

For example, an efficiency measurement is the number of accounts payable vouchers processed per employee per week. An effectiveness measure is the time it takes from the moment an invoice comes in until the time the voucher is processed correctly.

However, this pricing model will work only if the following conditions are met:

The requirements for appropriate inputs must be clearly defined and agreed to by the SBUs and the shared service operation, and must be adhered to by SBUs. At the same time, the shared service operation promises to deliver high value (as defined by the parties along the four dimensions of cycle time, quality, speed, and resource allocation).

This set of promises and requirements is defined within the service-level agreement (SLA) and shown as Figure 12-1. A model SLA appears at the end of the book as Appendix C.

PRICING METHODOLOGY INTEGRAL TO SLAs

The key to making any pricing model work is building an agreement between the business unit partners and the shared service organization. In addition, the pricing model will probably be different for different types of transactions, and different degrees of relationship between the business unit and shared services partners.

Figure 12-1 Principles of a Service-Level Agreement

Overriding Principles:

- Keep it SIMPLE
- Keep it brief
- Use to factually document the existing service/performance levels
- Evolve to a more simplified format as trust builds
- Ultimate goal being to have no NEED for a documented agreement

Some Cautions:

- Establish responsibilities and metrics for both the Shared Services center AND the SBU
- Limit the amount of time spent on this non-value-added activity
- Meet and communicate regularly to fix issues quickly

Initially a Standard Service-Level Agreement for a Shared Service Implementation Would Typically Contain the Following Elements

- Guiding Operating Principles - spirit of total cooperation
- Definition of Services to be provided by whom and to whom
- Timelines and effective dates
- Procedural split of responsibilities clearly laid out for both parties with timing
- Accountability identified
- Performance levels defined in the form of Metrics
- Pricing per transaction or unit and duration of price-list
- Discounts / Pricing to drive the right behaviors
- Payment procedures and extent of back-up provided to support billing

- Share and liquidation of Implementation costs
- Allocation of benefits and cost reduction
- Tax accounting vs Management accounting - treatment of mark-ups
- Help desk names, contact numbers and availability
- Disposition of errors and penalties
- Disaster recovery plans
- Dispute resolution procedures
- Escalation protocol
- Continuous improvement teaming and beneficiaries
- Signatures of both parties and date discussed

The goal of any pricing model is simplicity, but not at the price of unfairness. At first blush, "do nothing" would seem to meet this requirement. However, a "do nothing" model by its very nature lapses into pure centralization due to lack of accountability and lack of business focus. In the "do nothing" model, shared service management lacks the ability to "think like a business."

It can be saddled with increased volumes, inflation, and the costs of bringing on new infrastructure without having any flexibility to adjust pricing. The only virtue of being purely a cost center is that the shared service center is forced to constantly reinvent itself in order to maintain its volumes within its defined budget.

Figure 12-2 shows how the different pricing models might be used in different circumstances. The vertical axis shows the complexity of the transactions a shared service operation deals with. The horizontal axis shows the decision to be either a purely internal service organization or to open itself up to service outside clients. Remember, in Chapter 7 on outsourcing, we argued that every shared service organization should become good enough at what it does to be able to offer its services to the outside. That is not to say that every shared service

167

Figure 12-2   Service-Level Agreement Pricing Matrix

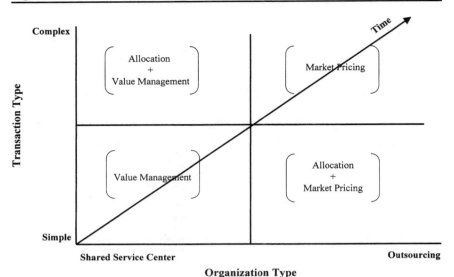

organization will eventually do so, but some no doubt will. The diagonal "time" line is not meant to imply that every organization should move in this direction, only that some will over time.

For simple transactions in a purely internal setting, creating a value management price should be relatively easy and is the preferred methodology (lower left box).

As transactions become more complex, it is possible that value management will not be able in and of itself to account for the differences in complexity among the many different types of transactions. You may need to allocate a portion of shared service center costs to all business units, in essence asking business units to "ante up" a certain amount to create an income base for the shared service organization (upper left box).

If the shared service organization moves into the realm of being a provider of outsourced services, it needs to form a market pricing strategy for external customers. If the transactions it handles for its business unit partners within the same corporate umbrella are simple, it may want to work on a purely allocation methodology or an allocation/market pricing methodology with them, while maintaining pure market pricing for its outside clients (lower right box).

If it is handling transactions for its business unit partners and its outsourcing clients that are complex, it will be easier to move to a pure market pricing methodology for both internal partners and external clients (upper right box).

The Effect of IT Systems

It should also be noted here that the level of information technology (IT) sophistication has a great impact on the shared service organization's ability to create variable pricing. In fact, until systems are fully rationalized, the variability in cost might be intertwined with the IT used. The shared service organization can use pricing to force a desired behavior change—migration by the business unit partner to the hardware platform of choice and the preferred software.

If a company already has gone to an enterprise resource planning (ERP) software system, both pricing and the elements of the SLA become far easier to arrive at. Enterprise resource planning enhances the ability to both create value management pricing and best-practice market pricing.

PERFORMANCE TRACKING AND CONTINUOUS IMPROVEMENT

Once the program is in place, the question becomes how the partners track their own performance and the performance of the other partner. For this, we use our continuous improvement model, shown in Figure 12-3.

This model will be more fully explained in Chapter 18 on performance measures for the entire shared service organization.

For our discussion here, it is sufficient to explain that each time there is an exception to the standards, as defined by the SLA, it must be captured, tracked, understood, and then fixed. The way this is done is by bringing it into the dispute resolution model.

The biggest fear of shared service organizations is: "What if my

Figure 12-3   Continuous Improvement Model

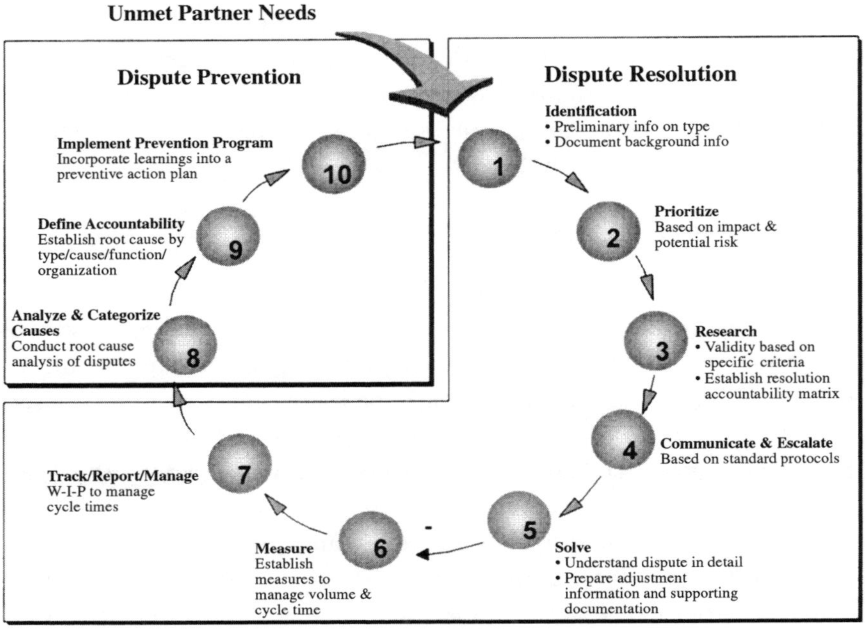

business unit partners send me stuff that is not what has been promised (messy input), but believe that I am still responsible for doing what I have agreed to do (value output)?" The answer is, the dispute resolution model needs to be used, and once it is determined where the problem lies, the value management model allows for either price adjustment or adjustment in the guarantees for output.

LUCENT'S SLAs AND PRICING (TOLD BY JIM LUSK)

Again, our model is simplicity. We want to focus people throughout the shared service operations on producing the ultimate value for the company. Right now, we are operating under the umbrella of all the transfer price arrangements that have previously been set up throughout the company. This includes normal overheads and everything else.

Now that we have more experience with our new processes, we

are beginning to look more closely at creating more formal SLAs and a different pricing policy. Currently, we are running shared services as a cost center with an annual budget.

CHECKLIST

- ☐ Set goal of shared service operations: breaking even
- ☐ Choose from among the following pricing strategies:
  - ○ Do Nothing
  - ○ Allocation
  - ○ Transfer pricing
  - ○ Market pricing
  - ○ Value management (recommended)
    Draft an SLA
       Define value in terms of
          Speed
          Resources
          Cycle time
          Quality
       Identify input criteria (timeliness and cleanliness of data)
       Identify output criteria (timeliness and quality of information)
- ☐ Take into account IT systems' impact on shared service center's ability to create variable pricing.
- ☐ Create a performance tracking process.
- ☐ Create a process for continuous improvement.

13

Final Business Case

- **Purpose**
- **Baselining—fact gathering**
- **Benchmarking—comparison and analysis**
- **Making the business case**
- **Costs**
- **Process**
- **Technology**
- **Facilities**

It has been stated a number of times throughout this book that there are tangible/quantifiable benefits to creating a shared service organization, as well as intangible benefits. It has also been stated that, if one were to create a cost–benefit analysis (a business case) based merely on the tangible benefits, creating a shared service organization would in almost all cases be a nonstarter. The effort must fit in with the company's overall strategy.

However, it is necessary to create a business case, in order not merely to justify the business change effort, but also to set some targets for quantifiable results, where they are possible to achieve.

Figure 13-1 shows the benefits over time of optimizing service delivery to maximize productivity (left), as well as the investment over time that is necessary to undertake the effort. Notice that the results accrue well after the majority of the investment has been spent. In real time, the two slopes usually converge between 18 and 24 months after the onset of the effort. Once this "payback" has been achieved, gains

Figure 13-1   Benefits and Investments from Optimizing Productivity

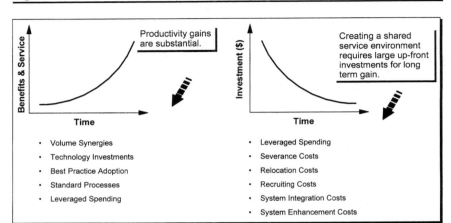

accrue rapidly. Because of this, the business case must show clearly the benefits that will accrue to executives, whose support is necessary for the effort to be successful.

Another clear value of doing a business case analysis before embarking on the effort is that it "sinks a stake in the ground" at the start of the program, defining the state of the business, processes, functions, and activities when the program began, and creating a vision for the end state. Because this will be a two- to three-year effort, and some individuals who play important roles within the effort will inevitably leave, it is important that an "institutional memory" be created. In order to fulfill such a roll, a business case must be a "living document" that takes a snapshot of a business entity at a moment in time, with the full realization that the business entity is organic and undergoes natural change over time as well as the change being imposed by this particular effort.

In order for the business case to fulfill all of these roles, it must be undertaken with complete honesty and designed to be pragmatic. Doing an honest business case means admitting up front that, because of the nature of the investment necessary, on a pure return on investment (ROI) basis, many other business projects will accrue greater and quicker returns—moving to shared services *cannot compete on ROI alone.*

Being pragmatic in the business case means breaking the paradigm of all-or-nothing programs, and being opportunistic by picking off low-hanging fruit.

DEVELOPING THE BUSINESS CASE

The business case is developed in three stages:

1. Fact gathering, or baselining
2. Comparison and analysis, or benchmarking
3. Interpreting the results

Proper baselining and benchmarking against other companies requires interpretation. Only looking at the raw data accumulated through these excercises has limited usefulness. Benchmarking provides directionally relevant information about competitors but should not be used as gospel. Benchmarking results are only data points. The entire set of analytical excercises—baselining, benchmarking, examining best practices, and analyzing gaps within your own processes between where they are and where they ought to be—needs to be undertaken.

Baselining and Benchmarking

In this stage of business case development, you need to gather both summary and process facts about your business as it is presently constituted. This is the so-called as-is analysis.

Summary facts include headcount, number of sites, ratio of supervisors to line employees at each site (the span of control); process and activity definitions and descriptions at each site, and how those definitions and descriptions differ by site; and process costs by activity at each site. Our "baselining cube" (Fig. 13-2) shows all of the variables.

Process facts include a detailed review of process costs and headcount, as well as which process activities fall within the purview of each individual. From this, a comparison of process performance between business units and sites can be made. Highlight those processes and activities that consume significant resources or look out of balance with other processes and activities.

Figure 13-2 Baselining and Benchmarking Tools

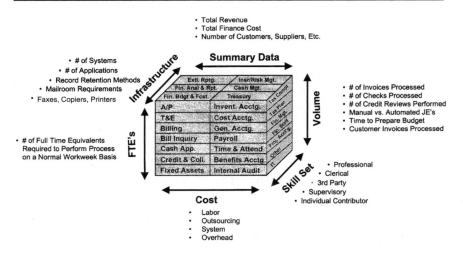

Summary facts and process facts give the baseline of the process and its costs in the as-is state.

There are two ways to benchmark. One is to actually make site visits to "best-in-class" companies and watch the way they perform a specific process or set of activities. This is often done in manufacturing and other core processes as part of a total quality management (TQM) or business process reengineering (BPR) effort.

However, in support service processes, benchmarking can be successfully accomplished by simply comparing objective measures (transactions per full-time equivalent [FTE] employee, e.g., FTEs per process, FTEs per supervisor, FTEs per $1 billion of revenue; number of pay slips per FTE; number of benefit transactions per FTE, etc). For instance, PricewaterhouseCoopers uses a benchmarking template for finance organizations that measures 26 different finance processes.

This kind of data has been gathered for hundreds of companies over time. You can get a pretty good idea of how good your process is by comparing the results of your baseline data against the 25th percentile (first quartile). The goal here is not to nitpick how you are different from companies in the top quartile, and how it might be difficult to achieve their kind of results, but rather to use first quartile rankings as a guide for the directions in which your company should be moving.

You can and should also benchmark each business unit against all others by each of these process measures, as well as by wage rates and some of the other criteria laid out in Chapter 10 (this can be done using the format we used for benchmarking potential locations in Figure 10-1).

The reason for this is because you want the ability to either design your shared service organization as a "greenfield" operation, starting anew; or to use your best-in-class operation as the starting point to build the organization. Whenever you have a process being performed to first quartile specifications inside your organization, use that as the foundation to build the organization, unless there are internal political reasons for going to a green field design.

It is important in this set of analytical excercises to VBPS (visit best-practice sites). Just reading about best practices does not give one the true "feel of the air" in an environment in which support processes hum along in a finely tuned manner.

Figure 13-3   Benefits to Creating a Shared Service Organization

- **Some Tangible**
  - Leveraging consolidated spending with vendors to negotiate better terms and prices
  - Working capital improvements from standardizing, centralizing, and netting treasury activities
  - Working capital gains from operating receivables, payables, and inventory management in a center of expertise
  - Reduction in business complexity, audit and statutory reporting fees
  - Consolidated transactions across common customers and vendors

- **Some Intangible**
  - Promotes the "one-company" approach
  - Drives the effort to more rapidly transition the business focusing on "added-value"
  - Enables the effective maintenance of standard "code-block" throughout the organization
  - Leverages and speeds the adoption of best practices
  - Improved accuracy and consistency of information
  - More sophisticated business controls from leveraging volumes and technology investments
  - When linked to a new system migration - better leverages learning curve

MAKING THE CASE

Remember, benefits are not limited to cost reduction. There are a number of revenue-positive benefits. In addition, benefits are not all tangible; many are intangible, as shown in Figure 13-3.

Making the Business Case: The Benefit Side

Once you have baselined and benchmarked, you can measure your potential savings by modeling an operation on first quartile productivity and employment statistics, or on your best operations.

Figure 13-4 shows a template that can be used to determine potential benefits.

Both benefits and costs, which will be discussed later, are identified in terms of people, processes, technology, and facilities.

People Benefits. People benefits include a reduction in FTEs through improved and standardized processes, as well as through more level loading of work. If there is enough work for 3.5 people at

Figure 13-4 The Business Case

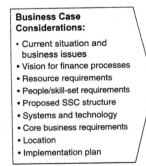
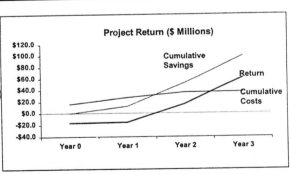

The business case will vary, but should be dependent upon and address management's vision and demonstrate significant improvement potential

each of four sites in one process, four people must be on the payroll to accomplish the work at each site. Simply consolidating the process will allow a reduction of two people, without any process enhancements.

It should always be noted that the goal is not to reduce headcount, but to reduce cost per activity, transaction, or process and free up business unit management to produce or sell more product. If more product can be sold, market share increases and transaction volumes may increase, which will, in turn, lead to more, different, and possibly better employment opportunities for those who have been reduced through FTE consolidation and process enhancement. This is a key concept to communicate to employees throughout the transition to a shared service environment.

A similar argument can be made for span of control. If a supervisor can effectively supervise eight people, but there are only 3.5 FTEs (four bodies) performing a process at each site, with one supervisor, consolidating into a shared service operation will allow the 14 process employees (reduction of two) to be supervised by two supervisors (also a reduction of two.)

Wages can be reduced if a shared service center can be established and the processes can effectively be performed by employees in a lower-wage location than is currently the case. While wage reduction is often a goal, this must be balanced against the increased costs (financial and social) of establishing a green field operation rather than building off the company's best efforts.

Moving to a shared service method of operation also affords support process managers a broader view of the business aspects of the services they provide. "Thinking like a business manager" means finding creative ways to deliver more value for less cost to the client, in this case a business unit partner. This benefit might be termed making transactional managers into business managers.

Process Benefits. Standardizing processes and implementing best practices, either from within or from outside the company, affords one the opportunity to both improve productivity and reduce the cost of quality. This occurs in part because all employees can begin to take an end-to-end process view of their work and see how their activities fit into the entire process.

Technology Benefits. The vast majority of programs undertaken to move to a shared service environment coincide with major implementation of new system software, and often hardware as well. More and more companies are moving to enterprise resource planning (ERP) software, which links activities throughout the company's recordkeeping.

At a minimum, moving to a shared service operation necessitates rationalizing the number of hardware platforms and software packages on which recordkeeping is performed. Processes cannot be truly standardized unless and until systems are standardized.

Moving to one hardware and software platform also reduces software purchases, license fees, and maintenance costs.

Facilities Benefits. The costs of facilities can be reduced if, in fact, facilities can be closed as operations are consolidated. If each operation is merely occupying space in a company-owned facility that has other operations, even total physical consolidation may not reduce facilities costs. However, most companies that embark on shared services are able to close facilities, and the more processes are consolidated into the shared service operation, the more facilities can be closed.

Making the Business Case: The Costs

On the flip side, there are costs associated with moving to a shared service organization. They are shown in the template in Figure 13-5.

People Costs. Before you can start realizing the savings from reductions in staffing, you need to pay the costs of trying to keep the staff you want and dismissing the staff you feel are not well suited to the new way of working. There are a number of costs associated with this effort.

For those you want to stay, even if it means moving, there are relocation costs, and often bonuses for staying. There is the cost of increased training to help them build all the skills necessary to take on the new process activities.

Figure 13-5   Costs Associated with Moving to a Shared Service
Organization

Costs	Benefits
People	
• Relocation • Stay bonuses • Training • Temporary staff • Severance packages • Customer Service—Help Desk	• Reduction in FTEs • Reduction in wages due to site selection • Maximized span of control • Minimized overtime
Processes	
• Reengineer processes • Establish metrics • Implement best practices	• Improved productivity • Implement best practices • Standardized processes • Reduced cost of quality
Technology	
• Hardware • New software • Upgrade infrastructure • Call center	• Enterprise-wide software • Platform scalability • Reduced software purchase price • Reduced license fees • Reduced maintenance fees
Facilities	
• Consolidate operations • Close old facilities	• Decreased rent • Decreased facilities management costs

For those you will not retain, there are severance costs including accumulated leave time payments, possible early retirement buyouts, outplacement, and possibly increased unemployment insurance costs for those laid off.

There are also costs associated with building the new staff in the new location. Even if everyone in the new operation comes from inside the company, there will be temporary staffing needs while they make the move and the transition. If there is a need to hire more staff, there are recruiting costs, as well as orientation and training costs.

Process Costs.   These are the costs of any process reengineering, process redesign, or new process design. Such costs are inherent in any consolidation to shared services, to one degree or another. In the simplest case, it is establishing new metrics and implementing best-practice processes from within the company. In the most complex case, it is an extensive BPR effort carried out either prior to or after consolidating the activities in a shared service center.

Technology Costs.   Again, there is always some degree of technological transformation inherent in the creation of a shared service operation. That means that there is always some upgrading of hardware and/or software. Carrying out service processes for many different physical locations and many business units also requires a heavy investment in telecommunications infrastructure.

Facilities Costs.   While closing facilities saves money in the long run, there are short-term costs. There are also costs to finding, taking possession of, designing and outfitting the new facility, as well as moving of whatever equipment and records are moved from the old facilities to the new facility.

THE LUCENT BUSINESS CASE (TOLD BY JIM LUSK)

For us, shared services was really a "no-brainer business case." The effort was going to be self-funded. There were really no trade-off decisions to make. But we still did go through many of the steps in the business case laid out in this chapter.

We did a lot of benchmarking. I found companies to benchmark partly through personal contacts, other controllers I know, and partially from suggestions by my consultants. From visits to places like Hewlett Packard, AlliedSignal, and others, we were able to see the kinds of added value that a shared service finance organization could deliver.

We saw and laid out for our own education the benefits that we could derive and that we thought we should derive as part of our vision for the shared service organization. Since we did not need to justify costs against other proposed projects, we did not do a full-blown business case.

CHECKLIST

Developing the Business Case—Three Stages

☐ Baselining—fact gathering
   ○ Collect Summary Facts
     Headcount
     Number of sites
     Ratio of supervisors to line employees at each site
     Process costs by activity at each site
   ○ Collect Process Facts
     Detailed review of process costs and headcount
     Which process activities fall within the purview of each individual
   ○ Highlight those processes and activities that consume significant resources or look out of balance with other processes and activities
☐ Benchmarking—comparison and analysis
   ○ Make site visits to "best in class"
   ○ Compare objective measures on paper
☐ Making the Business Case
   ○ Identify and Measure Benefits
     People—Reduction in FTEs via

Process—Improve productivity and reduce the cost of quality

Technology—rationalization of hardware platforms and software packages, standardized systems, standardized processes, reduction of software purchases, license fees and maintenance costs

Facilities—reduce costs due to consolidation of operations.

Value chain—support managers have broader view of business and thus find creative ways to deliver more value for less to the client/business unit partner.

o Identify and Measure Costs

People

 Keeping staff

  Relocation

  Bonuses

  Increased training

 Dismissing staff

  Severance

  Accumulated leave time payments

  Early retirement buyouts

  Outplacement

  Increased unemployment insurance

 Building new staff

  Recruiting costs

  Orientation

  Training

Process

 Process reengineering

 Process redesign

 New process design

Technology

Facilities

 Finding, taking possession of, designing and outfitting

 Moving equipment and records from old facility

Part Four

Implement

In this final part, we take readers through some of the major issues involved in the implementation of shared services.

Like both business process reengineering (BPR) and enterprise resource planning (ERP), implementation of shared services is a major organizational change effort. The entire effort must be defined and mapped out, and it is usually important to have outside consulting assistance.

Strong program and project management is integral to success, as are strong change management skills. We map out for readers the kind of teams that need to be created to undertake such a large implementation, and what is expected of them. We also explain how to find the proper consultant to match the in-house skills present in the organization.

In Chapter 18 we present a format for creating a set of integrated metrics by which to measure the success not only of the implementation program but of the shared service organization once it is established.

Finally, in Chapter 19 we look at the long-term implications of shared services. While no company has yet been successful in a truly global implementation, more companies are moving in that direction all the time. And as information technology (IT) advances, more and more previously manual activities within support processes are becoming completely automated.

14

Defining and Setting Up
the Project

- **Type of start: Fast or Deliberate**
- **Model of a SS organization**
- **Implementation program development (based on deliberate start)**
- **Keys to successful implementation**

Beginning with this chapter, we move from program design to implementation. The previous six chapters have looked at what the shared service vision should be and how to get there through the sizing of the opportunity and development of a clear, honest business case. We have discussed the importance of choosing appropriate processes and activities within those processes to coalesce into the shared service organization. We have highlighted the issues around choosing the geographic model and regional location selection, as well as specific site selection. The intricacies of legal and organizational variations have also been discussed.

ALTERNATIVE APPROACHES: QUICK START OR DELIBERATE APPROACH

Quick Start

This is often called *rapid deployment*, or *early adoption*, but might be termed the "grab them by their pocketbook and their hearts and minds will follow" approach. You simply declare everyone who performs certain activities to be a part of the shared service effort, no matter where they are located. For instance, everyone within the company who is currently in an accounts payable unit is now part of the shared service organization.

This establishes reporting lines immediately. Once this is accomplished, shared service management begins to define the standard process, the skills necessary to remain a part of the organization, and the physical migration path of employees within the organization.

The upside of this approach is that there is no beating around the bush. A declaration is made that this is the way it will be, with no ifs, ands, or buts. In an organization with powerful business unit leadership—"Business Unit Kings"—this approach may be necessary in order to simply bowl over political opposition and the push-back of business unit heads.

The downside to this approach is that it is often terribly disruptive to the majority of employees, and therefore to the actual day-to-day operations of work. Also, carving up which activities within a process are in the shared service purview and which are out is more difficult because the decisions are often made quickly and sometimes made in an atmosphere of "bargaining" with the business unit heads rather than in the context of long-term corporate strategy.

Deliberate Approach

A more deliberate approach is the way to proceed in most circumstances. With this methodology, you set up a program group (a set of teams described later in the chapter) and plan the approach carefully. While you change the context in which work is done quickly, actual process changes are made more slowly.

Processes, activities, and people are migrated into the organization over a period of time. This provides shared service management with a better opportunity to define the characteristics of the standard processes, as well as the appropriate skills necessary to carry out those processes and the best people to bring into the organization.

A more deliberate approach allows for a more organized process of human resource development—determining the proper staff size;

bringing the right people into the organization from business units and training them; recruiting, hiring, and training new people; and releasing those who do not have the skill set for the new way of working in the most considerate way possible.

A more deliberate approach also offers the opportunity to pilot the effort in one process, which is an invaluable learning experience. This allows people to understand more completely what they are doing, and allows you to "tease out" quick wins that might be overlooked if you were trying to "hit the ground running."

The downside of using the deliberate approach is that it invariably runs into more resistance, because people are in a state of transition for longer. Inertia and bureaucratic obstacles can take their toll. However, with proper change management (discussed in detail in Chapter 17), this approach usually works quite well.

CLASSIC MODEL OF A SHARED SERVICE ORGANIZATION

The classic model of a company working in a shared service environment has three components:

1. A corporate center
2. Independent strategic business units (SBUs)
3. A shared service operation with one or many locations

Corporate Center

In a company working in a shared service environment, the opportunity exists to make corporate center an incredibly lean operation, consisting of the chief executive officer (CEO) and his or her direct reports, as well as their immediate staffs.

The corporate center houses only the top-level business and technical expertise, and any activities that will remain centralized (research and development, for instance).

While we have spoken extensively about the virtue of shared services in freeing up the management time of business unit leaders to focus on their core processes, the same can be said about the time of corporate-level executives, who no longer have to manage the day-to-day activities of centralized service processes.

Business Units

A shared service model of operation allows the office of the chief financial officer (CFO), as well as the human resources director and the chief information officer (CIO) to become strategic partners to business unit leaders.

Financial, informational, system maintenance, and human resource transactions are all now the purview of the shared service management. This allows the SBU heads, CIO, CFO, and human resources head to work as a team to analyze business opportunities in terms of the need for financial management, information management, and management of human resources.

By freeing up business units from the unwanted burdens of performing transactional tasks, there is more time to focus on the business analysis needed to solve each business unit's particular problems and achieve competitive advantage. Business unit executives and managers are relieved of the "data chasing" they used to do and freed up to do more strategic and competitive business analysis.

Shared Service Operation

The shared service operation does more than simply pick up transactional activities within supporting business processes. It creates a more seamless career ladder for individuals in the supporting processes.

Many people find that moving to a shared service operation enhances both their current job and their career prospects. A well-designed shared service operation is set up to provide a training ground for individuals to move into management, and can even be a stepping stone into line management in a business unit.

TEN STEPS TO IMPLEMENTATION PROGRAM DEVELOPMENT

It is time to turn to the actual program of creating a new way of performing important supporting processes for the business units. There are 12 steps to the program. We base this methodology on a slower start. For a rapid deployment, some of these items are collapsed into each other, and many are performed concurrently.

1. Set up the program's teams.
2. Assess organizational readiness.
3. Identify quick hits.
4. Identify critical success factors.
5. Design an implementation phase-in.
6. Begin intense communications. (From here to the end, you will need to communicate, communicate, communicate.)
7. Find specialized shared service tools.
8. Develop business controls.
9. Run a pilot and assess lessons learned from it.
10. Develop a continuous-improvement plan.

Program Teams

Shared services, like all of the other members of the "process orientation family" of management techniques (just-in-time [JIT], total quality management [TQM], business process reengineering [BPR], and enterprise systems implementation) is a team-based activity. Teams used for implementing shared services must be self-directed, horizontal teams. These teams will manage all aspects of the implementation. In *Best Practices in Reengineering,* our colleagues David Carr and Henry Johansson listed "Create Top-Notch Teams" as Best Practice #5. They wrote:

> Dramatic change requires people with creativity, vision, and openness to innovation. Often they will already be some of the busiest people in a company because everyone recognizes and respects their talents. Yet they are made available to the . . . effort because company leadership gives this assignment its highest priority.[1]

Carr and Johansson remind us that "a team is more than a group." They developed a wonderfully concise graphic to show characteristics of effective versus ineffective teams (see Figure 14-1).

As previously stated, the program to convert to a shared service environment will be run by a number of teams. A small *core team*, made up of individuals dedicated full time to the effort, will run the day-to-day operations. Core team members are people with strong project skills, and can be taken from anywhere in the organization. They must have good general business knowledge; specific technical knowledge of any particular process is not as necessary. Most important, they must be people their managers *don't want to give up*. No dead wood allowed here.

A larger *project team* is a cross-functional group of experts in particular areas that will be coalesced into the shared service organization. Project team members are on call to the core team to provide technical insight and problem solving in particular areas. There are also some "all-team" meetings attended by all members of the project team to keep them up to speed on the total workings of the program.

Finally, a *steering committee* is a senior-management-level group made up of high-level individuals in the particular areas that will be coalesced into the shared service operation. These people maintain contact between the program and the executive suite. It is from this group that the program's *champion* must come.

Figure 14-1 What Makes an Effective Team?

Effective Teams:	*Ineffective Teams:*
Communication goes two ways.	Communication is one-way.
Members openly and accurately express all their ideas.	Members express their ideas, but keep their feelings to themselves.
Team members share participation and leadership.	Member participation is unequal: members who hold positions of authority tend to dominate.
Decision-making procedures are appropriate for the situation - teams discuss issues and try to reach consensus on them.	Decisions are always made by members who possess the most authority - there is minimal team discussion.
Constructive controversy and conflict enhance the quality of decisions the team makes.	Controversy and conflict are ignored or avoided, and the quality of decision making suffers.
Members evaluate the effectiveness of the team and decide how to improve its work.	The highest-ranking member of the team, or management itself, decides how to improve the team's effectiveness.

In addition to the teams, there will be program and project managers (discussed in Chapter 16), and more than likely outside consulting assistance (discussed in Chapter 15).

Figure 14-2 is a checklist to use in assessing the readiness of your organization to engage in the kind of transformation necessary to successfully implement a move to a shared service method of operating.

Quick Hits

It is important at the outset to look for quick successes. Quick successes accomplish two purposes. First, they accumulate cost reduction or revenue enhancement that can be used to "self-fund" the program. Remember, the early costs are enormous, and payback often does not come for 18 to 24 months or more. The earlier some cash can be generated to offset the costs, the better. Second, quick successes build confidence among team members, generate enthusiasm and build credibility outside of the shared service organization, and help maintain executive and senior management support for the effort.

Critical Success Factors

It is important to define critical success factors (CSFs) early in the implementation process. In order to do this, you must first define success. From the definition of success will come the definition of a set of drivers that force that success to occur.

A set of performance measures that monitor the drive to success, as well as milestones of success, should be created. Both measures and milestones help maintain a relatively straight path to success. Performance measurement, and by extension CSFs, will be discussed in greater detail in Chapter 18.

Phase-in Plan

There are a few different ways to phase in shared services. One is to phase it in by processes or subprocesses made up of groups of activities—for instance, consolidating all pension and benefits transactions first, then travel and expense, and moving along from one process to

Figure 14-2   Organizational Readiness: A 10-Point Checklist

Lack of organizational readiness is one of the largest inhibitors to success. Assuming you have a business strategy, an information technology (IT) strategy, and a vision for shared services that are all in sync, you should make sure the following 10 items are in place prior to beginning the implementation of a shared service operation.

1. Senior executive buy-in is achieved across the corporation, and senior executives agree to positively communicate their buy-in to those who work for them.

2. Senior executives are confident the company's culture is ready to absorb the stress from a massive change effort, involving both business process change and total system change.

3. The project's scope is clearly defined, and mechanisms are in place to assess any suggested expansion of that scope and make a quick decision, so that the scope does not metastasize on its own.

4. A strong senior project sponsor is in place. Program and project management (discussed in detail in Chapter 16) has been identified, is available, and is willing.

5. The anticipated business benefits are quantified and articulated across the corporation.

6. There is a solid understanding of existing systems.

7. Resources (the project team) have been identified, are available, and are willing.

8. Funding needs have been assessed, funding levels have been agreed to, and funding has been appropriated.

9. Consulting or short-term permanent staff have been identified, a decision on consulting versus short-term permanent staff has been made, and the source of that assistance has been identified and hired.

10. Clear decision making and issue resolution mechanisms are in place.

the next. A variation of this is to bring in all the processes in each type of services in order (i.e., finance first, then human resources, then materials management).

A second way is to focus on the largest business unit first, bringing successive business units into the shared service operations in descending order of size.

When deciding on the approach, take into account how the largest tangible payback will be achieved while causing the least disruption to the culture.

Communications

The most important single piece of any major business change implementation is communication. When a major organizational change is underway, people will always find out that something is going on. The less real information they have, the more rumor will be created; and rumor always focuses on potential bad things that can come about.

Throughout the SBUs, it is important to remind everyone, both those who perform supporting processes and those who are involved with core business processes, of why the change to a shared service environment is taking place. Talk to people personally; communication cannot just be by impersonal memos and intranet postings.

Sometimes, corporate leaders do not want to communicate with employees until they can announce an outcome. This is simply wrong. Major business change is as much about process as it is about outcome. Clearly, the outcome goals are what drive the process, but even if the outcome is not clear, people need to understand the process at every step of the way.

It is important to tell the staff that the decision process is still underway, as well as when you anticipate that the decision will be reached. Keeping people apprised of progress toward final decisions and time frames for reaching decisions lessens anxiety, reduces the possibility of rumors, and helps to create trust. Explain to people that throughout the change process, the vision will stay constant, although tactical decisions can and probably will change.

A special reward and recognition program should also be put in place to recognize a team's achievement, as well as contributions of individuals as they successfully modify their own behavior and the way they accomplish work.

A final word of caution: Corporate leaders and managers almost invariably underestimate the amount of resource (time and energy) clear and consistent communication entails.

Business Controls

In periods of rapid transition, the control environment in a company can be an afterthought. During implementation of major business change, controls often slip. It is imperative that during a transition to a shared service environment, the control environment is maintained at its highest level.

Business controls must be designed into the new processes; they cannot be put in after the fact. Controls need to be designed around systems and processes. There must be an individual whose focus is controls; this person makes sure that controls get embedded into systems and processes as they are designed.

Business controls are created in order to mitigate against risk; therefore, the opposite of good control is heightened risk. When moving from an organizational model in which each business process is performed in multiple places to one in which each process is performed in only one place, one must manage through potential risks.

Pilot/Lessons Learned

Whether pilots are necessary or not is a point of dispute. However, unless you are implementing your entire shared service operation in one "big bang," you are, de facto, running a pilot on the first process or business unit that is brought into the new operation.

It should not be necessary to run a "proof of concept" pilot, unless you are simultaneously implementing shared services and new technology, especially across borders.

Continuous Improvement Plan

Our experience, as well as much research in the business literature, shows that transformational business change cannot be maintained without a plan for continuous improvement after the change has been accomplished.

Again, we turn to our colleagues Carr and Johansson, who titled the final chapter of their book on BPR "Deming Was Right." They argue that the organization of the 21st century will be "fast, flexible, and obsessed with continuous improvement." They call this organization the "improvement-driven" organization, one that seeks both revolutionary and evolutionary change.[2]

Figure 14-3 shows a graphic representation of their improvement-driven organization. Clearly, shared services can fit in the central box labeled "business process improvement."

Figure 14-3   Improvement-Driven Organization

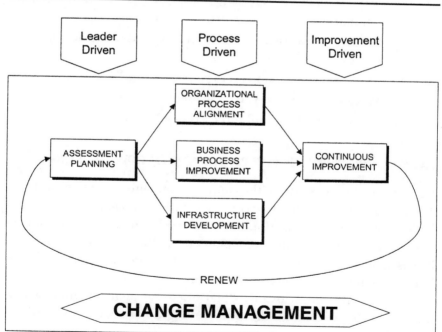

Again, we will discuss continuous improvement in more detail in Chapter 18, on performance measures and continuous improvement.

CONCLUSION

There are 10 keys to successful implementation. These are important for corporate management as well as program and project management to remember throughout the implementation:

1. Keep people focused on the reason why the company is moving to shared services: to solve a business problem.
2. Focus on lowest-hanging fruit.
3. Broadcast early successes.
4. Adopt special compensation programs to manage human resources.
5. Avoid bureaucracy and organizational layers.
6. Capitalize on teams; organize around teams.
7. Focus on processes, people, and organization, not on technology.
8. Build additional controls as you go.
9. Make metrics the key to fact-based discussions.
10. Agree on budgets and forecasts in advance.

HOW LUCENT SET UP THE PROJECT (TOLD BY JIM LUSK)

Lucent can clearly be put in the camp of companies that went with the "quick start" philosophy. It was done first by human resources, on a global basis. Then it was done in finance. Human resources and finance were really working independently. But as human resources learns new and better ways of accomplishing tasks, we transfer that knowledge into the finance organization.

We did not do a lot of formal organizational readiness assessment. Nor did we do a lot of formal setting up of teams. Our philosophy was much more of "just get on with it." But stepping back, we really did have all the pieces in place; a core team and project team. The leadership team acted as a steering committee, and we certainly had champions, but it was more intuitive and future led than formal planning.

Right before we moved to a shared service model, we were looking at ways to improve processes; we did this through something we called "Project Quantum Leap." This project really helped us identify opportunities for quick return.

We did not really have time for a pilot. We wanted to move quickly and felt that running a pilot would be like taking baby steps. We really wanted to go for the whole effort at once.

We have looked at the possibility of global delivery of these services, but it just is not practical, at least not at this point. For one thing, we are still working to develop a global mindset. What we are looking at is merging some of the human resources shared services and some of the financial shared services. We both do a lot of end-to-end value analysis, and there is probably some value to be gained by merging back offices.

Everything is so new in this area at Lucent, we are still debating whether to merge all at once now, or get things humming in both human resources and finance, and then merge them later. We see some real opportunities for further improvement there, some real synergies.

Much of this seeking of synergies and added value comes out of a very aggressive strategic plan we have at the company. We are in relentless pursuit of performance milestones, and we are constantly trying to improve processes and the way people carry out every activity within those processes.

This is especially important because we are in an acquisition mode and constantly looking to new venture development. We are constantly needing to integrate those ventures and those acquisitions, and handle more volume without adding people. This means continuous improvement and continuous rethinking, constantly asking ourselves if we are on the right track.

CHECKLIST

☐   Decide on quick start versus deliberate approach (checklist)
☐   Create a model of a shared service organization
    1. Corporate center
    2. Business units
    3. Shared service operation
☐   Implementation Program Development (based on slow start)
    1. Set up program's teams:
       Core team
       Project team
       Steering committee
       Champion
    2. Assess organizational readiness.
    3. Identify quick hits:
       Accumulate cost reduction or revenue enhancement that can be used to "self-fund."
       Build confidence among team members and help maintain executive and senior management support.
    4. Identify critical success factors:
       Define success
       What drives success?
       Create performance measures that monitor the drive to success.
       What are the milestones?
    5. Design an implementation phase-in plan:
       By process/in order
       In descending order of size
    6. Begin intense communications
    7. Find specialized shared service tools.
    8. Develop business controls:
       Business controls must be designed into and around the new systems and processes.
       Control should be the focus of one individual.
       Manage through potential risks.

9. Run a pilot and assess lessons learned.
10. Develop continuous improvement plan.
☐ Keys to successful implementation:
1. Focus on low-hanging fruit.
2. Broadcast early success.
3. Adopt special compensation programs to manage human resources.
4. Avoid bureaucracy and organizational layers.
5. Capitalize on teams, organize around teams.
6. Focus on processes, people, and organization, not on technology.
7. Build additional controls as you go.
8. Focus on end-to-end processes.
9. Make metrics the key to fact-based discussions.
10. Agree on budgets and forecasts in advance.

NOTES

1. David K. Carr and Henry J. Johansson, *Best Practices in Reengineering: What Works and What Doesn't in the Reengineering Process* (McGraw-Hill, 1995).
2. See note 1.

15

Partnering for Success: Proceed with Care When Choosing a Consultant

- Why use a consulting partner?
- Types of consulting partners
- Kinds of consultants
- Questions to ask when selecting a consulting partner
- Ten ways consultants can add value to your shared service implementation

Shared services is very new. The first company to use the technique, General Electric, began doing so only in the early 1980s. The first wave really took hold in the early 1990s, and as we enter the 21st century, there are still only in the neighborhood of 100 companies around the world that are truly operating in a shared service environment.

Until about 1995, there were few, if any, consultants who could provide not only advice on how to implement a shared service envrionment, but a database of practical experience that made that advice more than merely common sense.

Today, there are probably a dozen or more practitioners a company can turn to for expert assistance in this complicated implementation.

Although it it possible to implement shared services without assistance, by seeking out a consulting partner that best fits your needs, you can greatly increase your chances of a successful implementation, defined as on time, on budget, and providing your company with all the functionality you find necessary.

This chapter will describe how you can manage the process of partnering with consultants, and how you can manage the consultants themselves and draw the most value from them.

WHY USE A CONSULTING PARTNER?

Consultants have done it before and have seen both successes and failures in a number of different organizational contexts. You can learn from the mistakes of others by having consultants get you through the minefields that have damaged other companies and transfer their knowledge of best practices to you.

Consultants understand the logic and integration behind the shared service structure and its support systems, and can expedite your organization's going up the learning curve without adding to your permanent payroll. They can help you quicken the implementation cycle by focusing your company's decision making on the true issues. However, they cannot quicken the implementation cycle if your company's leadership has difficulty making decisions.

TYPES OF CONSULTING PARTNERS

There are three types of consultants that work with shared services:

1. All the Big Five accounting/consulting firms and some other large management consulting firms
2. Boutique, or specialist, consultants
3. Independents

The Big Five and Other Large Management Consultants

All of the Big Five accounting and consulting firms have practices in shared service implementation, as do some, but not all, of the larger general management consulting practices. Practitioners at all of these firms (of which three of the four authors' employer is one) look at shared service implementation as a business issue, not merely a technical issue. They know about business process reengineering (BPR) issues, as well as quality and change management. If they need help in these areas, they can turn to other practice areas within their firm. These firms are very strong on project management skills.

Also, these firms are global in nature, as are most of the businesses that are implementing shared services. In fact, the reason for the 1998 merger that consolidated the Big Six into the Big Five was the need for more global reach of services for clients. Another similar wave of mergers in management consulting may occur in the near future. This will narrow the number of firms to choose from, but should increase each firm's ability to handle the largest and most complex shared service implementation.

Boutiques

There are a few small consulting firms that specialize in solving the particular issues surrounding a shared service implementation. Although their hourly rates are about the same as larger firms, they can be less expensive because they do more leveraging of your staff than the Big Five and larger management consultants, and can be used very effectively for "handholding" by companies that want to do most of the implementation work with in-house staff. The downside to using these firms is their difficulty in assisting global projects because of their size.

Independents

There are also a few former executives who headed up shared service operations for early implementors who have gone out on their own to consult. These individuals are also much cheaper than large, global firms. However, in addition to their inability to provide the consulting staff necessary to help with a large, global implementation, they also often have a narrow focus of experience. They tend to look at things through the lens of the company where they worked and often do not have a wide breadth of experience with companies with varying cultures and needs from their shared service operations.

SEEK COUNSELING, NOT JUST CONSULTING OR IMPLEMENTATION

There are three kinds of consultants in the world: implementors, consultants, and counselors.

Implementors do the trench work. They are task oriented. Within any consulting project, there are a number of implementors working away. A lot of this work involves modifying and implementing software systems and documenting processes and procedures.

Consultants understand the business issues involved in a project. They are able to manage the implementors, spot problems, and discuss with you the various options for correcting problems. Although they have a much higher level of business knowledge, they focus their interactions with you around the task at hand.

Counselors give advice about a broad range of business issues. These may or may not have to do with the current project. They will give you their best advice even if is not always to their advantage. They may tell you to hire another firm to do a particular consulting job. They do this based on the relationship they have with you, and with the knowledge that you will turn to them for their expertise and hire them when you believe they can do the job as well as or better than a competitor.

Boutique firms often set themselves up as counselors. However, the best counseling often comes from a Big Five firm, which has personnel in all three areas—counselors, consultants, and implementors. The first place to look is the firm that does your company's auditing. Your auditing firm, especially if it is your long-time auditing firm, should have developed a network within your business. Complementing this with the network that any good consulting counselor has developed over the years, your audit firm should be able to provide you with good intelligence about what is going on both inside and outside your company as you undertake the shared service implementation.

This also adds to the value of the audit performed for your company. Your auditors know your business better, and that makes it easier for them to keep you out of trouble.

Another reason to look to your auditing firm as a natural consulting partner for your shared service project is that your auditor "has skin in the game." There is a relationship there, and a desire to make shared services truly work for your business. Your auditor has a way to go right to the chief financial officer (CFO) if there is a problem.

A strong consulting team should have within it at least one counselor, a handful of consultants, and numerous implementors.

The most consulting leverage one can achieve is on the high end of the scale, from the counselor who helps with vision, strategy, and planning. The counselor, because of his or her overview understanding of the company, is able to provide input into the day-to-day issues that crop up during implementation of the shared service operation as they pertain to the original vision, strategy, and plans.

Remember our *Figure 1-1*, with the goal of growth and the focus on the value chain. The counselor consults into those top two boxes, primarily working with the chief executive officer (CEO) and those who report to the CEO. Consultants also work on the value-chain box. Although conselors may help with the strategic thinking, over time implementation is the more difficult and time-consuming work. For this, strong consultants and often a small army of implementors are needed. This is so because, during the course of an implementation, it is important that some of the work be done by people outside the culture and the politics of your company.

The counselor also consults into the business problem box. While implementors and consultants consult into the process, which is the tools that solve the business problem, the counselor consults through the lens of the business problem, tying together larger issues as they affect the process implementation (see Figure 15-1).

KEY QUESTIONS TO ASK WHEN SELECTING A CONSULTANT

The major questions to ask when selecting a consulting partner fall into three categories:

1. Staffing
2. Track record
3. Fees

Figure 15-1   Business Problem Solution—Consultant's Role

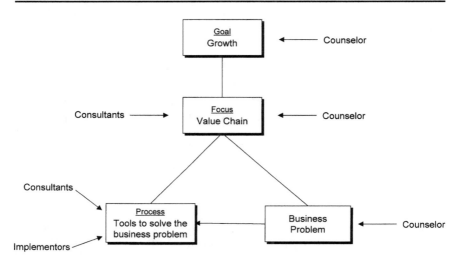

Staffing

Be sure that the people who make the sales call and close the deal are going to be involved in the project. At the meeting when you close the deal, you want the consulting partner to commit in writing to the project manager and some of the key staff people, and to the percentage of time they will devote to your project. *Have this confirmed in writing!*

It is also important to find out if the staff needs to travel or if they are local. Travel adds cost. Sometimes, you need to pay extra to get the most experience. Try to strike a balance between cost and experience.

Track Record

A potential consulting partner should be able to provide at least a handful of quality references that can show success in terms of a project completed on time, within budget, and providing the requisite functionality that was defined at the project's inception. At least some of those references should be from companies that are similar in size to yours and in the same industry.

Fees

Professional fees are charged (exclusive of expenses) on a daily or hourly basis. If hourly rates are proposed, be sure to cap the number of billable hours per day. And be sure to address travel time and overtime.

GETTING THE MOST OUT OF CONSULTANTS

The key to getting the most out of consultants can be summed up in two sentences:

1. Manage them; do not let them manage you.
2. Remember who is paying whom.

It is important not to let consultants take over a project. When this happens, you lose the necessary "buy-in" from your organization. It is equally as important to treat consultants as equals with your own employees (do not exploit them and do not dump on them).

Although you should never exploit them as people, you should always exploit their knowledge. After all, you are paying for their experience, and you should never hesitate to solicit their input. They can let you know both what is going on in various parts of the project and what went on in past projects on which they have worked.

Consultants can play a very useful role in keeping your company politics honest. Someone from the consultant's organization should be placed on the steering committee.

Finally, the goal is to complete the project and get the consultants out. This allows them to move on to their next job and allows your company to get on with its true business.

Figure 15-2 shows the ten most important ways consultants can add value to a shared service implementation. When you interview potential consultants, ask these questions, or include them in your request for proposals and ask for specific answers.

Figure 15-2   Ten Ways Consultants Can Add Value to Your Shared
Service Implementation

---

1. *Management Counseling.*   Putting shared services in the big picture
of a company's vision, strategy, and tactical implementation is the first step.
Management consultants, who work with CEOs, can help to bring the tactic
of shared services to the level of strategy for the CEO's benefit.

2. *Shared service benchmarking.*   Some consulting organizations have
done extensive benchmarking. They have an inventory of project/program
experience with other companies and have a "playbook" of best practices
that they can assist you to implement as part of your effort.

3. *Vision and strategy development for shared services.*   One of the key
first steps in any shared service implementation is to develop a vision of
what the company can and should achieve in the shared service initiative,
as well as a strategy for getting there.

4. *Business process reengineering.*   Instituting a shared service operation
often goes hand-in-hand with some degree of BPR.

5. *Barrier identification and change management.*   Creating a shared service environment is a major cultural change for an organization. Good consultants have seen the kinds of resistance to this change that have surfaced
in other organizations and have created change management programs to
help mitigate those barriers.

6. *Program and project management.*   Consultants can serve to keep the
effort focused, and maintain momentum between the executive suite and
those implementing in the trenches.

7. *Integration of shared services with information/support systems.*   The
linkage of the shared service processes with the supporting transaction and
information processing systems is critical to any implementation. Consultants can add a great deal of value, especially if the company is using an enterprise resource planning (ERP) software platform, such as SAP, Baan,
PeopleSoft, or Oracle.

8. *Implementation Assistance.*   Consultants have been there before in
the nitty-gritty of implementation, such as developing service-level agreements between shared service operations and business unit clients.

9. *International shared service deployment.*   International deployments
have some unusual characteristics. Consultants with international experience in given countries can buy you credibility when dealing with the organization within that country.

10. *Training.*   Consultants can either train those who will be a part of
the shared service organization, or they can train those inside your organization to then train your people. Either way, they can bring experiences from
other organizations, so that you do not just fall into doing things "the old way."

LUCENT'S USE OF CONSULTANTS FOR ITS SHARED SERVICE IMPLEMENTATION (TOLD BY JIM LUSK)

We have used four consulting firms on our shared service implementation effort: Coopers & Lybrand (now PricewaterhouseCoopers), Gunn Partners, Arthur Anderson and the London Perret Roche Group LLC (LPR). The first time I went to a consultant (Coopers & Lybrand's Jack Dunleavy) I did not know much about shared services, and I wanted some people with experience to help me think through some of the issues.

I was looking for some people who knew what worked and what did not, people with a very broad picture of how shared services fits in. I also wanted someone who knew Lucent and how we operate. I needed someone who could translate others' experiences into relevant terms for our business culture.

The concept of different kinds of consultants—implementors, consultants, and counselors—is very helpful. I really found the counseling role helpful at the beginning, having someone I could turn to and ask questions such as:

- Is this kind of effort doable for us?
- Does this kind of approach make sense for us?
- What have you seen that works and what does not work?

The counseling role was really critical for us at the beginning, in formulating a vision and translating that vision for the entire workforce in terms that are relevant for them.

Some consulting firms we interviewed wanted to just begin right at implementation—go do this to accounts payable, go do that to another area. It was a brute force approach: cut people out rather than create a compelling vision, create a future, create a way for people to add more value to the work they do, create a way for people to work smarter and do more without feeling that they are under a speed-up.

The consultants we finally chose are the people who I feel understand a central truth: that we in management and in consulting do not know how to do work better than the people who actually do the work.

The people who make change happen best are the people who actually do the work. Our job as managers and consultants is to change the context in which they do their work in order to allow them to work better, smarter, and faster.

CHECKLIST

☐   Why do you want a consulting partner?
- Consultants have done it before and have seen both successes and failures.
- Consultants allow you to learn from the mistakes of others.
- Consultants understand the logic and integration behind the shared service structure.
- Consultants can expedite your learning curve without adding to your permanent payroll.
- Consultants quicken implementation, assuming good decision making from the company.

☐   What type of consulting partner serves your needs?
- Big Five
- Boutiques
- Independents

☐   What role do you need the consultant to play?
- Implementors
- Consultants
- Counselors

☐   When selecting a consulting partner, ask about:
- Staffing
- Track record
- Fees

16

Program and Project Management

- **Program management**
- **Project management**
- **Project manager attributes**
- **Project structure**
- **Project planning**
- **Project execution and control**
- **Kind of people to fill these roles**
- **Importance of executive buy-in**
- **Risk management**
- **Varieties of risk**

As a general rule, the implementation of a shared service operation will require both program management and project management. Shared service organizations are generally characteristic of large, complex organizations. Because of this complexity of consolidating much of the supporting activity of many business units into the shared service operation, program management is required to oversee the efforts of all the individual projects that form the integration.

Figure 16-1 is a reprise of our Figure 8-2, which shows the governance model of the implementation program for shared services.

What is the difference between program and project management? Simply stated, there is one set of skills needed to run a discreet segment—a project—and another set of skills necessary to run

213

Figure 16-1   Governance Model

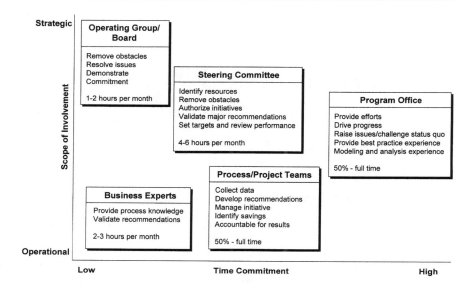

an overall program such as implementing a shared service operation.

Project management is:

The day-to-day responsibility for the planning, control, and execution of an individual project.

Program management is:

Coordination and integration of the goals, objectives, and results of individual projects to achieve the overall business objectives.

PROGRAM MANAGEMENT

Programs include a number of projects. The keys to program management are alignment and balance. A program manager seeks to align the objectives of each individual project with the company's overall objectives. He or she seeks to balance the resources going to individual projects so as to keep all projects on track, achieving deliverables in a relatively uniform fashion.

Remember, the goal of a shared service implementation program is to create a new business unit that supports particular service activities across strategic business unit (SBU) boundaries within the entire company. If some projects in some departments, functions, or business units are lagging other projects, it is more difficult to achieve this integration.

Finally, the program manager is responsible for conflict mediation and resolution as different projects within departments and functions jostle for resources and work to achieve their objectives.

Alignment of Objectives

What do we mean by alignment of objectives?

Think of a shared service implementation across departmental, functional, and business unit lines as an eight-man crew race. The eight rowers in a championship crew are each phenomenally strong and strong willed. They are capable of getting their boat from the beginning of the course to the end of the course no matter how they row.

However, the biggest and strongest team does not always win. It is the team that is most coordinated—most aligned—that gets to the end of the course first.

Think about it. The crew is rowing backward, so they really cannot see where their destination is. In many ways, those involved in each project within a shared service implementation program are "rowing backwards" also, unable to see where they are going. The program manager acts as the coxswain, calling out in rhythm for the projects to "stroke" together, making sure there are no obstructions in their way, and keeping an eye on the end of the course, as well as the intermediate milestone markers.

Of course, being program manager for a shared service implementation is more complex than steering a rowing crew. While crew members have a very simple mission and each individual knows the value of teamwork, departments, functions, and business units within a company often have more complex, and distinct, missions. There are different business drivers for each.

The implementation team members, as well as employees within each department, function, or business unit, have to be educated about the program's dependencies and the value of maintaining common scope and synchronized timelines.

Resource Allocation and Conflict Resolution

Program managers are most concerned with one central issue: Can all teams achieve their deadlines? To answer this question, the program manager must look at whether each team has the necessary resources to succeed in its project. It is his or her job to allocate often scarce internal business and technical resources, as well as consulting resources, across the spectrum of projects.

Only when resource allocation is done appropriately can each team be asked to achieve the same deliverables on the same time scales, so that the deliverables can be properly integrated into a workable system.

Finally, the program manager is responsible for resolving conflicts between the projects. These may take a variety of forms, including time lines, scope, perceived objectives, and limited or restricted resources.

Issue Resolution

It is also the program manager's job to identify issues across any and all of the projects that may impede the ultimate delivery of the program's objectives. These issues often revolve around conflicts between project managers seeking resources. Issues might be endemic across the entire program, and the program manager must assess the effect of each project on all of the other projects. This task of issue identification and resolution is a key to overall program success.

PROJECT MANAGEMENT

The project manager must perform a number of diverse tasks throughout the project life cycle. Good project managers possess a number of attributes and qualities:

- They are intelligent.
- They communicate well.
- They are respected throughout the organization.
- They are experienced.
- They are good cheerleaders.
- They are "helicopter thinkers," able to take a broad view from high above the playing field, then zoom down from one subject to another, getting into the detail of various parts of the action when necessary.

Remember, they are the external face of the project. They must present the project both to the employees within the department, function, or business unit within which they work, as well as to the rest of the company. A good project manager is able to evaluate the conflicts, seek a win–win solution, and, if necessary, make a decision that all parties can live with, even those who "lose." They must:

- Be flexible. Managing a shared service installation is akin to "herding cats." The shared service operation must support what are often viewed by business unit managers as "unique needs."
- Be determined. There are going to be a lot of hurdles in the project, some natural as part of a complex undertaking, but many of the organizational culture and resistance to change variety. Project managers must have the finesse of an American football halfback, weaving and dodging, as well as the toughness of a fullback, able to get "three yards and a cloud of dust" when necessary.
- Be enthusiastic. A shared service implementation is a long process, and the enthusiasm of many team members will wax and wane over time. A project manager cannot allow the down days to set the tone. He or she must leave the frustration in the office at the end of the day and come back the next day ready to do battle again.
- Be personable. Team members come in all shapes and sizes, and project managers must get along with them all. They need to be able to charm corporate steering committee members as

217

well as workers within the department, function, or business unit in which they are managing the project.

o Know the organization and how to maneuver politically through it.

It's difficult to find an individual with such a large and diverse set of skills. Sometimes, you must find a "second-in-command" with complementary skills to the project manager.

PROJECT STRUCTURES

Most companies are structured either hierarchically or in a matrix. Consequently, they tend to run their projects that way as well.

The hierarchical project structure is the most common approach. It tends to work well in most business cultures, even those that have more of a matrix management structure. It tends not to work in a culture that is a true "consensus" organization.

A hierarchical structure is favored for rapid implementation, as it favors chain-of-command decision making. Typically, subteams are created by their particular function. Each team is composed of the resources it needs to deliver the finished product; for instance, the finance team will have expertise in design, configuration, testing, conversion, documentation, and training. Because of this need for all specialties in each team, hierarchical structure often requires a lot of resources. The structure allows for the roll of each person to be defined; there is nowhere to hide. In a hierarchical structure, the program and project managers have a large integration role.

In a matrix project structure, there are functional teams and there are discipline teams. A true matrix project structure is very free flowing and allows for the most flexibility and free thinking.

It is possible for individuals to serve on more than one team within a matrix project structure. An individual can serve on a discipline team (e.g., change management) as well as a functional team (e.g., finance). The downside of matrix project management is that people are spread thin and there can be difficulty managing the intersections and crossovers. Also, since people's responsibilities often overlap, there are cracks within which people can hide.

The steering committee and the program and/or project manager still sit above the teams, as in a hierarchical structure. In addition, there are strong functional teams. It is important to maintain a strong functional structure.

However, as with the matrix organization, there are some process teams that cut across functional lines. Having these process teams in such areas as change management and integration allows for more effective leveraging of specialized, limited resources, because these specialties do not have to reside in each functional team.

Occasionally, there will be a project that runs in more of a "hub-and-spoke" type of structure, with an integration team in the center and functional teams around it.

In this scenario, project management resides in the integration hub. One client of ours used this unorthodox structure quite effectively. Weekly integration meetings were used to plan the short- and long-term project goals and activities. These were supplemented by daily issue meetings that were used to identify potential trouble spots for special attention. The project teams were tightly linked and the project was delivered on time and on budget.

Whatever overarching project structure is used, the detailed structure within should reflect the project milestones.

PROJECT PLANNING

Project planning is concerned with three main issues:

1. Targets
2. Scope
3. Resources

Targets

A shared service operation might be seen as akin to trying to eat an elephant. If you try to swallow it in one bite, it will stick in your throat. It is easier to digest if cut into bite-sized pieces.

It is helpful to use intermediate targets and milestones throughout a project as part of project management. Determining intermediate targets is, in effect, determining the number and size of the elephant pieces you will eat. Just as the size of a meal is determined by each individual, the targets should be tailored to the individual organization and project. Without setting challenging yet attainable intermediate goals (milestones), it is easy to lose sight of where the end state of the effort is. The light at the end of the tunnel seems to be a constantly receding train.

It is also important to understand the individual steps or activities needed to meet a milestone and the dependencies between targets. Only when this is done can a realistic scenario be created. Intermediate goals are important for maintaining a sense of achievement within the teams, and for maintaining realistic expectations on the part of executives who are not involved with the project on a day-to-day basis.

Everyone involved in the project needs intermediate goals, even the project support office. Early goals should be easy, and later goals more difficult, in order to "create wins" soon enough for teams to flex their muscles and develop their team strength.

Scope

Understanding the project's scope from the beginning is critically important. If the scope of the project and program has not been defined, agreed to, and signed off on by executive management, disaster awaits.

You should know up front the number of business processes that will be redesigned and whether they will be redesigned prior to or after moving to a shared service operation. In addition, you must know the number of legacy systems that will be turned off when any new system is up and running, and where those systems reside. You must know if there are geographic, divisional, and functional boundaries for the implementation.

The scope must be clearly defined and communicated for all those working on the project. Further, there must be a mechanism for project teams to make formal requests to expand the scope. They may not make unilateral changes, or else the project will get completely out of control. However, they must have a mechanism by which they can make business case arguments on the merits of their request to expand the scope.

Resources

Needless to say, a shared service implementation project needs the best and brightest a company can find for project teams. The teams must not be made up entirely of hotshots, however. There should be some veteran players as well—people with credibility in the company and who have been around long enough to know and understand the culture.

They must be willing to change the way business gets done, but they must also understand why business is done now the way it is done, and be able to articulate to the team the difficulties it will encounter when making changes. There can be no better advocate for change than the people who created the current systems and processes. However, these people often are not brought into the leadership roles, and they become the most vociferous resistors of change.

Some organizations have taken the approach of requiring that their high-potential people work at some point in the shared service organization to understand the business of many businesses.

PROJECT EXECUTION AND CONTROL

Milestones are meaningless without a way to monitor progress. Milestones cannot be achieved without a mechanism for conflict resolution. Progress monitoring and conflict resolution are what project managers will spend much of their time on.

Milestones must be measurable, discreet, and build toward the end state. The conflict resolution process must be clearly understood and agreed to from the outset. Monitoring must be regular, cross-functional, and based on achieving the milestones determined.

Figure 16-2 shows the stepped methodology for undertaking a program to implement shared services in your company. This methodology helps to ensure that the focus is on deliverables rather than on "process" itself.

WHAT KIND OF PEOPLE SHOULD FILL THESE ROLES?

The program manager has to be at a high enough level of the organization where he or she has a network of high-level contacts and can break

Figure 16-2 A Stepped Methodology Ensures Focus on Deliverables

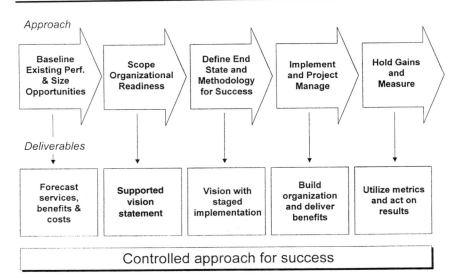

down barriers to the project's success. He or she needs to be the kind of person who can literally walk into any senior executive's office and say "We have a brush fire, and we need x, y, and z resources to solve it, now, before it turns into a conflagration." The program manager is responsible for seeing the big picture, for managing the cracks between the discreet projects, and for making things happen across the organization.

This person need not have ever implemented a shared service organization before—that would entail hiring from outside. However, this person should have had major responsibility for a large integrative project at some time before; he or she may have been key in building a new plant, developing a new product, or market development for a product line. Finally, this person should have more than a passing understanding of contemporary information technology (IT) issues, process management techniques, and operations.

For example, we know of one individual who could be a program manager for any business implementation effort. He was a program manager for construction of the airport in Dharan, Saudi Arabia. He was not an engineer, a contractor, or a financial analyst by training. His strength was his ability to understand sequencing, cost, and dependencies. He knew that the concrete for the easternmost runway couldn't be poured until the buildings on the eastern part of the airport had been constructed. He knew that electricians could not work until after plumbers had been into a facility to rough out plumbing. He knew when to delay the concrete, even if it meant paying a penalty to the contractor, rather than pouring on time and ruining sequencing.

In short, managing schedules, budgets, and human resources are the keys to program management. This means the need for someone who knows how to *communicate* effectively with those at all levels of the organization, as well as prime contractors and even subcontractors. The program manager also has to have an understanding of where all of the various business unit customers are coming from in their evolving relationship with the shared service organization.

For the project managers, find some people with general management experience, from the business units, as well as some people from the functions that are being incorporated into the shared service operation. Project managers should have prior experience in project or program management for a large effort.

Finally, if you can get someone with a prior shared service implementation, all the better. This is usually difficult to do, since there are only 100 to 150 companies around the world that have actually done this to date, and they have been trying to hold onto the people who have been instrumental in making their efforts successful.

Project managers should also have some system application experience, because much of the integration of the effort hinges on information systems.

WHY EXECUTIVE BUY-IN IS ESSENTIAL FOR SUCCESS

Before your company can truly "start the engine" for a shared services implementation, you must obtain buy-in from the entire senior executive team and from the executives of all the business units. For shared services to be truly worth the time, effort, and pain of the implementation process, a company needs to achieve true integration.

Without up-front buy-in, that integration will not happen. You will experience one or more of the following conditions:

- Feuding among functional executives (operations vs. finance vs. information systems vs. human resources). Everyone will be trying to steer the program to optimize their efforts, with the consequences of global suboptimization and lack of integration.
- Active subversion or terrorism aimed at the program or particular projects by those who do not get a clear message from their functional or business unit executive that he or she has bought into the effort.
- Narrowing of scope, as particular executives decided "not to play" midway through the effort. Having to pull back on scope after a fully integrated effort has been designed is almost as bad as a scope that keeps expanding.
- Failure by one or more business unit customers to accept the system after it is implemented, because they feel it was pushed down their throats by an outsider against the wishes of their senior executives.

Any or all of these leads to a reduction in the benefits the company achieves from the effort.

Buy-in across executive ranks must not be tacit, but rather explicit. Executives must continually communicate to those who work for them, their managers and employees, that they believe shares services is good for the functional or business unit organization.

One way to achieve buy-in across the organization is through strong sponsorship by someone near the top of the organization. The sponsor needs to be someone who commands respect from his or her colleagues across the executive ranks. A strong sponsor, working diligently among his or her executive colleagues, can reduce resistance, facilitate decision making, and mobilize resources. This person acts as the gatekeeper for the program manager just as the program manager acts as a gatekeeper for the project managers. The sponsor insulates senior executives from the need to be involved day-to-day in the machinations of the implementation effort, but keeps them fully apprised of the effort.

RISK MANAGEMENT

Every action taken in business entails some level of risk. A large task within any major implementation that creates organizational change is mitigating against those risks.

Although it is impossible to eliminate all risk from any business undertaking, least of all one so radical as creating a shared service operations unit, it is possible to manage risk in a way that allows a business to pursue its legitimate opportunities without endangering its survival.

Shared services, by its very nature, is fraught with risk. A shared service implementation is a major organizational change initiative. With proper focus, the risks can be managed, but first they must be identified.

Our definition of risk is:

> Any factor that can affect the ability of the project to deliver results that are on time and on budget, and that meet expectations.

FOUR STEPS IN THE RISK MANAGEMENT PROCESS

Risk is another way of saying uncertainty. Uncertainty can be described in a mathematical way. For instance, if you toss a coin, you are 50 percent certain it will come up heads. As the number of variables in the equation increases, the level of uncertainty grows. Therefore the number of possible risks grows. Risk management becomes more complex and more important.

Risk comes in one of seven varieties:

1. Executive risks
2. Project management and project plan risks
3. Technical risks

4. Organizational (end users in business units) risks

5. Decision-making risks

6. Functional risks

7. Business ecology risks (i.e., mergers and acquisitions)

Overlying these different varieties of risk are the four aspects of risk management, which, taken together, can be viewed as the risk management process:

1. Risk identification

2. Risk assessment and analysis

3. Risk control and mitigation

4. Risk avoidance

Risk management must be part of the implementation program from the beginning. It must also be participative and iterative, meaning that all participants in the undertaking know of the risk management plans, think about them, and add to them as time goes on, making the risk management effort better over time.

Risk management is an easily overlooked part of the program and project planning process. Risks can come from the "blind side" and envelop the effort in fire fighting. An aggressive risk management plan can nip such problems in the bud.

Not engaging in risk management from the start can be catastrophic. Conducting risk identification, assessment, and analysis early on provides an opportunity to achieve buy-in from all elements of the company—executives, project teams, and end users. This, in turn, avoids the "I told you so's" as the program progresses and runs against the unavoidable snags.

Figure 16-3 shows the top ten risks involved with shared services.

Risk Identification

Risk identification involves looking at risks on the seven dimensions listed earlier. When identifying each risk, specify within which business

Figure 16-3   Top 10 Risks to Shared Service Implementation

While risks come in a variety of forms, and each company's effort will encounter specific risks, a number of risks are common to all shared service implementations and can develop into significant problems with alarming speed unless carefully controlled. They are:

1. Inadequate sponsorship
2. Poor/slow decision making
3. Poor/no scope definition
4. Inadequate attention to change management
5. Lack of cooperation between business areas/departments
6. Poor use of consultants
7. Inappropriate resources
8. Unrealistic expectations
9. Inadequate knowledge transfer
10. Poor project management

area the risk lies, and at what organizational level. This assists in both clarifying the risk and developing actions to control and avoid the risk. Many risks are so bound up in the organization's culture that an outsider cannot find them and an insider is so used to them that they do not make an impression. Trying to get a comprehensive picture of all possible risks is difficult.

Risks inherent in the decision-making process are especially difficult to mitigate against. Process change and large-scale organizational change cry out for a clear, orderly decision-making process, one in which input is accepted by those with the authority and responsibility for the decisions, and the decisions are made in a timely way.

Long decision cycles, excess time arguing about the decision, and most of all, backing away from decisions, cause confusion, anxiety, and anger within the organization. This triggers other problems, which can drive an effort to failure.

Risk Assessment and Analysis

Assessing and analyzing risks means determining their potential impact on the program and project, as well as their likelihood of happening. The impact can be in terms of missed milestones, the need for rework, the need for reimplementation, and the level of acceptance the project will have after it is completed.

Executive risks are risks regarding executive commitment and support, including sponsorship, alignment with other business initiatives, and turf fighting. These risks have a high impact on both the project team and its work, as well as on delivery of the final program. Likelihood of occurrence is higher if there is less prework by the leadership team, and if the implementation is being carried out for unclear or conflicting reasons.

Project management and project plan risks are risks that affect the efficiency and effectiveness of how the project is run. Shared service implementation is one of the largest implementations a company will ever undertake. Such an effort cries out for effective program and project management.

The most apparent risks in this area include planning and execution of project steps, as well as knowledge transfer from experienced staff or outside consultants to those who will carry out the project and later retention of this newly knowledgeable staff. Other risks in this category are the "scope creep" of the project, adherence to methodology, and use of resources.

These risks can have a very high impact on both the project team and delivery. Likelihood of occurrence is high.

Technical risks are the real issues of hardware, software, and systems architecture involved in a shared service implementation, as well as the architecture of the human system. The organization must plan carefully how the information systems infrastructure will support the shared service operation. While the exercise must be driven by business needs and not by IT desires, the technical organization should remain part of the leadership team for the project. Technical risks include sizing, networks, and personal computing/network computing requirements. The impact of technical risks varies; it can affect end users from individuals to the entire organization.

Organizational (end users in SBUs) risks occur if the entire organization is not aligned with the project. Different functional areas may retain their old ways of doing business. These disconnects hurt the overall integration of the business process and lead to gaps in functionality.

Staff retention and training are also issues. If the most knowledgeable staff leave or have negative views of the effort, it is hard to keep the rest on track.

These risks have a higher impact on specific areas, but the risks also affect other areas. Likelihood of occurrence varies depending on how much attention is paid to understanding the organizational culture and creating viable ways to decrease resistance.

Decision-making risks occur if there is a poor decision-making process, slow decision making, or the inability to make crucial decisions. It is crucial to keep momentum going throughout the effort, and the only way to do that is to make decisions that move the project toward the next milestone.

These risks have a high impact on the entire organization. Their likelihood of occurring is low, but the impact for those occurrences that do happen is very high.

Functional risks are those that affect the system's ability to support specific users or user functions. Typically, functional risks occur where specific requirements or business processes are overlooked in the implementation. It is common for such risks to occur in limited areas of a shared service program, especially where the scope of the effort is wide or poorly defined. Their impact is high within limited areas.

Risk Control and Mitigation

Because a shared service implementation entails a host of risks, from the purely technical to what happens when the most basic of human emotions are triggered, a comprehensive risk-control strategy is important. Within this strategy can be detailed a number of actions to be taken to alleviate the risk in each of the six major risk categories.

Risk control must be constantly monitored. A good way to start is to step back when each project milestone is reached and assess the effectiveness of risk-control actions taken during the time it took to reach the milestone. Revisit identifying and assessing the risks that may dominate the next milestone phase, and determine whether the current risk-control strategy and actions will serve well during the next phase, or whether a new strategy needs to be developed and new actions outlined.

Risk Avoidance

It is possible to avoid some risks. This is mostly done by being brutally realistic about the nature and amount of resources it will take to successfully complete a project. Executives and key users must define up front their expectations for the project. Then, the project leader must be completely honest in telling those executives and key users what kind of costs and time commitment are necessary to undertake the project.

There are costs in people's time, dollars, and technology. These costs must be borne in order to avoid unnecessary risks. Trying to cut corners increases the likelihood of risks occurring, and magnifies the impact, and the cost, when they do occur.

LUCENT'S PROGRAM AND PROJECT MANAGEMENT (TOLD BY JIM LUSK)

We have very formal program management. We have a "war room" set up, from which the program management takes place. We have very detailed planning—names, dates, milestones. We keep track of everything in terms of how it supports the future operations. We believe a formal program plan is essential to risk management in a change effort of this magnitude.

There is a program manager, who works with the overall project plan manager. The two people in those leadership positions came from within Lucent. They are people who have very good leadership skills, are real visionaries, and could be counted on to make major changes.

These two people have a lot of credibility within the business, both with executives and with associates. They know the processes very well, but were able to step back, create a future and maintain the vision, and not let the current environment drag the effort down.

They were given a lot of responsibility, and a lot of accountability. They were also given full flexibility, carte blanche. They were told, "Whatever you think you need, just go ahead and do it." There were no rules, except to stay within the future boundaries we created.

However, there was responsibility. We set up an internal board, and these two program leaders reported to the board just as a senior management team of a business reports to a board. This takes none of the responsibility off my shoulders as the controller, but the two program leaders did not just feel accountable to me, but to a wider audience, and a larger constituency within the company—the board. It really helped them to set priorities and to determine what things they wanted to take up with me and the board not so much for a go-ahead, but for input, for some other heads working through a particular challenge. Board members include officers from several different parts of Lucent.

Even though they were not part of the formal chain of responsibility for the program, I also had the entire controller's leadership team working on this from the beginning. I said to them, "You need to give the program people input on what information you would like to have, and how you would like to receive it, to make your job easier."

Creation of executive "ownership" to an effort like this is absolutely critical. Having the CFO we do, Don Peterson, who has a vision for a more value-added CFO organization, really helped us a lot in that regard. He did not just talk, he really led; he went out and did road shows. He has the philosophy, "We'll work on this vision together, and then I'm holding you accountable for results."

Don Peterson and his CFO Leadership Team consisting of Bill Carapezzi, Vice President Tax and Tax Counsel; Gil Harris, Vice President and General Auditor; Meg Walsh, Vice President and Treasurer; and me. Along with our Human Resource partners, Maryanne DiMarzo, Human Resources Vice President - Corporate Centers, and Amy Acker, Human Resources Director, we worked to establish goals for the CFO organization. We worked closely with the Business Unit CFO team consisting of Tony Abrahams, Cathy DeBlasio, Wayne Edmunds, Ned Hayes, David Hitchcock, John Kritzmacher, Trent Mattern, Michael Montemarano, Charlie Peiffer, and Matt Riley. The shared services leadership team consisting of Danny Lanier and Cheryl

Nabholz were also an integral part of this process. The four major goals we established for the CFO organization were:

1. One hundred percent of our business partners acknowledge the CFO team as a strategic business partner in achieving Lucent's objectives by 12/31/98.
2. One hundred percent of the CFO team agree to live our values and purpose.
3. The total CFO budget should be less than or equal to 1 percent of Lucent revenues for calendar 1998.
4. Financial modules of SAP implemented fully by 12/31/98.

These four goals were in support of our CFO Strategic Vision— "Team CFO, Engine of Excellence, Powering Lucent."

We as senior managers were given that set of goals from the executive suite, and we in turn passed them on to the program directors, who in turn passed them to project managers throughout the effort, saying essentially: "This is where we are going; be innovative and do what you have to do to get there. In terms of risk management, always be aware that our goal is to add value for our business partners, never to degrade the current value we produce." The CFO leadership team took ownership of these goals and through an incredible amount of partnership and teamwork put Lucent in a position to achieve these goals.

CHECKLIST

☐ Choose a project manager with the following attributes:
  ○ Intelligent
  ○ Communicates well
  ○ Respected
  ○ Experienced
  ○ Good cheerleader
  ○ Helicopter thinker (broad perspective)

- ○ Flexible
- ○ Determined
- ○ Enthusiastic
- ○ Personable
- ○ Political
- ☐ Which type of project structure do/will you have?
  - ○ Hierarchical;
    Rapid implementation
    Subteams
    Requires much resources
    Role definition
  - ○ Matrix:
    Free flowing
    Flexible
    Free thinking
    Discipline teams
    People are spread thin
    Difficulty in managing intersections and crossovers
    Cracks within which people can hide
- ☐ Project Planning
  - ○ Set targets:
    Tailored to individual organization and project
    Understand the individual steps or activities needed to meet a milestone
    Understand the dependencies between targets
  - ○ Understand scope:
    Know the number of business processes that will be re-designed.
    Know the number of legacy systems that will be turned off.
    Know where the legacy systems will reside.
    Know whether there are geographic, divisional and functional boundaries.
    Define and communicate scope.

Create a mechanism to enable formal requests to expand the scope.

Create a mechanism to prevent unilateral changes.

- ○ Evaluate resources:

Best and brightest

Veterans

☐ Project execution and control:

- ○ Monitor progress
- ○ Resolve conflict
- ○ Manage expectations

Emphasize importance of executive buy-in

Risk management must be part of the implementation program from the beginning.

☐ Risk management involves:

- ○ Risk identification
- ○ Risk assessment and analysis
- ○ Risk control and mitigation
- ○ Risk avoidance

☐ Consider the varieties of risk:

- ○ Executive
- ○ Project management and project plan
- ○ Technical
- ○ Organizational
- ○ Decision making
- ○ Functional

17

Barriers to Implementation and Change Management Solutions

- Barriers to success
- Visionary leadership
- Active change management approach
- Risk in undertaking organizational change
- Validity of decisions made
- Effectiveness of the implementation process
- Mitigate risks
- Resistance to change
- Minimize resistance to change
- Approach to change management
- Plan
- Levels of culture

Barriers to implementation of a shared service operation are essentially the same barriers that would be found in any major organizational change initiative:

- People
- Policies and procedures
- Technology
- Corporate culture and organizational dynamics

- Controls
- Metrics

At a more fundamental level, the barriers all revolve around individuals, the business problem, and how groups work together. The three largest barriers to success are:

1. If people get hung up on *how* (the process) and forget about *why* (to solve a business problem)
2. If people get hung up on redefining the problem
3. If people are so wed to the status quo that they cannot look to the future

VISIONARY LEADERSHIP BREAKS DOWN BARRIERS

In order to break through these barriers, an individual who is willing and able to lead the charge is needed, a leader who creates a vision and drives it deep into the fabric of the organization. Creating a vision is best done when you find the desired end state, then work backwards to determine what is necessary each step of the way in order to get to that end state.

The visionary leader must both "stand in the future" and be willing to point out to people that they are spinning their wheels and not moving toward the goal. The visionary leader sets tone and direction and essentially says, "I don't care how you get there, but you always have to be moving in the direction of the vision."

The visionary leader must have a ruthless consistency to his or her vision, and must constantly remind people of why the organization is doing what it is doing: to solve business problems. The leader needs to constantly explain how the vision will make solving business problems easier, and will ultimately make people's work more challenging and more rewarding.

CHANGE MANAGEMENT: THE TECHNIQUES

Change management means the effort it takes to manage people through the emotional ups and downs that inevitably occur when an organization is undergoing massive change.

The implementation of shared services, and the business process changes that must simultaneously occur, necessarily affect a business's organizational structure and, more important, the individual roles that a number of people have within the organization.

An active change management approach helps to make a shared service implementation project successful by:

○ Building people's understanding of and commitment to changes associated with the implementation

○ Aligning key organizational elements (structures, roles, and skills) to support the implementation

○ Enabling continuous improvement to sustain the change

In surveys seeking to define the key elements of success for major projects, including shared service implementations, change management is always cited, as is communication, which we see as an integral part of change management. In *Best Practices In Reengineering*, communicating the vision and strategies for change was listed as one of those best practices.

Successful change management must provide each and every individual within the organization a sense of ownership in the vision of the "to be." Each individual must understand why the company needs to get from the "as is" to the "to be," and must understand what role he or she will be asked to play in that future state. At the same time, an organizational structure must be created that enhances how work gets done, and the organization that is in place at the end of the change effort must be more capable of managing future changes.

EASIER TO MANAGE CHANGE DURING GROWTH

Of course, many shared service implementations will lead to a need for fewer people than under the old way of doing business. In growing businesses, people can be offered the ability to move into other areas.

One financial services company that reengineered a lot of the back-office functions in its private banking unit retrained people to perform marketing and product development work and set up a new group of "middle office" people to act as liaisons between private bankers or their clients and the back-office processes. This, in turn, freed up private bankers from many routine chores, allowing them to find new clients and increase their financial productivity. The end result was that more clients performed more transactions, with better quality and service to the client, with the same number of people in the organization. The company increased its revenues and profit, and more people within the organization acquired upgraded skill sets, and jobs that paid better and were more challenging.

In companies with flat or declining market share, change management is often more difficult. As individuals realize that fewer people will be needed in the to-be state, their willingness to work through the change often wanes. Many times, the most marketable individuals with skills that will be needed after the change "head for the lifeboats," whereas those who fear that they may be asked to leave in the to-be state dig in their heels and resist the change.

RISKS TO ORGANIZATIONAL CHANGE

There are two broad categories of risks in undertaking organizational change; the validity of decisions made and the effectiveness of the implementation of those decisions. Change management focuses on implementation and the management of key organizational elements to align them with the desired change.

Successful change management can occur only when the first variable, the validity of decisions, is accepted by all concerned. This means that leadership must create both a "burning platform"—a reason for why change must occur—and a vision of what the organization will look like after the change occurs.

One way to try to mitigate these risks is to define clearly who within the organization falls into each of the four key roles of any change effort. These four roles are shown in Figure 17-1. The *change sponsor* is the individual or group who legitimizes the change. The *change agent* is the individual or group who is responsible for implementing the change. The *change target* is the individual or group who

Figure 17-1   Key Roles of Change Effort

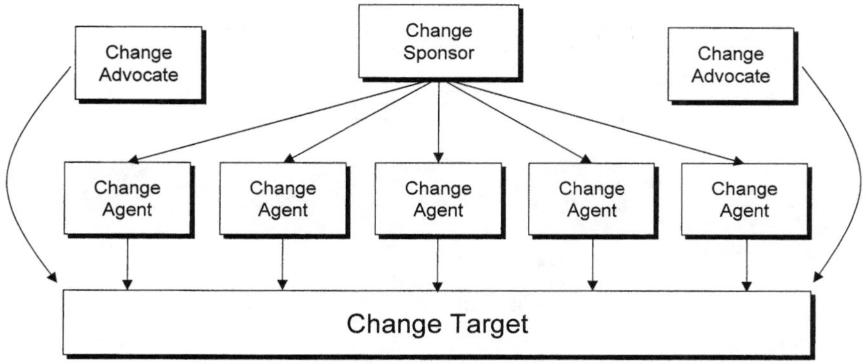

must actually change. The *change advocate* is the individual or group who wants to achieve a change, but does not possess the power within the organization to legitimize the effort.

CHANGE MANAGEMENT PROCESS

Change is a process. It is often the largest jeopardy to a shared service implementation project and is easily overlooked. An organization can undergo successful change only if those in the leadership are willing to let the natural process take its course. This process affects every individual in the organization. For some individuals, the change process is a wrenching experience; for others, it is something they embrace.

Figure 17-2 shows the change process.

Resistance to Change: Is It Manageable?

What is resistance to change? Is it inevitable? What causes it? How can it be managed?

First, recall changes that have affected you, either personally or professionally. Did the experience create stress? Anxiety? Uncertainty? How did you perceive the change? Was it positive and beneficial? Or was it unavoidable, unnecessary, and undesirable?

What determines how changes are perceived? To a large extent,

Figure 17-2   Change Process

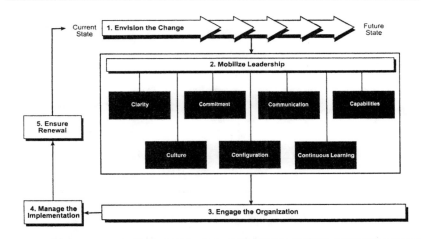

Throughout the implementation of shared services, consideration must be given to a number of change issues and potential barriers.

change is viewed in terms of its effects. Will I benefit? Will I be better off as a result of the change? What will need to occur during the change?

Figure 17-3 lists some of the characteristics of a negative or a positive response to change.

When the benefits and the payoffs associated with an upcoming change are evident, people "buy in" to the overall direction of the change.

Resistance stems from perceived loss—loss of the known and tried and loss of personal choice. Examples of fears held by employees that create resistance to change are job loss or other adverse impact, as well as a shift in communication patterns, organizational structure, influence, authority, and control. Whether the threat is actual or imagined, it should always be treated as real. Reduce fear by removing uncertainties, using education and demonstration.

People resist the imposition of change that is simply ordered to happen without everyone's prior involvement. To minimize resistance, seek involvement of those affected by the change in determin-

Figure 17-3   Characteristics of Response to Change

Negative	Positive
Immobilization • *Fearful, confused* • *Appear overwhelmed*	**Uniformed optimism** • *Positive feelings about the change* • *High confidence in themselves*
Denial • *Defending against a shift* • *See change as an unacceptable reality*	**Informed pessimism** • *Negative feelings about the change* • *Low confidence in themselves*
Anger • *Effort to regain control* • *Desire to present stability*	**Hopeful realism** • *Begin to perceive the change project as achievable* • *Reduced negative feelings about the change* • *Increase in self-confidence*
Bargaining • *Trying to minimize impact*	**Informed optimism** • *High levels of positive energy* • *Increased self-confidence brought by the approaching success*
Depression • *Frustration* • *Sense of loss* • *Low levels of coping*	**Completion** • *Strong support of the change* • *Willingness to help others through the transition* • *High self-confidence*

ing how or if a change should happen. This will lessen the feelings of lost control.

The degree of ease and success with which an organizational change is introduced is directly proportional to the amount of choice that people feel they have in determining and implementing the change. Communicating anticipated changes should incorporate the elements of personal choice, highlighting possible options instead of a singular predetermined path.

It is also possible that people believe the planned change is ill fated and will not work, or it may violate deeply held values and beliefs. This may stem from underlying value differences or intellectual/technical differences in approach and philosophy. The best response is to counter with well-conceived, influential explanations incorporating facts, anecdotal evidence, and data. Conclusions drawn from inadequate data and weak linkages invite opposition.

Encouraging overt resistance is one strategy for identifying and developing responses to individuals experiencing a values conflict. Overtly expressing resistance can help individuals surface and overcome resentments rooted in loss of control. Covert resistance is hazardous to the change project and should be transformed into overt resistance whenever recognized.

Finally, some people resist change because they have a low tolerance for change in general. Provide them with as much reassurance as possible as they move into a world of uncertainty. Time may also reduce anxiety as fears are proven unwarranted.

The key objective is to predict, or at least recognize, resistance; uncover the root cause; and act directly to minimize or overcome it.

OUR APPROACH TO CHANGE MANAGEMENT

Our approach to change management has five components:

1. Mobilize
2. Assess
3. Plan
4. Implement
5. Renew

Mobilize

During this phase, confirm the project's scope and outline the strategy for conducting change management. Change management teams are formed and team leaders chosen. Leaders of process change and system implementation teams, as well as the sponsors of these efforts, are trained in the concepts of change management. Leaders of process change and system implementation teams must be chosen based partly on their ability to be agents of change.

Assess

In this stage, you need to analyze the current human resource situation, and define the purpose and nature of the change as it affects employees. The entire change process as well as its implications for work, both human and technological changes, must be articulated to the entire organization.

A large part of this assessment is an assessment of the organization's readiness to change. A number of key organizational variables are relevant in a systems implementation.

The impact on the *external environment,* on suppliers, customers, and shareholders must be assessed.

Leadership is necessary to set direction for the change effort by clearly articulating both the reason the change is necessary—the burning platform—and the vision of how the company will enhance its competitive position through undergoing the change.

Both a *vision* and a *strategy* for change must be clearly articulated and communicated to the entire organization. It is not enough to say "I have a vision of scoring a touchdown." It is necessary to say, "We're going to run these types of plays, in this order, so we can score a touchdown."

The current *organization culture* must be congruent with such changes, or it must be willing and able to adapt to the desired changes.

Management practices must foster support and commitment to the change effort.

The *work-unit climate* must be receptive to change.

Finally, the organizational *structure* can be a facilitator or inhibitor of change. Current business process redesign and systems modernization efforts both work on the principle of flattening organizational hierarchy, leaving lean central organizations responsible for overall strategy and some general and administrative functions in a shared services environment. Most operating and tactical decision making is left to business unit officers. A rigid, hierarchical structure, with slow and cumbersome decision making at the executive management level, is a great inhibitor to change.

Motivation is a key factor for adopting an improvement.

The *skills* and *abilities* of individuals and the *task requirements* of the shared service implementation must be matched.

Individual needs and values must not be seen to be contradicted by the project. Areas of congruence should be highlighted to foster support. There must be clear mechanisms to report on both *individual* and *organizational performance* in relation to the change.

Plan

In this stage, develop strategies to bridge the gap between the as-is situation and the desired to-be state. This strategy is then translated into tactics for instilling change, including:

- Determination of process and job redesign needs
- A plan for organizational interventions
- Development of communications and awareness programs
- Creation of training curriculum content

Implement

During this stage of change management, build understanding of and commitment to change, as well as train the staff toward the new business goals and organizational outcomes, and establish new ways of working.

Both the change plan and the communication plan need to be implemented simultaneously. Sponsors, coaches, executives, and team members all have to be aligned in their activities.

Mechanisms need to be set up for cross-team learning, and training programs need to be piloted, then rolled out across the organization.

Renew and Sustain

In this final stage, develop a system of ongoing support for the workforce, as well as a system of measurement to assess the achievement of change and the learning that has occurred. It is possible to tinker with the change plan and redirect it as needed for a second round of organizational change.

Training and education programs need to be evaluated and modified as necessary for any future changes. The results of the effort need to be communicated. Individuals and groups should be commended for their work and their continuing efforts to enhance the business through achievement of the to-be state.

ORGANIZATIONAL CULTURE AND ITS RELATION TO CHANGE

Organizational culture is the "personality" of the organization: the collective pattern of beliefs, values, behaviors, and philosophy developed over time. According to the organizational dynamics author and consultant J. Steven Ott, there are five levels of culture that exist within an organization.[1]

- *Artifacts.* Artifacts are manifestations of the company's "heritage" and cultural activity (myths, ceremonies, jargon, and logos) that can be observed. It is important to know what these artifacts mean about the organization.
- *Patterns of behavior.* Patterns of behavior include customs, traditions, habits, and patterns of interaction, such as how decisions are made, what is done to fit in, and what is needed to get ahead.
- *Behavioral norms.* Norms are the "house rules," the unwritten but observed code for working. These include beliefs about acceptable and unacceptable behaviors such as cooperation and competition between and among departments, and the behaviors it takes to fit in and to get ahead.
- *Values.* Values are the shared beliefs regarding organizational identity and ethics, as seen in corporate ideologies and patterns. Values reflect the priorities assigned to particular behaviors.
- *Fundamental assumptions.* Fundamental assumptions are the glue that holds the organization together. They are shared by all, and members live by them.

The odds of successfully implementing change grow as the similarity grows between the existing culture and the behaviors and assumptions required by the change initiative, as well as those behaviors and assumptions that will be part of the desired state, as shown in Figure 17-4.

When current culture is in conflict with the necessary culture, three options exist for those leading the change effort:

Figure 17-4   From Existing Culture and Desired State

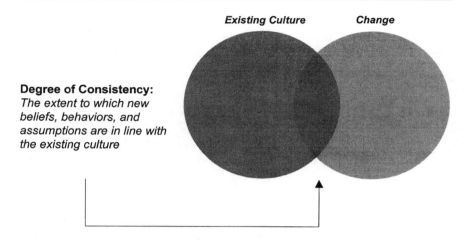

Degree of Consistency:
*The extent to which new
beliefs, behaviors, and
assumptions are in line with
the existing culture*

1. Modify the change to be more in line with the existing beliefs, behaviors, and assumptions of the culture.
2. Modify the beliefs, behaviors, and assumptions of the culture to be more supportive of the change.
3. Prepare for the change effort to fail.

The change methods outlined earlier can be used to accomplish either option 1 or option 2, or a combination of those two options.

LUCENT'S ACTIVE CHANGE MANAGEMENT (TOLD BY JIM LUSK)

Changing the context in which work is done is clearly the biggest change to the whole effort. It is a matter of articulating the vision for people and getting them to believe that what they do on a day-to-day basis is relevant to achieving that vision. It was integral that people understood the answer to the question: "How does the work I do every day add value to Lucent?"

Once they could understand that the work they did, if done within the new work context, really does add value, any resistance they felt to change was gone. There was resistance for sure, more at the beginning of the effort than later. It's about producing results, not just being busy.

We addressed this resistance by talking to people. We did innumerable road shows. We took every person in the chief financial officer (CFO) organization through a change management process, through strategic intent coaching sessions.

Another way to address resistance is to have the leadership be consistent. No matter who on the CFO leadership team an employee talked to throughout the implementation, the response was clear and consistent. Everyone said the same thing. This again was testament to the teamwork of Don Peterson, as well as others (Bill, Meg, and Gil), and was critical in changing the context.

I may not know exactly how you will take your area of expertise through the change process, the exact steps you will take, the ways you will be innovative; but I do know where you are going and the vision at the end of the journey, because it is also my vision. Therefore, I can "be a stand" for you any time you need backup.

Fear is clearly a large issue for all of us. There is a real fear that this is just another "program of the month." However, the consistent message, and the fact that this effort was part of the CFO's strategic intent, mitigated a lot of that fear.

The leadership team answered hundreds of questions from hundreds of employees from around the world. Basically, they were the same three questions being asked in innumerable different ways: "Why is this different? How is it going to be different? Are you committed?"

Leadership in business has too often left colleagues hanging out on a highwire with no net. Even if you have never done it, even if your company has never done it; even if a particular employee has never had it done to him or her, they have all heard stories and read articles, and they are afraid.

The message to us was clear: DON'T DO THIS BEHIND CLOSED DOORS.

The leadership team made a huge effort to "get in front" of people, not merely in the sense of standing in front of them to answer questions, but in terms of getting in front of them on the journey itself. The leadership team conducted global roadshows, where face-to-face dialogues were held with the people being affected. We all tried to be very open and honest. A lot of times this meant saying, "I don't know."

"I don't know" is a very scary thing for a leader to have to say, but you have to say it. You have to say, "The situation is fluid. This is the way I think it will happen, the way I hope it will happen." Then, you need to communicate as soon as something is solidified, and that often means that you have to go back and say, "Things have changed. We're not able to do it the way I said last week or last month that we would like to do it. Instead, we have to do it this way."

This is a big point. It is so easy to say something off the cuff because people want to get information *now*, even if things are not completed. You have to constantly tell people that things are not completed, that the situation is fluid.

That happened to me a few times. As a leader, it is not what you are used to doing, having to say "I don't know." But if you have been open and up front from the beginning, you have built trust. People accept that the world is full of surprises and business conditions do change, and I am only human and have to adjust and adapt. If they see you as a leader adapting and adjusting, admitting gaps in your current knowledge and the information you have and can give out, and stepping up to accountability, they are more willing to do so as well.

Originally, there was a varying level of commitment among business unit leaders. We dealt with that by getting the entire CFO team rallied around the idea. Then, each of the CFOs went and worked with their particular strategic business partners. They said: "Look, don't worry. We really need to try to make this work. If it does, your lives will be easier. If it doesn't work, we'll make it work together. But we really need to take the risk together. We'll guarantee that the value we provide will not in any way be reduced or degraded. It will get better." It is the same message that the company's CFO gave to us in the CFO leadership team. Because we ourselves had bought into a vision, it was much easier for us to be convincing in our discussions with our business partners.

CHECKLIST

☐ Three largest barriers to success are:
1. People getting hung up on *how* (the process) and forget about *why* (to solve a business problem).
2. People getting hung up on redefining the problem.
3. People so wed to the status quo that they can't look to the future.

☐ Emphasize importance of a visionary leader to break down barriers:
- Create a vision.
- Drive vision deep into the organization.
- Set tone and direction.
- Say: "I don't care how you get there, but you always have to be moving in the direction of the vision.

☐ Active change management approach:
1. Build people's understanding of and commitment to changes associated with the implementation.
2. Align key organizational elements (structures, roles, and skills) to support the implementation.
3. Enable continuous improvement to sustain the change.

☐ Identify risks in undertaking organizational change:
- Validity of decisions made
- Effectiveness of the implementation process of those decisions

☐ Mitigate risks by defining key roles:
- Change sponsor
- Change agent
- Change target
- Change advocate

Resistance to Change

☐ Resistance stems from perceived loss—loss of the known and tried and loss of personal choice. Reduce fear by removing uncertainties using education and demonstration.

☐ Minimize resistance by seeking involvement of those affected

---

by the change in determining how or if a change should happen, lessening the feeling of lost control.

☐ Communicating anticipated changes should incorporate the elements of personal choice, highlighting possible options instead of a singular predetermined path.

☐ Provide well conceived, influential explanations incorporating facts, anecdotal evidence and data to prevent opposition from conclusions drawn from inadequate data and weak linkages.

☐ Encourage overt resistance to identify and develop responses to individuals experiencing a values conflict.

☐ Provide reassurance to reduce anxiety for those who have a low tolerance for change.

☐ Approach to change management:
  ○ Mobilize:
    Confirm the project's scope.
    Outline strategy for conducting change management.
    Choose change management teams.
    Choose team leaders.
    Train leaders.
  ○ Assess:
    Analyze the current human resource situation.
    Define the purpose and nature of the change as it affects employees.
    Articulate to the entire organization the entire change process as well as its implications for work, both human and technological changes.
    Assess the organization's readiness to change
      External environment—impact on suppliers, customers, and shareholders.
      Leadership—set direction by articulating the reason change is necessary and the vision of how the company will enhance its competitive position through undergoing change.
      Vision—communicate.

> Strategy—communicate.
>
> Organization culture—must be congruent with changes or be willing to adapt.
>
> Management Practices—must foster support and commitment to the change effort.
>
> Work-unit climate—must be receptive to change.
>
> Structure—can be a facilitator or an inhibitor to change.
>
> Motivation—a key factor for adopting improvement.
>
> Skills and abilities—must be matched.
>
> Task requirements—must be matched.
>
> Individual needs and values—must not be contradicted by the project.
>
> Individual and organizational performance—create mechanisms to report in relation to change.
>
> o Plan:
>
> > Develop strategies to bridge the gap between the as-is situation and the desired to-be state.
> >
> > Translate strategy into tactics.
>
> o Implement:
>
> > Build understanding of and commitment to change.
> >
> > Train staff toward new goal and organizational outcomes.
> >
> > Establish new ways of working.
> >
> > Align sponsors, coaches, executives and team members.
> >
> > Set up mechanisms for cross-team learning.
> >
> > Pilot training programs.
> >
> > Roll out training programs.
>
> o Renew and sustain:
>
> > Develop a system of ongoing support for workforce
> >
> > Develop a system of measurement to assess the achievement of change and the learning that has occurred.

NOTE

1. J. Steven Ott, The Organizational Culture Perspective (Pacific Grove, CA: Brook Cole Publishing, 1991).

18

Performance Measures and Continuous Improvement

- **Relevant metrics**
- **Characteristics of best metrics**
- **Performance measures**
- **Strategic performance measures**
- **Creating strategic performance measures**
- **Balanced scorecard—dimensions**
- **Key questions**
- **Tying performance measures and metrics to compensation**
- **Embedding continuous improvement**

While designing a shared service operation in the abstract is well and good, when the implementation occurs, it is necessary to have a way to measure the operation's success. Measuring the success of shared services is not an easy task. There are a few reasons for this.

First, while shared services is not necessarily a strategic operation, it must always be undertaken as an integral part of a corporate strategy. Because of this, an entire pyramid of metrics must be developed, from discrete metrics at the activity level to macro metrics at the corporate level. At the top level are a few strategic performance measures on which the entire operation can be graded.

Second, because the relationship between the shared service organization and the business units is one of partnership and not customer/supplier, a different set of metrics than those traditionally used must be created to measure the relationship, one that measures partnership as well as value.

Third, because there is an end-state vision for the shared service operation that is different from the current state, a different set of metrics will be needed to measure success in the end state than the one used at the beginning of the shared service organization's life.

Many businesses have books of hundreds, if not thousands, of metrics that are tracked closely at all times, and that management is constantly seeking to fine tune. At any time, there are probably no more than 5 to 10 key metrics per work area that should be tracked closely, and those will change over a period of several months or a few years at most.

Although these metrics are not used on a day-to-day basis, it is important to be able to track them and to "audit" any one particular high-level metric occasionally by following the entire cascade of metrics to the discrete activity level. Also, it is important to keep track of all these metrics because they are what the rank-and-file employee is being measured by. Management cannot possibly keep track of that many metrics and digest them in a meaningful way in order to make rational decisions.

Thinking these metrics through is like trying to play chess in three dimensions. However, throughout this chapter, two-dimensional pyramids will be used to describe the metrics. We describe the relationship of metrics within one pyramid as cascading down from high-level strategic performance measures to more discrete metrics, or linking up from discrete metrics to higher-level performance measurements. We describe the relationship between the pyramids as being connected over time.

Figure 18-1 shows the pyramids of current and future metrics, illustrating the cascading and linking-up effects.

OF METRICS AND MEASUREMENTS

Too often, traditional metrics do not tie management actions to business strategy. It is possible to replace wrong metrics with correct metrics to create such a link.

Figure 18-1   Hierarchy of Metrics

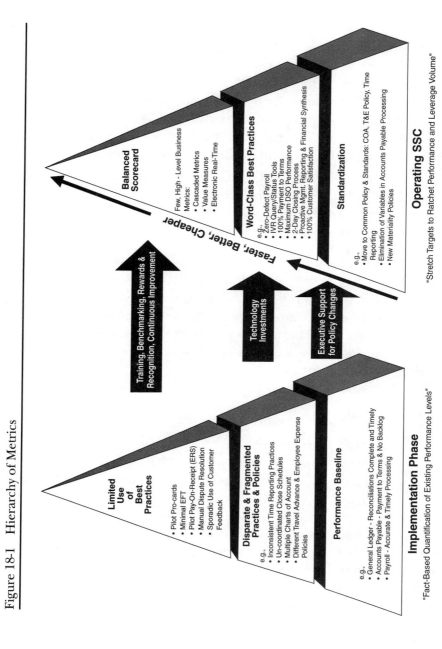

Relevant metrics must support management by focusing on activities and processes rather than functions. Understanding total process performance and the real contribution made by each activity in the process is the key to improvement.

In many companies, people are working hard, but at the wrong things. There is too much non-value-added work, and too much time wasted fixing problems that should not have happened in the first place. Too much time is spent looking backward, trying to create short-term fixes, rather than looking forward and creating an environment in which the organization can attain peak performance.

Before going any further, we will explain exactly what is meant by the terminology *metrics and measurements,* specifically strategic performance measurements.

Metrics are quantitative calibrations of performance along a single dimension, such as time, cost, or accuracy. How many rings it takes to answer the average call coming into a call center is a metric. The time it takes to make a change of beneficiary on one's group life insurance policy is a metric. The accuracy with which a travel and expense voucher is processed is a metric. The cost of a service call to fix a networked printer is a metric.

The best metrics are:

o Discrete (they measure a single item)
o Quantitative (they can easily be compared)
o Comprehensible (anyone should understand a metric)
o Visual (represented by a bar graph, pie chart, or other simple graphic)

Performance measures are like metrics, or metrics that measure the same activities, that are grouped together into an area of focus. Performance measures give one the ability to compare different locations against one another by "rolling up" metrics into performance measures that are meaningful in a macro sense.

Strategic performance measurement takes as its basic tenet that establishing base controls is necessary but in no way sufficient. Management today often works with a set of metrics that is overly complex, yet does not answer questions about how the organization is performing strategically. It is harder to create a set of simple metrics that tie operational performance to strategy than it is to simply measure everything.

Strategic performance measurement seeks to create a set of simple, well-thought-out and hierarchical metrics that drive success along three critical dimensions:

1. *Strategy.* Performance measures provide an ongoing mechanism for measuring the organization's success in channeling its energy into meeting strategic goals.

2. *Processes.* Performance measures provide actionable, real-time data and use targets for operational excellence in critical processes to create the incentives for improvement and proper resource allocation.

3. *People.* Performance measures align the objectives of individuals with the overall organizational strategy, ensuring a universal commitment to common goals.

STRATEGIC MEASUREMENTS LEAD TO KEY METRICS

Each organization must create a somewhat customized set of strategic performance measurements based on its internal and external value chain. The "balanced scorecard" approach is a good place to start. Creating such a set of strategic performance measurements will in turn help the organization to create a set of metrics that looks forward rather than backward and can act as an early-warning system for potential problems.

Creating a set of strategic performance measures and supporting metrics is a three-step process:

1. Start with the strategy.
2. Design the performance measures, then the metrics.
3. Plan and implement the design.

Strategic Key: A Balanced Scorecard for Shared Service Organizations

The balanced scorecard concept was first laid out by Robert Kaplan and David Norton in a 1992 *Harvard Business Review* article.[1] The balanced scorecard is an approach by which a company can see the impact that activities today have on critical dimensions of corporate performance.

In the traditional balanced scorecard, three dimensions are almost always used—financial, customer, and internal. The fourth dimension is left open to give a company some flexibility in defining a key dimension of its business. Kaplan and Norton use the term *innovation* in this dimension.

Creating the appropriate balanced scorecard dimensions is where the organization's strategy is linked to the measurement system. If the strategy addresses objectives and key stakeholders, highlights the organization's core competencies and core processes, and has enough focus that people understand both the short- and long-term objectives, strategic performance measures should fall into place.

For shared service organizations, the four dimensions should be

Figure 18-2   Balanced Scorecard for Shared Service Organization

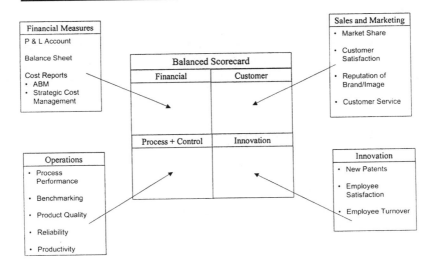

financial, partnership, operation, and innovation. Figure 18-2 shows the standard balanced scorecard matrix with these dimensions.

Design Key: Choosing the Right Top-Level Metrics

A key to creating a well-integrated and appropriate set of metrics is to choose the right top-level metrics. If executive management is looking at the right metrics, they will drive the connection between these top-level metrics and the physical things in the trenches that are being measured.

Top-level metrics should measure the end-to-end processes within the shared service operation. They should measure the operation from the partner's perspective, not from an internal perspective. The best way to look at the end-to-end process is from the partner's perspective.

The entire set of metrics for the shared service organization must both cascade down and roll up, linking tightly with the metrics both above and below on the pyramid.

Take a critical look at every prospective metric and ask a series of questions:

- Does the metric support the strategy?
- Does the metric support business processes?
- Is the metric easy to understand?
- Can the metric be presented clearly in vision terms?
- Can the metric be calculated from obtainable data?
- Is the metric relevant, is it a good indicator of company performance?

Implementation Key: Questioning a Metric

Take the metric "speed of monthly financial closing." The goal is "one day."

Now ask the six questions of the metric.

1. Does it support the strategy?
2. Does it support processes?

3. Is it easy to understand? The answer here is yes, it is easy and straightforward, at least on the surface. But you might ask the question: What is meant by one day?

4. Can it be clearly shown in vision form? Metrics are most powerful when they are presented visually, in graphic form, and displayed prominently throughout the business.

5. Can it be calculated from obtainable data? Again, the answer is yes.

6. Is it relevant, and is it a good indicator of performance? Here the answer begins to get murky. Is the information within a monthly closing worthwhile, or is it too much detail? Is it forward looking, or backward looking?

You might also ask a couple of questions about the information in the closing, such as: Is it accurate? If the closing is fast but inaccurate, it could be more harmful than helpful to the company.

TYING PERFORMANCE MEASURES AND METRICS TO COMPENSATION

This is a delicate subject. If compensation is tied to specific metrics, it must be tied to a limited number of metrics, and those metrics must be simple and clear. What is happening in some companies is that they are setting bonus compensation on a growth target, with some portion determined by the return on controllable assets.

EMBEDDING CONTINUOUS IMPROVEMENT

The establishment of appropriate cascading and linking metrics creates an environment in which continuous improvement can flourish. A shared service organization, almost by definition because of its focus on partnership and service, is an organization that must focus on continuous improvement.

A number of companies that have long-standing continuous improvement programs, as part of total quality management (TQM) work done in the 1980s or business process reengineering (BPR) work done in the 1990s, have also moved into a shared service model for carrying out many supporting processes. For them, continuous improvement is a natural process.

Others should use the same dispute management model discussed in Chapter 12 on service-level agreements and shown here as Figure 18-3. As stated in Chapter 12, the continuous improvement dispute reconciliation methodology should be explicitly part of the service-level agreement. If an incident or exception occurs that is outside the acceptable parameters of the agreement, it is not looked at in a vacuum, but rather in the context of the entire universe of incidents or exceptions.

Errors are tracked, analyzed, and researched. Simultaneously, the individual occurrence is fixed and the occurrence is put into the shared service organization's database. Each individual occurrence is tracked for both its "reason" code and its "cause" code. The reason is

Figure 18-3 Continuous Improvement Model

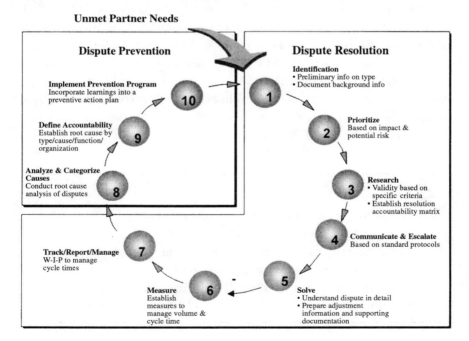

why it was an exception (the symptom), while the cause gets closer to the root of the problem. To do this properly, it is necessary to have sophisticated data warehousing capabilities.

MEASURES & METRICS AND LUCENT (TOLD BY JIM LUSK)

Lucent has five corporate metrics that the chief financial officer (CFO) measures:

1. Grow the top line at or above the industry and maintain best-in-class growth margins.
2. Reduce sales, general and administrative (SG&A) expenses by 4 to 8 percentage points.
3. Increase research and development (R&D) spending to 11 percent of revenues.
4. Double the return on assets from 5 percent to 10 percent.
5. Reduce taxes by 2 to 4 percentage points.

We drive these metrics in order to power the business. At the CFO level, we have the vision of creating an organization that adds value to all our business unit partners in order to help them to help the company hit the targets articulated in these metrics.

In order to drive toward these metrics, we have some very focused shared service metrics. These include cycle time, error rates, cost as a percentage of revenue, the number of days to close books, and the number of invoices paid electronically.

CHECKLIST

☐ Relevant metrics must support management by focusing on activities and processes rather than functions.

☐ Make sure the metrics have the following characteristics:
  ◦ Discrete (they measure a single item)
  ◦ Quantitative (they can easily be compared)
  ◦ Comprehensible (anyone should understand a metric)

---

    o Visual (represented by a bar graph, pie chart, or other simple graphic)

Performance measures

☐ Establish strategic performance measures for:
- Strategy
- Process
- People

☐ To create strategic performance measures:
- Start with strategy.
- Design the performance measures, then the metrics.
- Plan and implement the design.

☐ Create a balanced scorecard—dimensions:
- Financial
- Partnership
- Staff
- Innovation

☐ Be able to answer "yes" to all of the following key questions:
1. Does the metric support the strategy?
2. Does the metric support business processes?
3. Is the metric easy to understand?
4. Can the metric be presented clearly in visual terms?
5. Can the metric be calculated from obtainable data?
6. Is the metric relevant, is it a good indicator of company performance?

☐ If tying performance measures and metrics to compensation, make sure that compensation is tied to a limited number of specific metrics that are both simple and clear.

☐ Embed continuous improvement.

NOTE

1. Robert S. Kaplan and David P. Norton, "Balanced Scorecard: Measures That Drive Performance," *Harvard Business Review,* Jan./Feb. 1982.

19

The Global Potential and the Virtual Potential

- **Envision gains through globalization**
- **Potential drawbacks**

Much has been written about the business of the distant—or possibly near—future, a "factory-less" or "product-less" environment, where virtual organizations made up of many entities populate the supply chain, adding value through narrowly focused core competencies, and goods and services magically appear at the consumer's behest.

This environment is seen as one in which:

- Every interaction with an outsider (vendor, customer, potential employee) is met with a "wow."
- There is seamless process execution, no hand offs, and no artificial "functional" or even "company" boundaries.
- Products and services are bundled in a way that focuses on the end user (the customer) to provide "one-stop shopping."

In this vision's office of the future, workplaces will be devoid of people, and many employee activities will be simplified and "self-service." Technology will be abundant and visible. Workstations will be portable to home, customer, or vendor location. E-mail will be rapid, with no delays for downloading. Log-on will be automatic, driven by retina-recognition security systems when the user is within range. Cellular technology will provide a wireless office environment both at home and in collective workstations (the office).

265

If this vision holds true and extends, organizations will at some point in the future have no physical office as such. All communications will take place via Web technology. Very few employees will work for a company; those that do will work from their homes or "on the road." All administrative activity will take place automatically—electronically. Finally, everything other than a company's core competencies will be outsourced.

Business decisions will be boiled down to the answers to three questions:

1. Inside or outsource?
2. How large a volume?
3. At what price?

In this model of the future, shared services will eventually become passé. A small group of world-class companies will have as their core competency delivery of what are today's shared services. For instance, transactional accounting services, from procurement to payment or from credit to collection, will be delivered on an outsource basis to companies around the world. Others will provide global human resource capabilities in payroll, benefits administration, and so on. The role of each individual company's management will be to manage the relationships with outsource service providers, and to set policies and procedures for establishing outsourcing relationships.[1]

EXPANDING SHARED SERVICES' HORIZONS IN THE REAL WORLD OF TODAY

At the same time as this vision of small, lean, core-competency-driven businesses is being created, corporations are growing by rapid and, at times, voracious acquisition. Is there a way to reconcile these two seemingly disparate trends?

Shared services is a major piece of that reconciliation, at least for now. Shared services can allow a corporation to position itself to enter the world of virtual corporate identity in the future, if it so desires. In the short term, shared services across the organization provide the company with the ability to show one face to the customer, to be "easy to do business with," and to provide clear and efficient communication with those outside the company.

Today, shared services are provided in the following areas:

- Accounting
  - Transaction processing
    - Travel and expense
    - Accounts receivable, including credit and collection
    - Accounts payable
    - Financial reporting
    - Business solutions (analysis)
- Human resources
  - Payroll
  - Benefits administration
  - New hires pool
  - New employee orientation
- Logistics
  - Procurement
  - Materials management
  - Fleet administration (transport of finished goods)
- Information technology
  - Desktop maintenance
  - Systems maintenance

Companies on the cutting edge of shared services are beginning to move into such areas as:

- Tax planning (execution and compliance)
- Treasury planning (execution and compliance)
- Legal services
- Insurance services
- Facilities management

- Travel agency and services
- Conference, executive and corporate travel, and administration
- In-house medical, jet, and catering

On the near horizon, there are companies looking to provide even the following services within a shared service model:

- New IT systems selection, development, and implementation
- Electronic data interchange (EDI) and E-Commerce standards and development
- Global code-block maintenance (incorporating a chart of accounts)
- Company-wide document management
- Management of the portfolio of outsourcing contracts
- Manufacturing and plant management
- Potential acquisition due diligence
- Internal control and risk management

Throughout all of this, shared service operations are one of a number of organizations interwoven with the company that focus on effective and efficient delivery of end-to-end processes.

GLOBAL POTENTIAL IS STILL NOT FULLY REALIZED

Before the virtual vision can be realized, companies must find a way to harness the global potential of shared services. A few companies are moving in that direction. For instance, both Swissair and British Airways carry out global ticket clearinghouse activities in India. American Express processes accounts payable vouchers 24 hours a day on a global basis by utilizing three worldwide shared service hubs (Phoenix, in the United States; Brighton, in the United Kingdom, and New Delhi, in India). In addition to taking advantage of time differences, the company also uses a workload-balancing distribution model across its three centers.

A number of companies are experimenting with call center technology and training that allows any call to be answered at any center that is open at that hour of the day. Intelligent switchboards can help overcome language difficulties by directing the call to the appropriate competence. Furthermore, as discussed earlier, the tumbling price of telecommunications can only increase interest and takeup in this area.

The global software development industry and pharmaceutical research and development pioneered 24-hour around-the-world production.

Pros and Cons, and Barriers to Success

Despite these successes, most companies are finding it extremely difficult to process all transactions of global customers from one physical shared service center. There are a few challenges; paper flow, legal documentation requirements of various countries, multiple processing systems, and a resistance to change on the part of individuals throughout the organization as well as a sense of losing control.

Companies often envision the gains that can be achieved through complete globalization:

- Control of process standardization
- Consistent and available data and information
- Savings in systems maintenance
- Leveraging of investment in technology
- Potential for recruiting the absolute best to work on an incredible challenge

However, when all is said and done, they are often drawn back from the brink of choosing a truly global solution by a number of factors:

- Risk of having all of that data and information in one physical location, and the complexity of disaster recovery and backup plans

- Fear of becoming "oversized" beyond any real gains in efficiency (is there any real difference between processing 10 million transactions in one location or in three?)
- Document management issues, relating again to backups and risk of disaster
- Human factor issues

This is an especially potent issue in Europe, where individual countries often have very disparate business practices. In the United States and Canada, business practices are nearly the same. Throughout the Spanish- and Portuguese-speaking Americas, there is also more standardization of business practice than there is difference. The same is true throughout Asia. In Europe, today and probably through much of the first quarter of the 21st century, business practices will still be disparate.

It is still a cultural stretch to ask an Italian, French, German, or Spanish business leader to allow the company's transactional processing to be done in another European country, although over time the European Monetary Union will serve to break down some of these barriers in addition to unifying currency. It still will be difficult to ask that same leader to allow the company's processing to be done in Mexico or India or Singapore.

FUTURE OF SHARED SERVICES

Here are a few predictions for the first quarter of the 21st century:

- Technology will continue to eliminate the need for many manual transactions and the human effort it currently takes to perform them.
- The logical conclusion to internal shared services is outsourcing of transaction-based supporting processes. A handful of giant, global service-providing companies will perform all of these processes for most large companies.
- The global economy will continue to coalesce, breaking down language and cultural barriers.

To some, this might seem frightening—a major threat to thousands if not millions of jobs. However, rather than eliminate jobs, such a revolution will create jobs. In that way, shared services supported by enterprise resource planning (ERP) technology will be no different than any other technologically based revolution in the history of commerce.

Every business revolution has increased employment rather than decreasing it. Every technological revolution has created the need for not only those who can work with the technology but those who will take the technology to its next height.

The technological and business service revolution we are entering as we cross over the millennium will provide more people with more interesting, rewarding, and enjoyable work opportunities than has ever been the case.

And we are only at the beginning of the journey.

POTENTIAL FOR SHARED SERVICES AT LUCENT (TOLD BY JIM LUSK)

Shared services has incredible potential as a tool for making our strategic business unit partners very successful with their end customers, and in turn helping them all to meet the company's growth targets, and therefore provide value to our shareholders'.

It is also a powerful tool to get the chief financial officer (CFO) organization to constantly innovate and reinvent itself. It helps us to be comfortable with each wave of business change and technological change that occurs. We are, in a shared service model, a real learning organization and an innovating organization. That is not something that can be said generally about finance and CFO organizations in the past.

It is often said that people can accommodate only so much change at one time. We at Lucent have seen that change is a constant because of the rapidity of external changes being thrown at us. By going through a shared service implementation, we have changed the mindset of our organization in terms of how it deals with change and uncertainty. We have actually increased the capacity of both individuals and the organization to accommodate change.

We now agree with the concept that "gaps are good." If you really want to be the best in the world at what you do, you have to be constantly reinventing your future and yourself. That means looking at the next level of gaps and working to fill those gaps. That is an enormous change in culture, from one that says gaps are bad to one that says gaps are good because they show you where to put your effort to improve.

Will our company ever move to a fully global shared service organization? It is possible, but we have much to learn about activities and processes around the globe and how to do them better.

Will our company ever move to a virtual shared service organization? Again, it is possible, though it certainly will not happen any time soon. There is still far too much value added to these activities and processes by the human contact that goes into them. With computing changes and telecommunications changes, clearly some more human activities will be eliminated and more will be done through automation. That will give more people an opportunity to do more "business" and "analytical" work rather than transactional work.

I close the Lucent story with three thoughts.

First, almost everybody that made the changes we are talking about in this story came from AT&T. Therefore, it clearly is not about changing people, but rather about changing the concepts people have of their work and the context in which people work. It is about creating a compelling vision and allowing people to be as innovative and creative as humanly possible in how they get themselves, their peers, and their organizational units into alignment with that vision.

Second—and this is a message I now take to our associates and business unit partners whenever I am asked to make a formal presentation—It is an enormous culture change I have seen in the CFO organization, and we are helping to drive that change in other organizations around the company. That change is not about waiting around to be asked to be strategic partners. We now envision ourselves as strategic partners and behave that way from the start. We go into a relationship with the mindset of a strategic partner, and have developed a partnership and service head. That is an incredibly gratifying change to watch take place, and it is wonderful to see people go into a situation with enthusiasm about the value they add to the relationship and to the company's entire effort.

Lastly, it's about a great team. The implementation of shared services and our shift in context and culture could not have occurred without Don Peterson's vision and the partnership and teamwork of Bill Carapezzi, Gil Harris, Meg Walsh, Danny Lanier and Cheryl Nabholz of the shared services leadership team, and our Human Resource partners, Maryanne DiMarzo and Amy Acker. I feel honored to be part of that team.

CHECKLIST

☐   Envision the gains that can be achieved through globalization:
- Control of process standardization
- Consistent and available data and information
- Savings in systems maintenance
- Leveraging of investment in technology
- Potential for recruiting the absolute best to work on an incredible challenge

☐   But do not forget to consider the potential drawbacks:
- Risk of having all of that data and information in one physical location, and the complexity of disaster recovery and backup plans
- Becoming "oversized" beyond any real gains in efficiency (is there any real difference between processing 10 million transactions in one location or three?)
- Document management issues, relating again to backups and risks of disaster
- Human factor issues

A

Bibliography of Related Books by PricewaterhouseCoopers Authors

In Search of Shareholder Value; Dr. Andrew Black, Philip Wright and John E. Bachman; Financial Times Management, 1998

SAP: An Executive's Comprehensive Guide; Grant Norris, Ian Wright, James R. Hurley, John Dunleavy and Alison Gibson; John Wiley & Sons, 1998

Straight From the CEO; G. William Dauphinais and Colin Price; Simon & Schuster, 1998

CFO: Architect of the Corporation's Future; The Price Waterhouse Financial and Cost Management Team; John Wiley & Sons, 1997

Reinventing The CFO: Moving From Financial Management to Strategic Management; Thomas Walther, Henry Johansson, John Dunleavy and Elizabeth Hjelm; McGraw-Hill, 1997

The Paradox Principles; The Price Waterhouse Change Integration Team; Irwin Publishing, 1995

Best Practices in Reengineering: What Works and What Doesn't in the Reengineering Process; David Carr and Henry Johansson, The Coopers & Lybrand Center of Excellence for Total Quality and Change Management; McGraw-Hill 1995

Beyond Business Process Reengineering: Towards the Holonic Enterprise; Patrick McHugh, Giorgio Merli and William Wheeler III; John Wiley & Sons, 1995

Business Process Reengineering: Breakpoint Strategies for Market Dominance; Henry Johansson, Patrick McHugh, A. John Pendlebury and William Wheeler III; John Wiley & Sons, 1993

B

Greenfield Site-Decision Matrix

SSC Location Criteria*	Weighting Factor %	Europe				Australasia					United States				South America			
		Belgium	Holland	Rep. of Ireland	UK (N. England)	India	Hong Kong	Malaysia	Singapore	Sydney	Atlanta	Dallas	Greensboro	Phoenix	Uruguay	Venezuela	Brazil	Argentina
Quality/Skill of Workforce	___%	●	●	●	●	○	●	◐	●	●	●	●	◐	●	●	○	●	●
Availability of IT Skills	___%	◐	●	●	●	◐	●	●	●	●	●	●	●	●	○	○	●	●
Cost of Workforce	___%	○	◐	●	◐	●	○	●	○	●	○	◐	●	●	●	●	●	◐
Workforce Flexibility	___%	◐	●	●	●	◐	●	●	●	●	○	◐	●	●	●	○	○	◐
Availability of Govt. Grants	___%	○	○	●	●	◐	○	●	○	◐	◐	◐	●	●	○	○	○	○
Tax Considerations	___%	●	○	●	○	○	○	◐	○	○	◐	●	●	●	○	○	◐	○
Cost of Communications	___%	○	○	◐	●	○	○	◐	○	◐	●	●	●	●	○	○	○	○
Communication Infrastructure	___%	◐	◐	●	◐	○	●	●	●	●	●	●	●	●	○	○	●	◐
Real Estate Cost	___%	○	◐	●	●	●	○	◐	○	◐	◐	○	●	●	●	●	○	○
Statutory/Legal Requirements	___%	○	◐	●	●	○	◐	◐	●	◐	●	●	●	●	○	○	◐	○
External Infrastructure	___%	●	●	◐	●	○	●	●	●	●	●	●	●	●	◐	○	○	●
Travel Accessibility	___%	●	●	●	●	○	●	◐	●	●	●	●	●	●	◐	○	●	●
Political Stability	___%	●	●	●	●	○	◐	◐	●	●	●	●	●	●	●	○	◐	◐
Linguistic Ability	___%	◐	●	◐	○	◐	◐	◐	◐	◐	○	◐	○	◐	●	◐	●	●
Company Infrastructure**	___%	To be completed according to each organization's profile																

* Assessment of comparison is within region, not between regions
** Concentration of organizational presence

Key

● Recommended   ◐ Neutral   ○ Unfavorable

277

C

XYZ Shared Accounting Service Center ("SASC") Accounts Payable

Service Delivery Agreement between SASC and _____
_____ [Date]

XYZ's Shared Accounting Service Center operates as an accounting service provider to _____ and its affiliates. The SASC is located at _____. Services that are provided by SASC Accounts Payable include:

- Vendor Setup and Maintenance
- Tax Reporting and Compliance (1099 Statements and W-9 Forms)
- P.O. Invoice Processing
- Non-P.O. Invoice Processing
- Fleet Invoice Processing
- Contract Payments
- Purchasing Card Services
- Archival of Paid Documents
- Travel & Expense (T & E) Voucher Processing
- Check Disbursements
- Duplicate Payment Recovery
- Payment Discounts
- Performance Reports

This agreement includes _____ [all of, only] the above Accounts Payable services [except for, as follows] _____, _____, _____, _____. The SASC will provide vendor setup and maintenance for all of XYZ.

The SASC has agreed to provide service for Accounts Payable activity to _____ (entity/company) as of _____, 199__. The agreement will continue on a month to month basis and will only terminate upon the client providing ____ day notice of termination.

Service Delivery Agreements

Hours of Operation

The SASC will operate between the hours of 7 A.M. to 5 P.M. MST. Teams are assigned on a regional basis in parallel to the operational structure in XYZ (i.e., Central, Great Lakes, West, Southeast) and will arrange their work hours to match as closely as possible to the time zones of the systems or regions they are servicing. The _____ [Central, Great Lakes, West, Southeast, Corporate, etc.] team will provide coverage between the hours of _____ A.M. and _____ P.M. The customer service team will provide coverage between the hours of _____ A.M. and _____ P.M. MST.

Activities Performed

For Accounts Payable, the SASC will be responsible for the following [sample selection]:

Select	Activity
X	Receiving Mail from vendors/employees/systems
X	Validating approval codes and account codes
X	Entering vendor invoices and employee T&E vouchers into the A/P system
X	Approving/posting the transaction in the A/P system
X	Filing paid invoices
X	Printing and disbursing checks
X	Maintaining vendor maintenance tables; setup of new vendors

X   Compliance for W-9 and 1099 reporting; minority vendor reporting

X   Interfacing and posting to the General Ledger

X   Interfacing and posting Purchasing Card Activity

X   A/P daily and month end reporting

X   Sales and Use tax reporting and compliance in partnership with Tax Department

X   Support and Training for remote access to TAP or Oracle

Emergency Checks

Bank Reconciliation, Positive Pay, Stop Payments, Voids

Performance

Specific Service Agreements that Performance Measurements will be measured against are:

1. Setup of new vendor requests at SASC within a 24-hour period of receipt of the request.

2. Keying of invoices into the A/P system within 3 days of receipt at SASC.

3. Keying T&E vouchers within 3 days of receipt at SASC.

4. Providing copies of requested support within 24 hours of receipt of the request. If the request is for invoice copies from the previous calendar year, the SASC will provide copies within 15 days of receipt of the request. If requesting more than 10 copies of invoices at one time, special arrangements should be made with the A/P SASC leadership team.

5. Provide performance reports within 10 days after month end.

6. Provide 24-hour turnaround on Emergency Payments/special handling requests (overnight mail time included).

The SASC will provide a monthly report card to the Controllers or Business Finance Lead that will detail performance against the agreed-upon service-level agreement. Measurements will include actual results and monthly volumes of activity provided to the entity.

Customer Service Focus

The SASC will provide dedicated personnel in servicing requests for information over the telephone. For phone inquiries, please call the dedicated customer service team at phone _____. The goal for the customer service team is to respond to telephone inquiries within 2 hours.

When requesting copies of invoices, please fax all requests to _____ or mail to _____, attention: Documentation Management Team. The dedicated team will either fax back a copy of the invoice/T&E or send a copy interoffice within 24 hours if the request is for information in the current year. If the written request is for invoice copies that were paid in the previous year, please allow 15 days.

Cost of Service

Because the SASC will be operating independently of Corporate or any Division Finance department, the costs of running the SASC will be allocated and shared by the entities/divisions in which services are provided. Costs are defined as a fully loaded expense which include but are not limited to wages and benefits, real estate lease/depreciation, equipment costs, office supplies, check print and bank fees, CPU charges, training and education, and travel expenses.

The costs will be allocated on a per unit basis for the defined activities of the SASC. In 199_, costs will be allocated on a per invoice/voucher basis on an average unit cost. T&E vouchers will be charged a different rate than invoices. In 199_, activities included for a unit charge will include: Purchasing Card transactions, manual checks, P.O. supported invoices, non-P.O. invoices, merchandise invoices, EDI invoices, electronic T&E vouchers, manual T&E vouchers, and (others defined as material).

The cost of an invoice will be $_____ and will not exceed $_____ per unit during the terms of this agreement. The cost of a T&E voucher will be $_____ and will not exceed $_____ during the terms of this agreement. The costs will be reviewed and adjusted on a semi-annual basis. Adjustments will be made as part of the monthly billings in July and December for the prior six months. The adjustments (credit or debit) will be made back to the internal clients based on the volume processed during the six-month period.

For those entities which only have checks printed, they will be invoiced for the cost of check disbursement only. The cost for check disbursement only will be $_____ and will not exceed $_____.

Processing costs will be invoiced on a monthly basis no later than the _____th of the month. Settlement of these costs will be booked through the General Ledger/Intercompany process. The Controller should review the internal cost and discuss with the Director of SASC any discrepancies in the billing. This review process should be completed no later than 30 days from the internal invoice date.

This Service Agreement has been reviewed and approved by:

_____   _____
[Internal Controller Name]   [SASC Representative Name]

_____   XYZ Shared Accounting Service Center

_____ [date]   _____[date]

D

Summary of Future Finance Delivery Models

Decentralized (Business Unit)	Centralized (Corporate)	Shared Services Center
Credit & Collection Sensitive collections Extension of credit decisions		Non-sensitive collections
Taxation Providing supporting records Where legal entity consolidation not complete, certain taxation activities need to continue to be done at SBU	**Tax Department** Filing of consolidated U.S. tax returns Resolving tax litigations Tax planning Divestiture & acquisition due diligence Tax Dept./Corp. Controllers Tax package review/approval	VAT recovery on employee expenses VAT consolidation and reporting coordination and sign-off (including audit) Tax packages preparation (local statutory & U.S. incl. FAS 109)
Treasury Generate cash forecasts Exposures forecast & hedging plan decisions Absence of country cash-pools: SBU responsible for Cash Management	Strategic treasury direction Divestiture & acquisition due diligence	Consolidate cash & foreign exchange forecasts Bank liaison & fee negotiation Cash pool management
Corporate Accounting	Review & approval reported results	AIMs reporting for Corporate (Group holding company entities) Group consolidations
Statutory Accounting Subsidiary reporting Support local statutory audit reviews	**Local Board of Directors** Final approval on filed statutory accounts **Corporate Controllers** Ultimate responsibility for filing of accurate & timely statutory accounts	Auditor coordination & assistance Statutory accounts preparation and sign-off Supporting acquisition & divestiture decisions
Company Secretarial Communicate issue of legal significance	**Legal Department** Resolving legal litigations **Shared Services** Close coordination between legal department and/or external legal counsel	Company secretarial activities and legal compliance Required legal filings Legal contract administration Pension scheme trusteeship

E

Shared Service Decision Tree

Mobilize

What Is Shared Services	Compelling Business Reason	Is It Right for You?	International Challenges
-Enhance corporate value	-Customer demands	-Desire to minimize G&A	-Cultural Boundaries
-Strategic growth	-Business partner demands	-Desire to free up SBU to focus	-Complexity
-New management responsibility	-Globalization	on customer facing activities	-Infrastructure
-Customer service focus	-Transactional efficiency	-Desire for critical mass for	-Time zones
-Client support focus	-Support process effectiveness	support activities	-Legal issues
-SBU focus on strategy	-Consolidate activities	-Must tie infrastructure together	Government
-Secondary activities become	-Rationalizate lower value added	-Must have management time	-Stability
core processes	activities	and commitment	-Security
-Resource concentration	-Service to "internal" business	-Must address issues around	-Weather
-Service multiple internal entities	unit partners	responsibility	-Currency
-Higher service levels	-Benefits outweigh costs		
-Lower service cost	-Business units partner with the		
-Leverage technological	Shared Service operation		
investments	-Partners help define service		
-Continuous improvement	levels		
	-Free up SBU management		
	-Focus on customer facing		
	activities		
	-Better career progression		

Assess

Reengineering/Redesign	IT	Outsourcing
-Requirement	-Leverate technological	-Strategic relevance
-Worthwhile?	innovation	-Current performance level
-Pick low hanging fruit	-ERP	-Future required performance
-Incremental improvement	-SAP	level
-Timing	-Eliminate 100% verification	-Goal: Good enough to sell
-Corporate culture	by management	
-New HR structure	-Paperless, streamlined process	
-Reengineering upstream	-Rapid handling of information	
-Reengineering downstream	-Minimal human interference	
-New staff	-Cost savings	
-Existing staff	-Call centers	

Appendix E

Design			
Getting Started	**Planning and Approach**	**Setting Up the Infrastructure**	**SLAs and Pricing Issues**
-Develop business case	-"Burning Platform"	-Key principles	-Goal: Breaking even
-Develop support for initiative	-Appropriate model	-Legal entity	-Pricing strategies
-Organize initiative	-Path of least resistance	-Billing SS costs	-Effect of IT systems
-Communicate intent and plan	-Decision making process	-Funding the SS organization	-Performance tracking
-Identify desired skill set	-Influential factors	-Tax issues	-Continuous improvement
		-Physical infrastructure set up	
Selecting the Location	-Influential factors upon flexibility	-Tax considerations	-External infrastructure
-Quality/skill of work force	of work force	-Cost of communication	-Travel accessibility
-Availability of IT skills	-Work force flexibility - openness	-Communications infrastructure	-Political stability
-Cost/flexibility of work force	to new ideas	-Real estate cost	-Language suitability
	-Government grants	-Statutory/legal requirements	-Company infrastructure
Final Business Case	-Baselining	-Costs	-Technology
-Purpose	-Benchmarking	-Process	-Facilities

Implement			
Defining and Setting up the Project	**Choosing a Consultant**	**Program/Project Management**	**Barriers to Implementation and Change Management Solutions**
-Type of start	-Why use consultant	-Program management	
-Model of a SS organization	-Types of consultant partners	-Project management	-Barriers to success
-Implementation program development	-Kinds of consultants	-Project manager attributes	-Visionary leadership
-Keys to successful impleentation	-Questions to ask	-Project structure	-Active change management
	-Ways consultants add value	-Project planning	-Risk in change
Performance Measures and Continuous Improvement	-Balanced scorecard	-Project execution and control	-Validity of decisions
-Relevant metrics	-Key questions	-Kind of people to fill roles	-Effectiveness of implementation
-Characteristics of best metrics	-Tying performance measures and metrics to compensation	-Importance of executive buy in	-Mitigate risks
-Performance measures	-Embedding continuous	-Risk management	-Resistance to change
-Strategic performance measures	and metrics to compensation	-Varieties of risk	-Minimize resistance to change
-Creating strategic performance	**Global Potential vs. Virtual Potential**	-Gains through globalization	-Approach to change management
measures		-Potential draw backs	-Plan
			-Levels of culture

Business Processes	**Who's In/Who's Not**	**Business Controls**	-Schedule of Approvals
-Finance	-Businesses	-Business Case	-Banking Concept
-Human Resources	-Legal Entities	-Audit Implications	-Internal Controls
-Data Centers	-JV's/Associates	-Disaster Recovery	-Systems/EDI
-Logicstics	-Cost Increments	-Government Compliance	-Record/Retention
-Real Estate/Travel	**Communications & Change Management**	-Culture	-Celebrate Success
Candidate Activities		-Risk Ownership	-Customer Satisfaction Surveys
-Transaction Processing	-Vision/Objectives	-Baselining As-Is	-Exhaustive Communicaton Plans
-CTRS of Expertise	-Roll-Out	-Critical Success Factors	-New sletters/Videos/Pay-Slips

288

Index

Index

Index